'I have always admired Dr Leo Ruickbie's comprehensive expertise in the paranormal'
– Rosemary Ellen Guiley, bestselling author

Described as 'a young Van Helsing' in *The Ghost Club Journal*, **Dr Leo Ruickbie** has been investigating, writing about and experiencing the bizarre side of life – from vampire epidemics (there really was one) to sightings of angels – for most of his professional career. He has a PhD from King's College, London, on modern witchcraft and magic, and is the author of *Witchcraft Out of the Shadows*, *Faustus: The Life and Times of a Renaissance Magician*, *A Brief Guide to the Supernatural*, and *A Brief Guide to Ghost Hunting*, as well as being published in *Fortean Times*, *Paranormal* magazine, academic journals and the national press. He is also the co-editor of *Little Horrors: Interdisciplinary Perspectives on Anomalous Children and the Construction of Monstrosity* with Dr Simon Bacon, and *The Material Culture of Magic* with Dr Antje Bosselmann-Ruickbie. His work has been mentioned in the media from *The Guardian* to Radio Jamaica, and his expertise has been sought by film companies and the likes of the International Society for Human Rights. He is an Associate of King's College, London, and a member of Societas Magica, the European Society for the Study of Western Esotericism, the Society for Psychical Research and the Parapsychological Association. He is a committee member of the Gesellschaft für Anomalistik (Society for Anomalistics) and is the editor of the *Paranormal Review*, the magazine of the Society for Psychical Research. As a Scotsman, the impossible zoo has always been a living folk memory: he has stood on the banks of Loch Ness and stared into those sullen waters. Visit him online at www.ruickbie.com.

Also by Dr Leo Ruickbie

A Brief Guide to the Supernatural
A Brief Guide to Ghost Hunting

THE
IMPOSSIBLE ZOO

DR LEO RUICKBIE

Robinson • London

ROBINSON

First published in Great Britain in 2016 by Robinson

1 3 5 7 9 10 8 6 4 2

A CIP catalogue record for this book
is available from the British Library.

ISBN: 978-1-47213-644-2

Typeset by Basement Press, Glaisdale
Printed and bound in Great Britain by CPI Group (UK), Croydon CRO 4YY

Papers used by Robinson are from well-managed forests and other responsible sources.

MIX
Paper from
responsible sources
FSC® C104740

Robinson
An imprint of
Little, Brown Book Group
Carmelite House
50 Victoria Embankment
London EC4Y 0DZ

An Hachette UK Company
www.hachette.co.uk

www.littlebrown.co.uk

Every effort has been made to trace the copyright holders and to obtain their permission for the use of
images. The publisher apologizes for any errors or omissions in the above list and would be grateful if
notified of any corrections that should be incorporated in future reprints or editions of this book.

To Bill and Bernice who made it all possible.
To Antje, Morgana and Melissa who make it all worthwhile.

I write that which is reported; and nothing is impossible.
– Herodotus, *The Histories*, IV.195, fifth century BCE.

... and nature breeds,
Perverse, all monstrous, all prodigious things,
Abominable, inutterable, and worse
Than fables yet have feign'd, or fear conceiv'd,
Gorgons, and Hydras, and Chimeras dire.
– John Milton, *Paradise Lost*, Bk II, 1667.

Introduction

'He who does not expect the unexpected will not find it,' said the Ancient Greek philosopher Heraclitus, 'since it is trackless and unexplored.' Unexpected certainly, yet it is not altogether trackless nor unexplored. We have folklore, mythology, legend, travellers' tales, even news stories of today all describing animals that cannot be and have never been scientifically catalogued. This is the world of what I call 'parazoology': para- because it is beyond the range of normal zoology; para- because it makes us think of paranormal and parapsychology. It is not cryptozoology, the study of hidden ('crypto-') animals, because I do not suppose that any of them can be found. It is the biology of the supernatural; a study of the life of things that never lived. It is the world of mermaids and unicorns, confined now to fantasy, but once believed to exist; a world of the imagination that can still affect us today. Included are all the creatures of legend, beasts of fable and monsters of mythology, but not the transient products of modern culture. This is not *Fantastic Beasts and Where to Find Them*. This is the 'real' thing. Here are the things that made the woods wild and the night fearsome; the things that made cartographers of old write 'Here be dragons' on their maps. Here in this collection are the things that natural science has ruled out, yet still find their role in history and the social sciences. This is the Impossible Zoo.

It is a vast world and these monsters are legion, so how should we choose which of them to study? If these things truly existed, which of them would we put into a real zoo? The short answer is nothing too much like ourselves. In the possible zoo we may gawp at primates, but not pygmies, for example. So it is in the impossible zoo. Thus we will find fairy animals, but not the fairies themselves; we will find Alien Big Cats, but not Little Green Men or Greys; we will find animalistic Egyptian gods, but not anthropomorphic Ancient Greek ones. In a sense, it is a catalogue of our imaginings of the animal world.

As in a real zoo the cages must all vary in size, but here it is the importance of the animal rather than its physical dimensions that determine how big that cage is. Although one must concede that dragons are both large and important, consequently they will occupy a proportionate space in these pages. The labels to each cage will attempt to convey as much information as is known about the creature in question as far as is possible and are structured to provide details on etymology, name variants, description and sources.

As with any zoo, the primary purpose is entertainment, but again real zoos also serve more serious purposes. Here you will have the opportunity to study these fabulous beasts in more detail through the many illustrations provided, as well as the text, and the sources give a guide to further study and exploration.

In general, the fabulous, mythical and legendary beasts can be divided into four sorts: a) normal animals of extraordinary size; b) mostly normal animals that can become other mostly normal animals; c) composite animals that create new forms not found in nature; and d) misidentification and misdescription of existing animals. In class a) are all the giant fish (whales), giant snakes, and giant this and that. In class b) are those, usually, fairy creatures that can be one thing and then another: the black dog that can also be a pig or a bull, or even a human, for example; they are often also of extraordinary or at least remarkable size. In class c) are the classic monsters – the griffin, the harpy, Pegasus and so on – that are made up of different bits of real animals; the addition of birds wings to terrestrial beasts is the most frequently found motif. Finally, class d) contains things like the unicorn, which was really a misdescription of the rhinoceros that acquired mythical proportions. You will immediately ask, where does the dragon fit into this? The answer is that the dragon begins as a serpent of extraordinary size and then acquires composite character-istics, that is, wings; and becomes more lizard-like with the addition of four legs until it begins to look like a misdescription of an actual creature, particularly the crocodile. So we see that animals can display characteristics of the different classes and even move from one to another over time. The giant animals are similar to the misdescribed ones; the shape changers are similar to the composite ones. The first group represents humanity's endeavour to understand the natural world; the second group its struggle to represent the supernatural world. Before the advent of science these were not always seen as different things. Normal things, such as storms and the raging sea, have god-like power to destroy and acquire supernatural interpretations: the harpies are personifications of the destructive force of the wind, for example. This means that we are constantly shifting perspective between natural history and theology where superstition and allegory rather than evidence and analysis are the principal authorities. Then there are also magical and ritual aspects to consider. Odin's eight-legged horse, Sleipnir, for example, represents Odin's power to move between the worlds of the living and the dead, and is comparable to the spirit-horses found in shamanism where the shaman's journey is facilitated by such beings.

Finally, we should add class e) which comprises all those absurdities cooked up by unscrupulous individuals to dupe their fellow man and extract some of his coin. These are collectively known in the trade as Jenny Hanivers and comprise everything from makeshift mermaids to fraudulent fossils. The practice became such a nuisance to naturalists that the great ornithologist George Gray, FRS, complained in 1841 that 'continental preparers of objects of Natural History still continue the shameful practice of endeavouring to deceive the zealous collector by false means, as in bygone days, when several such were published in splendid works, that have since been discovered to be manufactured for the purpose of obtaining large sums of money from amateurs who were struck by their magnificent appearance' (*Annals and Magazine of Natural History*, 237). The celebrated Carolus Linnaeus, the father of modern scientific taxonomy, had been taken in by the Legless Bird of Paradise and *Papilio ecclipsis*, for example. Not to be left out, I have added a *Lepus cornutus* to my personal collection. They, too, are impossible and, whether stuffed, embalmed or fossilised, we would want them in our zoo.

There are some aspects of selection to note. I could have filled considerably more paper on the Egyptian gods, for example. But this is not the place to read about them in depth. Everyone has heard of Anubis, few of the Antelope Hodgsonii; the latter merits a longer entry precisely because of that. Furthermore, the mostly human, or sometimes human, characteristics of the Egyptian gods present a moral problem for our zoo that Hodgons's Antelope does not. Also, being a Scot from a long line of Scots (despite the odd name, we go back to 1066), I could not shake off an affinity for all things Celtic, and by further ancestral connections, all things Nordic, and that, I think, shows in the foregoing, but I make no apologies for it. I have skimmed stones on Loch Ness and searched for runestones and petroglyphs on Bornholm; I have not, more's the pity, left footprints in the Valley of the Kings.

So what of the status of this new-fangled thing, parazoology? For example, there is much debate over whether cryptozoology is a science or pseudoscience. For cryptozoology the answer is that it can be both depending on how well it adheres to accepted scientific method. As the study of hidden animals it is no more worthy of approbation than, say, cryptography, both can be done well or badly. It is an established fact that several creatures formerly considered to be legendary have in fact been discovered. But this is not a book of cryptozoology. If any of these creatures could be considered to be 'crpyto', hidden, then it is in the collective mind that we should search for them, not the jungles of Borneo. We live in a shared and constantly negotiated social reality that is something other than the world described by physics. We live in a world delimited by the capabilities of human physiology and psychology: we see black ravens; ravens see themselves as something else, much more colourful – you can see the hint of that on the plumage of ravens in strong sunlight. Religion proves that the world of the imagination is far more influential in human affairs than the world of facts and figures.

And beneath all this oddity of flying horses and world-encircling sea monsters, we see nature, as much of it as we can, as a fabulous thing. The crocodile is no less amazing than the dragon. The eagle is no less amazing than the griffin. We search for wonder, sometimes, most times, in the wrong places: it is already all around is. What this book did for me, and I hope that it will do for you, is rekindle my amazement at the natural world. Most of us go through a 'dinosaur phase' – the dinosaurs were far more 'impossible' than anything I am about to describe – we need to get back to that phase, because that state of wonder in respect of the natural world is uniquely human, therefore, it is what makes us human. Much of what you will read here comes from other people's amazement as they relate tales of creatures or search for the truth of legends. As children we were in love with nature; as adults we just buy it in the supermarket and eat it. The choice is yours – and think on this: much of what exists today will become impossible tomorrow unless we rekindle that love; remember the dodo. This is much more than a book of weirdness: it is a call to arms, a call to humanity.

In writing this book I have read many similar books and hope to have learnt from them. In general, I found the most unsatisfying approach was to merely state that 'this was that' without reference to the source material. Consequently, wherever possible I have sought to find the sources and quote from them. For example, where some might say under Abada, 'a small African unicorn', or some such thing, by looking for the sources we find a whole world of context that takes us from Portuguese traders to British explorers. This makes this both a richer book and a more useful one. I hope that the reader will equally be able to sit down and enjoy reading through this book, as well as write a term paper or essay using it.

A NOTE ON SOURCES

In the references listed for each entry I show where I have derived my information. In general, I prefer the earliest or most authoritative, but include recent research where illuminating. For reasons of space, the sources are not a bibliography of all works on the subject. When citing ancient authorities the standard form of referencing is used, rather than the specific edition, as this is always the most useful method, if, at first glance, the most perplexing to readers not used to this approach.

It is also as well here to introduce some of the sources used, since in the course of reading they will become familiar names, if they are not so already. Among the Ancient Greeks, the principal sources of monsterology are Homer, Hesiod and Herodotus. Homer is the traditional author of the *Iliad* and the *Odyssey* – the stories of the Trojan War and

Odysseus' return home afterwards – as well as the so-called *Homeric Hymns*; although, there is much debate on his identity and authorship.

Many of the writers may seem gullible from a modern perspective – some day we will seem gullible, too, no doubt – but accurate information was then scarce and the rest difficult to judge. Herodotus, for example, was only occasionally sceptical, but he qualified his position by saying 'I write that which is reported; and nothing is impossible' (*Hist.*, IV.195) and he did not even know about the dinosaurs.

Among the Romans, Pliny the Elder is foremost, but also important are Lucan and Aelian. Pliny should have an entry in this book himself – he is just as amazing as all the rest. Born in 23 CE as Gaius Plinius Secundus, this Pliny the Elder, as we now know him, was a soldier and philosopher. He saw action in Germania as a young man and was procurator of Gallia Belgica at Trier, and much else besides, before writing the *Naturalis Historia*, his last work, and one that we will refer to frequently. It was a monumental encyclopedia in thirty-seven books of all that was known of the world at that time; it is only a pity that we will focus on so much that was inaccurate or exaggerated. He died in Pompeii during the eruption of Vesuvius in 79 CE. If you are wondering who the Younger might be, it was his nephew, Gaius Caecilius – Pliny had no children and in his will adopted 'the Younger' as his heir. Lucan was Marcus Annaeus Lucanus (39 CE–65 CE), the most highly regarded poet of his time; all his peculiar natural history comes from his epic poem *Pharsalia* about the civil war between Julius Caesar and Pompey. Where Pliny kept his head down during the reign of Nero, Lucan stuck his out too far and was obliged to commit suicide. Aelian – Claudius Aelianus (*c.*175 CE–*c.*235 CE) – wrote much later, took much from Pliny in preparing his *De Natura Animalium*, but was still influential. It was not only read but translated by the important Swiss naturalist Conrad Gessner (1516–1565), for example – and Gesner's five volume *Historiae Animalium* (1551–1558, 1587) is widely considered to mark the birth of modern zoology.

The Christian writers took much of what they knew from these ancients, but added much else besides, often of a religious nature; Isidore of Seville (*c.*560–636 CE) is their leader, but attention must be paid to the many bestiaries that were written and circulated in the

Middle Ages. Finally, there is the class of travellers and explorers. Their tales were often no less bizarre than the tales of those who stayed at home. Here Marco Polo (*c.*1254–1324) and Sir John Mandeville, the supposed author of *The Travels of Sir John Mandeville* around 1357, will be our guides.

With regard to modern authors, we must use them warily. For example, a much-quoted entry in similar books is the 'Á Bao A Qu', a tedious creature that, to no particular effect, supposedly followed people up the 'Tower of Victory in Chitor' – this must be the imposing tower known as 'Vijay Stambha' in Chittorgarh Fort, Chittorgarh, Rajasthan, western India – but the creature is said to have originated from the Malay Penninsula. I checked books on Indian folklore and Malay folklore: nothing. It appears to have been invented by the Argentine fiction-writer Jorge Luis Borges in his *Book of Imaginary Beings* (1967), possibly as a joke aimed at one of his acquaintances who is named in the sources for this, and has no basis in local folklore. Not only that, the joke was not even funny. There is also the mysterious case of the Attercroppe, said to be a snake with human arms and legs, that has found its way into many recent collections, however, no reliable sources for this could be found. So, in many cases, when an entry is not included, it does not mean that it has not been researched. A book is always just the tip of an iceberg of research.

A

A'NASA

The supposed African **Unicorn**. Whilst in Cairo, the French explorer Antoine d'Abbadie wrote to the *Athenaeum* magazine in London, relating how a certain Baron von Müller had made the most astonishing discovery. Returning from Kordofan (also Kurdufan, a former province of central Sudan), the baron reported that on 17 April 1848 he had met a dealer in animal specimens in the town of Melpes, who offered him an a'nasa: 'It is the size of a small donkey, has a thick body and thin bones, coarse hair, and tail like a boar. It has a long horn on its forehead, and lets it hang when alone, but erects it immediately on seeing an enemy. It is a formidable weapon, but I do not know its exact length. The a'nasa is found not far from here (Melpes), towards the south-southwest. I have seen it often in the wild grounds, where the negroes kill it, and carry it home to make shields from its skin.' The baron added that the dealer was familiar with the rhinoceros, which he called *Fetit*, and distin-guished it from the a'nasa. In June whilst at Kursi, also in Kordofan, the baron had met a slave-trader who claimed to have eaten an a'nasa recently: 'its flesh was well flavoured'. Philip Henry Gosse, an important naturalist and Fellow of the Royal Society, brought this account to wider notice (Gosse, *Rom. Nat. Hist.*, 290) and it was widely repeated (e.g., Gould, *Myth. Mon.*, 346–7); it was first published in the *Athenaeum* (January 1849). See also **Abada**.

AATXE

Basque, meaning 'bullock': a super-natural bull or bullock of Basque legend. Also known as *Aratxegorri*, 'Red Bullock'. Related: *Txaalgorri*, 'Red Bullock'; *Zezengorri*, 'Red Bull'; *Beigorri*, 'Red Cow'. It lives in caves, particularly that of Leze near Sare (Basque, Sara) in the French Pyrenees, and is said to punish naughty children, grant the wishes of parents and carry off those who do not fulfil their religious duties. The creature is also believed to come out on stormy nights and force people to return to their homes. In several caves – Istúritz, Goikolau, Santimamiñe, Sagastigorri, Covairada and Solacueva – Roman coins have been found attesting to ancient practices intended to appease cave-dwelling spirits. (Barandiarán, 'Prähist. Höhlen'.)

ABAASY

A term for an evil spirit among the Yakut (Sakha) people of Siberia; variations include *abaahi, abacy, abasi,* or *abasy, abassylar.* In the epic poems (*olonkho*) of these people, they are described as having only one eye, one arm and one leg, sometimes riding on horses having two heads, eight legs and two tails. They are divided into three sorts: the 'Upper' who live in the western sky; the 'Middle' who live on the earth; and the 'Lower' who live below it. They are all considered to be harmful to men and, in particular, devour one of the three souls, the *kut* (the physical soul), upon death. They are ruled by Ulutuyer-Ulu-Toyon ('Onmipotent Lord'), who himself may not be wholly evil, but also has the power to protect people from the abaasy. Formerly, the Yakut sacrificed horses to the upper abaasy and horned cattle to the lower abaasy. Whilst the abaasy themselves are human too, we would certainly like to include their horses in our impossible zoo. (Czaplicka, *Sham. Sib.*; Hatto, *Essays*, 128; Eiichirô, '"Kappa" Legend', 114.)

ABADA

Also *abath*; *bada*, of doubtful etymology, being either from Malay *badak*, 'a rhinoceros', or Arabic *abadat*, *ābid*, fem. *ābida*, meaning, amongst other things, 'a wild animal', via Portuguese *badas*, 'rhinoceros'. An African word for a single-horned animal, seen as cognate with the **Unicorn** by early writers. Descriptions come from Portuguese Angola and old Abyssinia (Ethiopia). The name is first recorded in the seventeenth century by the Capuchin missionary Giovanni Antonio Cavazzi da Montecuccolo (1621–1678). Another Capuchin missionary, Girolamo Merolla da Sorrento, stated that in Angola: 'Here is also the unicorn, called by the Congolans abada, whose medicinal virtue, being sufficiently known, needs not to be taken notice of. These unicorns are very different from those commonly mentioned by authors; and, if you will believe what I have heard say, there are none of that sort now to be found' (*Breve* quoted and trans. in Pinkerton, *Gen. Col.*, 211). A story attributed to a Portuguese man who had spent some time in Abyssinia is quoted by Father Balthazar Tellez (1596–1675), who himself had never been to Abyssinia. He distinguished the *abada* from the unicorn proper, principally on account of its having two horns, quite contrary to expectations: 'The *abada* has two crooked horns, which are not so sovereign, although they will serve as antidotes against poison' (*Travels*). See also **Abath**. (Gould, *Myth. Mon.*, 347; Reade, *Savage*, 372–3.)

ABAIA

In the mythology of Melanesia, an eel with god-like powers who tries to destroy humankind by causing a catastrophic flood: 'One day a man discovered a lake in which were many fish; and at the bottom of the lake lived a magic eel, but the man knew it not. He caught many fish and returned the next day with the people of his village whom he had told of his discovery;

and they also were very successful, while one woman even laid hold of the great eel, Abaia, who dwelt in the depths of the lake, though he escaped her. Now Abaia was angry that his fish had been caught and that he himself had been seized, so he caused a great rain to fall that night, and the waters of the lake also rose, and all the people were drowned except an old woman who had not eaten of the fish and who saved herself in a tree.' (Dixon, *Ocean. Myth.*, 120.)

ABATH

The female African **Unicorn**: in the Strait of Malacca in 1592 on his voyage to the East Indies, the Elizabethan privateer Sir James Lancaster sent commodities to the King of Junsaloam 'to barter for Ambergriese and for the hornes of the Abath, whereof the king only hath the traffique in his hands. Now this Abath is a beast which hath one horn onely in her forehead, and is thought to be the female Unicorne, and is highly esteemed of all the Moores in these parts as a most soveraigne remedie against poyson'. It is usually interpreted as the rhinoceros. (Shepard, *Lore*, 218.)

ABOMINABLE SNOWMAN, SEE YETI

ACHLIS

A species of jointless elk mentioned by the Roman writer Pliny the Elder in the first century CE, alongside the normally jointed *alces*. In other editions of his *Natural History* the word *machlis* is also given, as in the first English translation from 1601: 'A certaine beast, called the Alce, very like to an horse, but that his eares are longer; and his necke likewise with two markes, which distinguish them asunder. Moreover, in the Island Scandinavia, there is a beast called Machlis, not much unlike to the Alce abovenamed: common he is there, and much talk we have heard of him, howbeit in these parts hee was never seene. Hee resembleth, I say, the Alce, but that hee hath neither joint in the hough, nor pasternes in his hind-legs: and therefore hee never lieth downe, but sleepeth leaning to a tree. And therefore the hunters that lie in await for these beasts, cut downe the tree whiles they are asleepe, and so take them: otherwise they should never bee taken, so swift of foot they are, that it is wonderfull. Their upper lip is exceeding great, and therefore as they grase and feed, they goe retrograde, least if they were passant forward, they should double that lip under their muzzle.' No one has been able to adequately explain what Pliny meant or where he got this word. Brooks ('Nail of the Great Beast', 317–21) ingeniously connected old folklore associated with the elk that once it has fallen it cannot get up again because, or in addition to, its suffering from falling sickness to the word *achlys*, from the Greek, meaning the 'mist which comes over the eyes of the dying or swooning, gloom, darkness'; and compares the explanation of the German *elend* given by Jacob Grimm that it can mean both 'elk' and 'epilepsy'; *machlis* was simply a copyist's error. The zoological name for the European elk is, after Pliny, *Alces alces*, known in North America and older literature as *Alces machlis*. The words 'Alces Machlis', said to mean 'large wild beast' and 'leader' were included on the emblem of the Moose Legion degree of the American Freemasonic organisation the Loyal Order of Moose (part of 'Moose International') up until 1992.

Adar Llwch Gwin

The Welsh **Griffin** (*griffwn*), from *adar*, 'birds' (sing. *aderyn*), *llwch*, meaning both 'dust' and 'lake', and *gwin*, 'wine' (Richards, *Antiquæ*, 5, 247, 296); hence, 'birds of the wine lake'. They were three marvellous birds of Drudwas ab Tryffin: he sent them to kill the first person to appear at a certain spot, having challenged King Arthur to appear there; but his wife, who delayed Arthur and Drudwas, curious to see what had become of his victim, was the first to arrive and consequently torn to pieces by his birds. The story dates to a letter of Robert Vaughan, dated 1655. (Guest, *Mabinogion*, 270.)

Adar Rhiannon

Welsh, the 'birds of Rhiannon': three birds who sang so sweetly that the knights listening to them stood enchanted for either seven or eighty years, depending on the tale. Their singing sounded distant, although the birds themselves were nearby. In another version, a man called Shon ap Shenkin comes upon them one summer morning and sits down under a tree to listen to them. When he rises the young tree has grown old and withered. Returning home he finds an old man on his doorstep, the new owner, and his own mother and father whom he had left but a moment ago, long gone – the old man is his nephew; and as he realises this, Shon crumbles into dust. (Sikes, *British Goblins*, ch. VII.)

Afanc

Also *Addanc*, the monster of Llyn yr Afanc, 'the Afanc's Pool', on the river Conwy in Wales, although other locations are given, including Llyn Llion. It was supposed to have been lured from the pool by a beautiful maiden and then chained whilst it slumbered on her bosom. This version and the association with Llyn yr Afanc can be traced back to a letter of Edward Llwyd, dated 1693. The creature itself dates from the medieval *Mabinogion*: the 'Addanc' sequesters himself in a cave with a stone pillar set before it, he sees everyone who approaches, though none see him, as he hides behind the pillar and slays them with poisoned darts; Peredur (Percival) sets out to fight the Addanc, but a fair lady he encounters on the way gives him a magic stone with which he can overcome the beast in return for a pledge of his undying love towards her (Guest, *Mabinogion*, 107–9). Other versions include the monster being dragged from the lake by Hu Gadarn and his large horned oxen; or by King Arthur on his destrier, or war-horse. The monster has been variously interpreted as a crocodile or a beaver, but the earlier tales contain no description, save for its strength and attraction to comely damsels. (Rhys, *Celtic Folklore*, 130–2.)

AHÄST, SEE BÄCKAHÄST

AHUIZOTL

In Mexican folklore, the Ahuizotl was 'an unheard-of animal' described by the Spanish Franciscan Bernardino de Sahagún in the sixteenth century: 'Its size is that of a small dog; its hair is very slippery and short, it has small pointed ears, and its body is black and smooth. It has hands and feet like a monkey, and a long tail at the extremity of which there is what is like a human hand'. It lived in water and would use this hand to pull the unwary into the depths. Some days later the victim's body would be found 'without eyes, without teeth, and without nails, for all these were taken from him by the Ahuizotl. The body itself exhibits no wounds, but is all covered with bruises or livid spots' (Nuttal, 'Note', 123). Ahuizotl was also the name of an Aztec king.

AJATAR

Plural, in the Finnish translation of the Bible, the word is used in Leviticus (17:7) for 'the hairy ones'; in English translations the words 'devils', 'he-goats' and 'satyrs' are used. (Abercromby, 'Magic Songs', 44.)

AKHEKH

Also *Axex*, a fabulous beast of Ancient Egypt. It has the body of a winged antelope with a bird's head crowned with three uraei; in appearance somewhat like the **Griffin**. It is associated with the god **Set** and therefore a symbol of darkness. (Budge, *Gods*, 247.)

ALCE

Also *Alice*, in heraldry, the male **Griffin**. (Elvin, *Dict.*, 4.)

ALERION

Also *Avalerion*, the king of the birds, according to Pierre de Beauvais (*Bestiaire*), writing sometime before 1218 CE. It is the colour of fire, larger than an eagle, with wings of razor sharpness. Only one pair exists. When the female reaches the age of sixty she lays two eggs that take sixty days to hatch. Once this happens, the parents fly to the sea and dive in, drowning themselves, and the chicks are raised by other birds. Pliny the Elder (*Nat. Hist.*, 10.22) said that only one pair of ravens was to be found around Cranon in Thessally in Greece, because the parents flew away as soon as their young were old enough to look after themselves. In heraldry the alerion is usually depicted as a bird with no beak or feet, as in the old coat of arms of Alsace-Lorraine, for example, which is itself derived from the ancient noble House of Lorraine.

ALIEN BIG CAT

Term used for various alleged sightings of large cat species in places without historical populations of such species, hence 'alien'. They are usually described as black in colour, with reports from across Europe, including the 'British Big Cat', such as the Beast of Bodmin, the Nottingham Lion and the Surrey Puma. Animal attacks and killings have been attributed to them, but as such no specimens have been caught, except one female puma in the Highlands of Scotland in 1980. (Eberhart, *Myst. Creat.*, I, 42–5, 100–3.)

ALLOCAMELUS

The ass-camel described by Conrad Gessner (*Hist. Anim.*) in the sixteenth century. It is also found in heraldry (Elvin, *Dict.*), although solely in the crest of the East Land Company, incorporated in 1579. It was already identified as the llama in the eighteenth century (Buffon, *Nat. Hist.*, 275).

ALPHYN

Also a composite beast with the forelegs of an eagle, the hind-legs and head of a lion with tall ears and a long knotted tail. It appears in English heraldic use from the late fifteenth century. It was at first depicted with cloven hooves and a straight tufted tail around 1470, but by the sixteenth century had assumed its now standard form. The word, as *alfyne*, was used in Sir Thomas Malory's *Morte d'Arthur* (1485) to mean 'lubberly fellow (equivalent to *elvish*); a sluggard' (Wright, *Dict. Ob.*, 51). That aside, the word is usually connected with the Middle English *alfin*, the name given to the bishop in chess, as in William Caxton's *Game and Playe of the Chesse* (1474), which was taken from Old French, itself derived from the Arabic for 'elephant', *al-fil*. However, the

alphyn could never be mistaken for an elephant, an animal; what is more, that is already attested in heraldry, and although potentially elvish in nature could hardly be thought lazy. Another origin has been suggested by Williams, deriving it from the hypothetical Irish word *anfaill, which he relates to *enfild as the origin of the **Enfield**. The alphyn is the badge of the Lords de la Warr, although nobody can say why that is. (Williams, 'Beasts and Banners', 69–70.)

Alphyn

ALU

One of the six chief demons of Sumerian mythology, but also the 'bull of heaven'. Its early representation is of a demon that hides in dark places, ruins and abandoned buildings. It waits to attack passers-by, to 'envelop him as with a garment'; it prowls the darkened streets, and torments the night hours, bringing nightmares and attempting to smother sleepers, causing night-paralysis. In this aspect it is described as having no mouth, limbs or ears, being something between a human and a devil in form. At other times we read of it as a storm-demon in the shape of a bull, like Gallu, another of the six demons. (Thompson, *Devils*, xxiii–xxvi, xxxv; Mackenzie, *Myth. Bab.*, 65, 68–9.)

AMMUT

Also *Ammit*, in Ancient Egyptian mythology, the 'devourer of the dead': a female demon with the head of a crocodile on a body composed of the front half of a lion and the rear half of a hippopotamus. She waited beside the scales where the hearts of the dead were weighed and devoured those whose evil lives had made them heavier than the feather of Maat. (Shaw and Nicholson, *Dict. Anc. Eg.*, 30.)

AMPHISBAENA

A type of fantastic snake with a head at each end of its body. Lucan mentioned 'dread Amphisbaena with his double head' in the first century CE (*Phars.*, 9.843); it was more fully described by Pliny the Elder: 'The amphisbaena has a twin head, that is one at the tail-end as well, as though it were not enough for poison to be poured out of one mouth' (*Nat. Hist.*, 8.35). By the seventh century CE, Isidore of Seville (*Etym.*, 12.4.20) was able to add a few more spurious attributes: 'named because he has two heads, one in the normal place, the other on its tail. The circular course of its body flows from each head. Only this one ventures into the cold, advancing first of all snakes [...] Its eyes shine like lamps.'

ANCHU, SEE ONCHÚ

ANIMALIA PARADOXA

'Contrary Animals': in the first edition of his *Systema Naturae* published in 1735, Carolus Linnaeus included a number of animals (*animalia*) under the heading of *Paradoxa*. These were, in the order given: **Hydra**, with reference to the 'Hydrae Apocalypticae' of the Book of Revelation (see **Beast of the Apocalypse**); **Rana-Piscis**; **Monoceros**; Pelecanus (pelican), which had become a fabulous bird in Christian legend and the medieval bestiaries; Satyrus (see **Satyr**); Borometz s. Agnus Scythicus, the **Vegetable Lamb of Tartary**; **Phoenix**; Bernicla s. Anser Scoticus and Concha Anatifera (see **Barnacle Goose**); Draco (see **Dragon**), which he described as having a serpentine body, two feet and two wings like those of a bat but identified as an artifically manipulated lizard or ray (see **Jenny Haniver**); and Automa Mortis, the deathwatch beetle, which, although a real insect (*Xestobium rufovillosum*), has the folk reputation as a harbinger of death. In the second edition of 1740, Linnaeus included several more creatures under this heading: Manticora (see **Manticore**); Antilope (sic); **Lamia**; and **Siren**. He did not specifically include the **Kraken** in his taxonomy as is sometimes thought: this seems to have arisen from a misreading of a footnote in an article published in *Blackwood's Magazine* in 1818 (W., 'Remarks', 646).

ANT

There are several species of impossible ant: for the ant-lion, see **Formicoleon**; for the giant ant, see **Myrmex Indikos**; for the ant in the Middle Ages, see **Pismire**; for the art in heraldry, see **Emmet**.

ANTELOPE HODGSONII

The Himalayan or Tibetan **Unicorn**, called *serou* in Tibetan, also *tchirou* in southern Tibetan dialect; *kere* in Mongolian; *tou-kio-chieou* in Chinese. The French traveller, Évariste Régis Huc (1813–1860), commonly known as the Abbé Huc, reported that 'The unicorn, which has long been regarded as a fabulous creature, really exists in Thibet. You find it frequently represented in the sculptures and paintings of the Buddhic temples. Even in China, you often see it in the landscapes that ornament the inns of the northern provinces' (*Travels*, II, 267). A certain Mr Hodgson, resident in Nepal, managed to secure a specimen of the skin and horn of a unicorn reputed to have once graced the menagerie of the Rajah of Nepal. It had been brought from the province of Tsang in southern Tibet where the aimals are found in herds. It has the reputation of being 'extremely fierce', although 'they do not let any one approach them, and flee at the least noise. If you attack them, they resist courageously'. Its description is specific: 'The form of the tchirou is graceful, like that of all the other animals of the antelope tribe, and it has likewise the incomparable eyes of the animals of that species; its colour is reddish, like that of the fawn in the upper parts of the body, and white below. Its distinctive features are, first a black horn, long and pointed, with three slight curvatures, and circular annulations towards the base; these annulations are more prominent in front than behind; there are two tufts of hair which project from the exterior of each nostril, and much down round the nose and mouth, which gives the animal's head a heavy appearance. The hair of the tchirou is rough, and seems hollow, like that of all the animals north of the Himalaya that Mr. Hodgson had the opportunity of examining. The hair is about five centimeters long, and so thick that it seems to the touch a solid mass' (Huc, *Travels*, II, 269). A certain Doctor Abel proposed the scientific name *Antelope Hodgsonii* in honour of Hodgson's discovery. In a footnote to this, Huc's translator, William Hazlitt, offers the explanation that this animal is 'the oryx-capra of the ancients [...] still found in the deserts of Upper Nubia, where it is called Ariel' (see **Oryx**), which should be differentiated from the unicorn described in the Bible and by Pliny (*Nat. Hist.*).

ANUBIS

Also *Anpu*, the jackal-headed god of the dead in Ancient Egyptian mythology, so named 'being thought to watch and guard the Gods, as dogs do mankind' (Plutarch's 'Mythological History of Isis and Osiris', XIV, in Budge, *Gods*, 189). According to some, he was the son of Set. He was symbolised by the jackal because the jackal, attracted by the smell of decomposition, might be seen prowling the cemeteries. (Budge, *Gods*, 261; Shaw and Nicholson, *Dict. Anc. Eg.*, 34–5.)

ANZU, SEE ZU BIRD

APEP

Also *Apophis*, a great Serpent representing evil in Ancient Egyptian mythology. A creature of **Set**; the enemy of **Horus**, Ra and Osiris. It wages war on gods and men, and sends forth serpents to destroy them. (Budge, *Gods*, 377; Shaw and Nicholson, *Dict. Anc. Eg.*, 36.)

APIS

The sacred bull of the Ancient Egyptians, seen as the herald or physical manifestation of the god Ptah, although observers, such as Pliny (*Nat. Hist.*, 8.46), believed that the bull or ox was itself worshipped as a god. Herodotus recorded the belief that the Apis was born of a lightning flash and could be distinguished by the white spot on its forehead (it had a black hide), the vulture shape on its back, the scarab form under its tongue and the double hairs on its tail. (Shaw and Nicholson, *Dict. Anc. Eg.*, 35–6.)

ASPIDES

A semi-legendary species of **Serpent**. Pliny the Elder (*Nat. Hist.*, 8.23) described this animal in the first century CE: 'The Aspides swell about the necke when they purpose to sting: and no remedie is there for them that are stung or bitten by them, unlesse the parts that are wounded, bee cut off presently. This pestilent creature, as venomous as hee is, hath one point yet of understanding, or affection rather: you shal not see them wandering abroad but two and two together, the male and female, as if they were yoked together; and unneth, or not at all, can they live alone without their mate: so that if the one of them bee killed, it is incredible how the other seeketh to bee revenged. It pursueth the murderer, it knoweth him againe amongst a number of people, be they never so many: him it courseth, and laieth for his life: notwithstanding what difficulties soever, it breaketh through all, be it never so farre thither, and nothing may impeach this revenging humor, unlesse some river be betweene to keepe it backe, or that the partie make speed and escape away in great hast.' The reference to swelling about the neck may be a distorted impression of the cobra fanning out its hood before striking.

ASPIDOCHELONE

Also *fastitocalon*, a giant fish found in medieval bestiaries derived from the earlier Greek work of allegorical natural history known under the name of its Latin translations as the *Physiologus*: 'one among the race of fish, | The great asp-turtle. Men who sail the sea | Often unwillingly encounter him, | Dread preyer on mankind. His name we know, | The ocean-swimmer, Fastitocalon. | Dun, like rough stone in colour, as he floats | He seems a heaving bank of reedy grass | Along the shore, with rolling dunes behind, | So that sea-wanderers deem their gaze has found | An island.

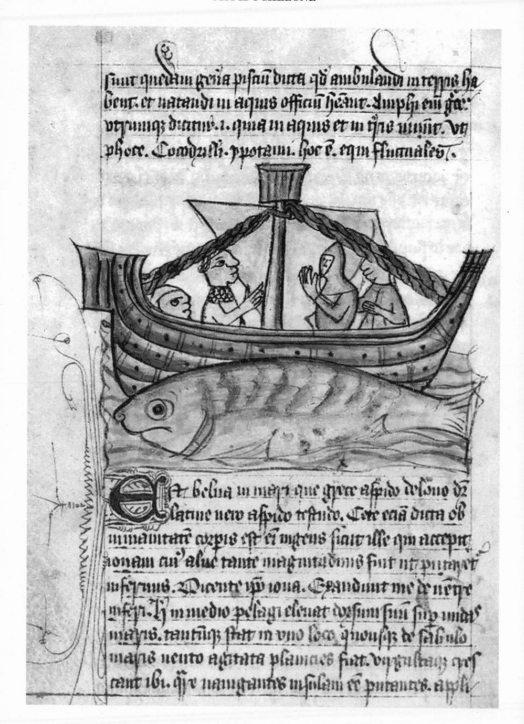

siunt quedam gria psau dicta qd ambulandi in teris ha
bent et natandi in aquis officiu habent. Ampsin eu gra
vtriusq dicatur .i. quia in aquis et in tie uiuit. Vt
phoce. Corodzilli. ptotam. hoc e. eqm fluuiales.

At belua in mari que grece aspido dosmo dr
latine vero aspido testudo. Cete etia dicta ob
inmanitate corpis est ei ugteus siaut ille qm accepit
ionam cui aluc tante magnitudonis fuit ut putaret
inferuus. Dicente ipo iona. Exaudiut me de uentre
inferni. Hi in medio pelagi eleuat dosum suu sup undas
mariis. tantuq stat in uno loco quouisq de sabulo
maris uento agitata psamates fiat. Vngulaiq cres
caunt ibi. q̃v nauigantes insolam ee putantes. apsi

Boldly then their high-prowed ships |
They moor with cables to that shore, a
land | That is no land. Still floating on
the waves' (Cook and Pitman, *Old
Eng. Phys.*, 13–14). In the Latin versions
it was also known as the *aspidochelone*
(or *aspidocalon*), from Greek *aspis*,
'shield', and *chelone*, 'turtle' – hence the
'asp-turtle' in the quotation – because
its back, when exposed above water,
was thought to resemble the shell of a
huge turtle; the Old English *fasti-
tocalon* is thought to be a scribal error.
Following a common theme, the
sailors disembark upon the strange
'island' and start a fire, whereupon the
monster is roused and dives into the
depths, carrying sailors and ships with
it: 'such is the way of demons, the
wont of devils: they spend their lives
outwitting men by their secret power'
(ibid.). Another trait was ascribed to
the monster: when seeking food it
would open its maw to vent 'a ravishing
perfume' that draws other fish to it,
swimming down into its belly. This
power was also attributed to the
Kraken. For sailors mistaking giant sea
creatures for islands, see also **Island
Fish**, **Jasconius** and **Pristes**.

Aspis (Thirteenth Century)

ASPIS

A type of fantastic snake (or snakes)
described by Isidore of Seville (*Etym.*,
12.4.12): 'Asp is named aspis because
it injects and sprinkles, *spargit*, poisons
with a bite. Ἰός is poison in Greek,
whence aspis, because it kills with a
poisoned bite. There are various kinds
and species, and different ways of
killing. It is said that the asp begins to
allow a sorcerer to call it out of its hole
with certain chants. But when it does not
wish to come out, it presses one ear to
the ground, and covers the other with its
tail and refuses to listen. Thus not
hearing the magic words, it does not
come out to the sorcerer.' The source of
the story seems to be Augustine of Hippo
in the fifth century CE (*Sermo* 316:2).

AUGHISKY

The Irish **Water-Horse**, equivalent to
the Scottish **Each-Uisge**. Its distribution
is prominent in Munster and Connaught,
where most lakes are said to have their
aughisky. It has been suggested that the
idea comes from the habit of the wind
whipping up peculiar waves that take on
a spectral appearance in the gloaming.
(Kinahan, 'Aughisky', 57–63.)

AVALERION, SEE ALERION

AZI DAHAK

Also *Azhi Dahaka*, *Azdahak*, *Zahhak*,
an ancient Iranian **Dragon**, from
Avestan *azi*, meaning 'serpent, dragon',

and the pejorative *dahaka*, hence the 'evil dragon'; probably the same as the earlier Indo-Iranian Ahih, the evil serpent defeated by Indra in the Vedas. It was a formulaic description of the monster to say that it had three mouths, three heads, six eyes and a thousand ears, although it was also referred to as a human, especially in later writings. It carried off the daughters of Yima and, after a reign of one thousand years, was enchained by Thraetona. On the Last Day it will break free and be finally defeated by Sama Keresaspa. In the *Shahnameh of Firdousi*, Dahaka is a young man who makes a pact with the Evil One, Iblis; as a sign of this, two serpents grow out from his shoulders. He is connected with Deioces, the King of the Medes, mentioned by Herodotus. (Ananikian, 'Armenia', 799–800; Sheldon, 'Herod.', 175, 178.)

B

BÄCKAHÄST

Scandinavian **Water-Horse** known variously as *bäckahäst*, *ahäst*, *dammhäst*, *sjöhästen* and *vattenhäst* (Swedish). Under the heading of 'Dam-Horse', Thorpe (*North. Myth.*, 208) recorded the following story. Some farmers' children from the village of Hirschholm near Copenhagen in Denmark were playing by Agersø (an island) when a large white horse – a dam-horse – sprang up from the waters and galloped to and fro. The boys all ran after it and one managed to climb on its back. As he did so the horse took off towards the sea with every intention of diving into it. In alarm the boy cried out 'Lord Jesus' cross! I never saw a larger horse!' At this it vanished and

Bäckahäst (*c*.1900)

sent him tumbling to the ground. Swedish folktales often involve several children mounting the horse, which miraculously elongates to accommodate them. To make matters worse the children find themselves stuck to the beast until one of them, generally the youngest, shouts out something that breaks the spell. This ejaculation is usually something Christian, as in Thorpe's example, or is the creature's own name, or something approximating it, the hearing of which causes it fright (the Rumpelstiltskin effect). In other folk tales, the water-horse is caught and put to work, usually ploughing the fields, before some incident allows it to escape and sometimes destroy its captor (Almqvist, 'Waterhorse', 107–20). A Danish equivalent is *Den lange hest*. See also **Kelpie**, **Shoopiltee**.

BAGWYN

A fabulous beast seen in European heraldry resembling the heraldic antelope, but with the tail of a horse and long backwards-curving goat's horns. A bagwyn may be found supporting of the arms of Carey, Lord Hundson, in Westminster Abbey, London. (Vinycomb, *Fict. Sym.*, 216.)

BALAENA

Plural *Balaenae*, huge, hairy fish that could spout rain storms. Pliny (*Nat. Hist.*, 9.3) introduces us to this giant sea animal: 'The Indian sea breedeth the most and the biggest fishes that are: among which, the Whales and Whirlepooles called Balænæ, take up in length as much as foure acres or arpens of land.' Herman Melville quoted this line in his ultimate whaling adventure *Moby-Dick* (1851). Elsewhere Pliny (9.6) writes: 'Balænæ have a certaine mouth or great hole in their forehead, and therefore as they swim aflote aloft on the water, they send up on high (as it were) with a mightie strong breath a great quantitie of water when they list, like stormes of raine.' He also thought that it had hair (9.13), although what he meant was that it was a mammal before this terminology had been introduced. Linnaeus named a genus of whales *Balaena* in 1758; this initially included the right whales, but now only comprises a single species, the bowhead whale (*Balaena mysticetus*) found in Arctic waters.

Balaena ((Thirteenth Century)

BARGHEST

Is it a black dog, a white cat or a headless man? 'The most dramatic and awesome of all the boggarts is the north-country Barghest' (Wright, *Rust. Sp.*, 193). Sir Walter Scott (*Letters*, 95) derives the name from *Bhar-geist* and argues that it is 'a deity, as the name implies, of Teutonic descent': *Bahre*, meaning 'bier', and *Geist*, 'spirit, ghost'. Other suggestions include similar derivations from *bam-ghaist* and *bier-ghaist*; or even from its habit of sitting on the top bar of the gate or fence. As to its exact form, Wright informs us that 'Sometimes the Barghest takes the shape of a large dog, donkey, pig, or calf; sometimes only its terrifying shrieks are heard, as it passes by at midnight, boding death to any one who happens to hear the sound.' Henderson had a personal report from a friend that Glassensikes near Darlington was 'haunted by a Barguest [sic.], which assumes at will the form of a headless man (who disappears in flame), a headless lady, a white cat, rabbit, or dog, or a black dog'. Other accounts placed barghests 'in a most uncannie looking Glen' near Throstlenest between Darlington and Houghton, and at Oxwells, a spring between Wreghorn and Headingly Hill outside Leeds. Here, 'On the death of any person of local importance in the neighbourhood, the creature would come forth, a large black dog with flaming eyes as big as saucers, followed by all the dogs of the place howling and barking. If any one came in its way the Barguest would strike out with its paw and inflict on man or beast a wound which would never heal. My informant, a Yorkshire gentleman, lately deceased, said he perfectly remembered the terror he experienced when a child at beholding this procession before the death of a certain Squire Wade, of New Grange' (Henderson, *Notes*, 274–5). 'To roar like a Barghest' was once a popular expression.

BARNACLE GOOSE

The barnacle goose (*Branta leucopsis*) is a perfectly possible sort of goose, but it has some quite impossible folklore connected with it. In the twelfth century, Giraldus Cambrensis wrote: 'There are likewise here many birds called barnacles, which nature produces in a wonderful manner, out of her ordinary course. They resemble the marsh-geese, but are smaller. Being at first gummy excrescences from pine-beams floating on the waters, and then enclosed in shells to secure their free growth, they hang by their beaks, like seaweeds attached to the timber. Being in process of time well covered with feathers, they either fall into the water or take their flight in the free air, their nourishment and growth being supplied, while they are bred in this very unaccountable and curious manner, from the juices of the wood in the sea-water. I have often seen with my own eyes more than a thousand minute embryos of birds of this species on the seashore, hanging from one piece of timber, covered with shells, and already formed. No eggs are laid by these birds after copulation, as is the case with birds in general; the hen never sits on eggs in order to hatch them; in no corner of the world are they seen either to pair, or build nests' (*Topographica Hiberniae* (1187) published as Cambrensis, *Hist. Works*, 34). This curious story was taken up by some 'bishops and men of religion' as an excuse to eat barnacle geese 'on fasting days, as not being flesh, because they are not born of flesh'. Giraldus repudiated this practice: 'But these men are curiously drawn into error. For, if any one had eaten part of the thigh of our first parent, which was really flesh, although not born of flesh, I should think him not guiltless of having eaten flesh.' Carolus Linnaeus included the barnacle goose under the names *Bernicla s. Anser Scoticus* and *Concha Annatifera* as one of the **Animalia Paradoxa** in the 1740 edition of his *Systema Naturae* (66).

BASILISK

From the Greek βασιλίσκος (*basilískos*), meaning 'little king'. First described by the Greek poet Nicander of Colophon (*Theriaca*, 396) in the second century BCE: the basilisk is the king of serpents, not on account of its size (it is only 23 cm (9 in) long), but on account of the fear it inspires in all other animals because of its extreme poisonousness; its victims cannot be handled due to the power of the poison within them. Lucan tells the story of a soldier called Murrus who runs a basilisk through with his lance: 'Swift through the weapon ran | The poison to his hand:

The Medieval Basilisk (Thirteenth Century)

he draws his sword | And severs arm and shoulder at a blow: | Then gazed secure upon his severed hand | Which perished as he looked. So had'st thou died, | And such had been thy fate!' (*Phars.*, book 9, ll 970–975). Pliny the Elder gave a detailed account in his *Naturalis Historia* (8.21): 'the serpent called a Basiliske: bred it is in the province Cyrenaica, and is not above twelve fingers-breadth long: a white spot like a starre it carrieth on the head, and setteth it out like a coronet or diademe: if he but hisse once, no other serpents dare come neere: he creepeth not winding and crawling by as other serpents doe, with one part of the bodie driving the other forward, but goeth upright and aloft from the ground with the one halfe part of his bodie: he killeth all trees and shrubs not only that he toucheth, but that he doth breath upon also: as for grasse and hearbs, those hee sindgeth and burneth up, yea and breaketh stones in sunder: so venimous and deadly is he. It is received for a truth, that one of them upon a time was killed with a launce by an horseman from his horseback, but the poison was so strong that went from his bodie along the staffe, as it killed both horse and man: and yet a sillie weazle hath a deadly power to kill this monstrous serpent, as pernicious as it is [for many kings have been desirous to see the experience thereof, and the manner how he is killed.] See how Nature hath delighted to match everything in the world with a concurrent. The manner is, to cast these weazles into their holes and cranies where they lye, (and easie

Voorzienighen raedt,   Boosheyt wederstaet,

Basilisk Attacked by a Weasel (Seventeenth Century)

they be to knowe, by the stinking sent of the place all about them) they are not so soone within, but they overcome them with their strong smell, but they die themselves withall; and so Nature for her pleasure hath the combat dispatched.' In the second century CE, the famous Roman physician Galen (*Ther. Pis.*, viii) thought it remarkable that so much should be known about a creature that killed on sight.

By the time Isidore of Seville got hold of it in the seventh century CE, the basilisk had shrunk to 15 cm (6 in), acquired more white spots and

could kill by its general smell and not just its breath. Isidore also added some more unexpected details: 'They are like scorpions in that they follow dry ground and when they come to water they make men frenzied and hydrophobic. The basilisk is also called *sibilus*, the hissing snake, because it kills with a hiss.' (*Etym.*, 12.4:6–9.) Bartholomaeus Anglicus vividly recounted all of this and more in his thirteenth-century CE work *De proprietatibus rerum*, book 18, but he had a new detail to add: 'His ashes be accounted good and profitable in working of Alchemy, and namely in turning and changing of metals.'

Aldrovandi's Basilisk (1640)

The reptile first described by Nicander has been identified as either (or both) of two cobra species: the Egyptian Cobra, *Naja haje*; or Black-Necked Spitting Cobra, *Naja nigricollis* (Alexander, 'Ev. Bas.', 170–81). Although able to grow over 2 m (6 ft 6 in) in length, making it considerably larger than the basilisk of Nicander and Pliny, the Egyptian Cobra matches most of the rest of the description: the weasel-like Egyptian mongoose is its predator; its venom remains dangerous to others even in the dead bodies of its victims; the flaring hood may be sufficiently crown-like to account for its regal reputation. Any of the African species of spitting cobra could also account for the basilisk's ability to kill at a distance. In addition, representations of the cobra in Ancient Egyptian art may explain characteristics such as the upright moving posture, crown derived from the solar disk frequently seen, and the small size from a literal interpretation of its depiction. Horapollo first identified the basilisk with the **Uraeus** in the fifth century CE (*Hieroglypthica*, i. I.).

Representations of the basilisk up to the seventeenth century were simply imaginative renderings of what the artist thought the monster would look like and there was considerable variation, with some examples looking more nearly like the **Cockatrice**. Thus in Johann Stabius' *De Labyrintho* (1510) we see a fierce cockatrice-type. By contrast, in Topsell's *Historie of Foure-Feeted Beastes* of 1607 we see a fairly unremarkable serpent wearing a crown and a mean look. The basilisk legend received apparently confirmatory evidence with the publication of the 'Basilicus ex raia effictus' in Aldrovandi's *Serpentum et Draconum* of 1640 – the frontispiece of the book is even decorated with basilisks (or dragons). As the Latin description indicates, this was a basilisk made out of a ray; evidence of a fraudulent **Jenny Haniver**, certainly, but a fraud that was widely perpetrated and exhibited under various names such as dragon and basilisk, as well as **Sea Eagle**, **Sea Bishop** and **Sea Monk**. Aldrovandi had shown a Jenny Haniver before in his book of 1613, but this was the first time he called one a basilisk. In fact, he called two of them basilisks: the first is a typical manipulated ray with a wonderfully developed head on an ovoid body; the other is more unusual in having a crown and eight legs, and a particularly surly expression. Francis Maximilian Misson saw a basilisk in Italy towards the close of the seventeenth century and described its manufacture: 'The invention is prettily contrived and has deceiv'd many; for they take a small Ray, and having turn'd it after a certain manner, and rais'd up the fins in the form of wings, they fit a little tongue to it, shap'd like a dart, and add claws and eyes of enamel, with other little knacks dextrously piec'd together; and this is the whole secrecy of making basilisks' (*New Voyage*, I, 134–5). (Gudger, 'Jenny Hanivers', 511–23.)

BAŠMU

The 'venomous snake' spawned by **Tiamat** in the Babylonian Creation Epic, *Enuma Elish*. After being defeated by the god Marduk (Ninurta), Bašmu became a beneficent demon used to guard doorways against evil influences. A clay figure would be buried at the threshold with an inscription such as 'go out evil, enter peace'. (Wiggerman, *Mes. Prot. Sp.*, 49.)

BEANNACH-NIMHE

A Scottish 'horned monster', or 'venomous horned beast'; in Socts Gaelic literally, 'horned poison'. Its blood had magical properties. There is a curious tale collected from Donald MacPhie on South Uist, concerning the hero Manus (Mhannis, or Magnus) and the Beannach-Nimhe. The son of the King of Light, called the White Gruagach, is dying. Manus asks him what the cause is and he replies that he should live as long as there are three trouts under a stone in the burn, and that Manus' wife has one of them now cooking over the fire. 'Is there anything in the world,' asked Manus, 'that would do thee good?' The White Gruagach replied that 'The King of the Great World has a *beannach-nimhe*, and if I could get his blood I would be as well as I ever was.' As they reach the house, the White

Gruagach finally expires; and Manus discovers that his ship – 'the speckled ship' – has been stolen. One of his foster brothers says that Brodram, son of the King of the Great World, has taken it. Manus goes to Brodram and asks him why he had taken his ship. 'He said that he had stolen her himself before, and that he had no right to her. He said that his father had a venomous horned (creature), and that while the Beannach Nimhe was alive that his father would be alive, and that if the Beannach Nimhe was slain that he would have the realm.' Accordingly, Manus goes with Brodram and they discover that 'the venomous horned beast was in a park'. They set loose a lion on it 'and he put his paw into the hollow of the throat of the venomous horned beast. The venomous horned beast fell dead, and the king fell dead within. Then Brodram was King over the Great World, and Manus got the blood, and he returned back, and with it he brought the White Gruagach to life.' ('The Lay of Magnus' in Campbell, *Pop. Tales*, III, 378–9.)

BEAST OF THE APOCALYPSE

This famous biblical monster from the Book of Revelation is, in fact, two beasts: the beast of the sea or abyss; and the beast 'out of the earth'. Both end up being thrown into a lake of fire and brimstone. The general consensus is that the beasts are allegories of the Roman Empire and the special number given to the beast – 666 – is interpreted as a code for Nero Caesar, Roman Emperor from 54 to 68 CE – Revelation was written in the latter

The Beast Out of the Earth (Thirteenth Century)

part of the first century CE. That there are two beasts is taken to mean, first the Roman Empire, second the religion of Rome, specifically the imperial cult – Nero claimed to be the solar-god Apollo and was worshipped as such. However, interpretations have varied. In the Middle Ages, Pope Innocent III, for example, argued that the beast out of the earth was the Islamic prophet Muhammed – as we also see in the *Master Bertram Apocalypse Altarpiece* from about 1400, now in the Victoria and Albert Museum in London. In some medieval depictions the monsters are given the additional faculty of vomiting frogs. Whilst the allegorical aspect of the beasts is clear, there is also an older mythological prototype underpining the Satanic majesty of the 'Beast Out of the Sea', that of the Babylonian sea-dragon **Tiamat** (Barton, 'Tiamat', 26–7; O'Hear, *Pict. Apoc.*, 131–54).

BEAST OUT OF THE SEA

This beast is first announced in Revelation 11:7 as coming out of the abyss, or hell: 'the beast that ascendeth out of the bottomless pit shall make war against them, and shall overcome them, and kill them'. By Revelation 13:1–10 this monster has become the beast 'out of the sea'. The supposed author of Revelation, John of Patmos, stands upon a beach and sees 'a beast rise up out of the sea'. It has seven heads with ten horns upon which it manages to balance ten crowns, with the additional distinction of having 'upon his heads the name of blasphemy', whatever that might be.

The Beast Out of the Sea (1805)

John described the monster as a leopard with the paws of a bear and the mouth of a lion. It takes its power directly from 'the dragon', i.e., the Devil. The beast shows off some self-healing powers and the people fall to worshipping it. The beast is also able to talk, 'speaking great things and blasphemies'. For forty-two months he rules the earth, waging war against the saints. An angel later explains to John in Revelation 17:7–18 the symbolic meaning of the beast: the seven heads are seven mountains, as well as seven kings – 'five are fallen, and one is, and the other is not yet come' – and the crowns are also kings 'which have received no kingdom as yet'; the water represents the people. When he later appears being ridden by the Whore of Babylon, his colour is described as scarlet. From the Middle Ages onwards, this beast began to be called the Antichrist.

BEAST OUT OF THE EARTH

In Revelation 13:11–18, John 'beheld another beast coming up out of the earth; and he had two horns like a lamb, and he spake as a dragon'. There is no other description of what shape he takes, although later artists usually gave him a human form, or made him entirely a lamb but able to stand upright, as in the so-called *Flemish Apocalypse* of *c*.1400 where a demonic looking lamb wears the habit of a Franciscan monk. He performs various marvels with the general intention of making sure that everyone worships the first beast, such as having them make an image of him and giving the infamous 'mark, or the name of the beast, or the number of his name'. It is at this point that John reveals the number to be 666, or 616 in some other versions. This beast is also described as the 'false prophet'.

BEAST OF THE CHARRED FORESTS

In Sutherland in Scotland, the disappearance of the ancient forests that once covered the regions is blamed upon 'a fierce and powerful monster, which roamed over the north of Scotland, breathing fire wheresoever he went. As proof of this, the more elderly inhabitants point yet to the charred stumps of pine-trees embedded in the peat-mosses. The entire populace fled for safety whenever the monster was reported to be stalking the land.' And so he came to be known among the people of Sutherland as the Beast of the Charred Forests. (MacGregor, *Peat-Fire Flame*, 83.)

BEAST OF GÉVAUDAN

'The Napoleon Bonapart of wolves', according to Robert Louis Stevenson (*Travels*, 42): a large wolf believed to be responsible for a series of attacks in the region of Gévaudan (Lozère) from 1764 to 1767. Some one hundred deaths were attributed to its attacks. The reign of terror finally came to an end when Jean Chastel shot a large animal on 19 June 1767. It was stuffed and sent to Paris to be examined by the famous naturalist the Comte de Buffon. The body was kept in the Museum d'Histoire Naturelle in Paris until 1819. (Eberhart, *Myst. Creat.*, I, 74–5.)

BEHEMOTH

A monster named in the Book of Job (40:15–24): 'Behold now Behemoth, which I made with thee; he eateth grass as an ox. Lo now, his strength is in his loins, and his force is in the navel of his belly. He moveth his tail like a cedar: the sinews of his stones are wrapped together. His bones are as strong pieces of brass; his bones are like bars of iron. He is the chief of the ways of God: he that made him can make his sword to approach unto him. Surely the mountains bring him forth food, where all the beasts of the field play. He lieth under the shady trees, in the covert of the reed, and fens. The shady trees cover him with their shadow; the willows of the brook compass him about. Behold, he drinketh up a river, and hasteth not: he trusteth that he can draw up Jordan into his mouth. He taketh it with his eyes: his nose pierceth through snares.' In the Old

Testament Behemoth is mentioned only in Job, significantly in the company of **Leviathan**; he also appears in the later Book of Enoch (1 Enoch 60:7–8) where Leviathan is the primordial force of the sea, **Ziz** of the sky and Behemoth of the land, living somewhere east of the Garden of Eden in an invisible desert. Behemoth has been variously identified as the elephant or hippopotamus.

Behemoth (1863)

BEITHIR

Scottish Gaelic (*beithir*, also *beathrach*; plural *beithrichean* and *beathraichean*), pronounced 'beir': a bear, a serpent, a wild animal, a thunderbolt, a strong gust of wind, or the Scottish **Dragon**; also *beithir-nimh*, 'venomous serpent', and *uile-bheist*, 'dragon'. Several dragons occur in the legends of the Celtic heroes. Finn fights the Winged Dragon of Sheil with two serpent heads ('Finn in the House of Blar-

Buie'). Alastir, son of the King of Ireland, fights the Great Fiery Dragon of the Seven Serpent Heads and of the Venomous Sting from the 'Gloomy Castle' ('The Bare-Stripping Hangman'). According to Carmichael (*Carm. Gad.*, II, 334–5), there were once giant snakes at large in Scotland: 'The serpent is now small and rare, though once large and numerous, in the Highlands. One was killed at Bailemonaidh, in Islay, in the early years of the century, measuring nine feet in length and eighteen inches in circumference. Much warm milk was abstracted every night from the milk-cot attached to the summer sheiling. After much searching, traces of milk were found leading to a grassy knoll in the neighbourhood. On the summit of the knoll a serpent lay coiled sunning itself in the summer sun and fast asleep. It immediately awoke, and, poising its head high in the air, hissed and lunged about in great fury. When shot, its enormously distended stomach was found to contain several twites, buntings, pipits, larks, and thrushes, and an incredible quantity of milk. Only a few years ago a larger serpent than this was killed in a turnip-field in Easter Ross. The presence of the reptile was indicated by the fear and anxiety displayed by a pair of well-trained horses working in the neighbourhood. Nothing could be seen, but the horses trembled violently, and, with nostrils distended and eyes staring, showed symptoms of great fear and could hardly be kept from running away from the men about them. When after some delay and difficulty the serpent was found and killed the horses quieted down, but for some days showed the effects of their fear.' What was known as a 'river dragon' was called *Croghall mor*. (Campbell, *Celt. Dragon*, passim; MacDougall, *Waifs*, 62, 98–9; MacDougall and Calder, *Folk Tales*, 95–8.)

BENNU

'I am the bennu bird which is in Annu, and I am the keeper of the volume of the book of things which are and of things which shall be' (*The Book of the Dead*, ch. 17, trans. Budge, *Egypt*, 282). The Ancient Egyptian bennu, also *benu*, was a symbolic representation of the sun, depicted in hieroglyphs as a heron, sometimes also as a heron standing upon a pyramid. The word was also used for the date palm as another symbol of rebirth because the palm was seen to continually regenerate. Just as the sun lives again after night, so the dead live again after death as the bennu. The bird figures in *The Book of the Dead*, dating from the New Kingdom period of Ancient Egypt, roughly from 1600 to 1200 BCE, firstly in chapter 17, then in 'The Chapter of Changing into a Bennu' (ibid., 339). The bennu is considered to be the prototype for the Ancient Greek **Phoenix**.

BIASD-NA-SCROGAIG

The Scottish **Unicorn**, called *beisd* or *biasd-na-scrogaig* (Skye), *buabhall* or *buabhul*; also *aon-adharcach*, *aon-bheannach*. As we read in Forbes (*Gaelic Names*, 224): 'This beast of the towering horn was said to be peculiar to Skye under the name "Biasd na sgrogaig", and indeed to the Outer Hebrides generally, having, as it is generally portrayed, one horn on the forehead, and dwelling in certain sea lochs (some accounts add long legs, clumsy and inelegant, tall and awkward). Now it is shrewdly surmised to be a narwhal strayed from the Arctic seas, and which is called in some places the "unicorn of the sea", having the horn shown in that animal. The unicorn is the right hand supporter of the MacGregor arms.'

BIGFOOT

The trail of the Bigfoot begins in 1869 when a hunter saw a pair of monkey-like animals about 150 cm (5 ft) in height near Orestimba Creek, California; but the name itself dates from 1958 when large footprints were found near Bluff Creek, California, and received their epithet from a local newspaper. Various reports describe it as a large primate or some sort of hairy human sub-species, with height estimates up to 275 cm (9 ft), and feet measured at 50 cm (20 in). Numerous theories have been advanced, although the misidentification of bears, especially when seen walking upright, and numerous hoaxes over the years would seem to account for the mystery; the debate, however, will continue for some time. Sasquatch is an anglicised form of the word used by the First Nations people of British Columbia for a similar creature. See also **Yahoo** and **Yeti**. (Eberhart, *Myst. Creat.*, I, 84–9; II, 495.)

BLÁ-GÓMA

The ugliest fish in the sea, according to Icelandic folklore. Davidson reports: 'this disgusting creature is said to have been a queen, who persecuted her stepdaughter in every conceivable way, and was thus transformed by way of punishment. The west-coast fishermen regard it with so much aversion that when they find they have caught one they will rather cut the line than take it on board' ('Folk-Lore', 329). Davidson identifies it as *Lophius piscatorious*, the scientific name for a type of monkfish, commonly called an angler, found in European waters. They can grow over 2 m (6 ft 6 in) long and certainly have a look that does not arouse affection.

BLACK DOG

Across the British Isles and Ireland, stories are told of a monstrous black dog. Its general habit is to haunt lonely byways and, if seen, is taken as an omen of impending death. Regional names include **Barghest** (North Country), **Black Shuck** (Norfolk), **Capelthwaite** (Westmorland/Yorkshire), **Gally-Trot** (Suffolk), Mauthe Doog or Moddey Dhoo (Isle of Man), Skriker and **Trash** (Lancashire); as well as simply the 'black dog' of some locality, such as the Black Dog of Kinlochbervie (Eskdale). As well as being supernatural, the naturally occurring black dog could also have supernatural effects: 'perfume made of the gall of a black dog, and his blood, besmeared on the posts and walls of the house, driveth out of the doors both devils and witches' (Scot, *Disc. Witch.*, 151–

2). (Dyer, *Ghost World*, 111; Seymour and Neligan, *True Irish*, 216ff.)

BLACK SHUCK

Also *Shuck Dog, Old Shuck*; a supernatural **Black Dog** of Norfolk, particularly, but also Essex, Suffolk and some parts of Cambridgeshire. It is described as a large dog, as big as a calf, with a shaggy black coat and huge yellow eyes, sometimes only one eye and occasionally headless. To meet it is always a portent of death. They say that if one afterwards examines the place where it was seen it will be found scorched and smelling of brimstone. (L'Estrange, *East. Count. Coll.*, 2; Hartland, *Eng. Fairy*, 237–8.)

BONASUS

Also *Bonnacon*, in an ancient land called Paeonia (nowadays Macedonia and parts of northern Greece and south-western Bulgaria), the Bonasus was a bull with a horse's mane, inward pointing horns and the unusual ability to squirt burning dung at his pursuers. According to Pliny the Elder 'There is (they say) a wild beast in Pæonia, which is called Bonasus, with a maine like an horse, otherwise resembling a bull: marie, his hornes bend so inward with their tips toward his head, that they serve him in no steed at all for fight, either to offend, or defend himselfe; and therefore, all the helpe that he hath, is in his good footmanship; and otherwhiles in his flight by dunging, which hee will squirt out from behind him three acres in length. This ordure of his is so strong and hot, that it burneth them that follow after him in chase, like fire, if haply they touch it' (*Nat. Hist.*, 8.15). Under the name Bonnacon, the creature appears in medieval bestiaries, such as the twelfth-century manuscript known as the 'Aberdeen Bestiary' (fol. 12r) and the thirteenth-century 'Rochester Bestiary'. The scientific name for the European bison is *Bison bonasus*.

Bonasus (Medieval)

BOOBRIE

A variation of the **Each-Uisge** or **Kelpie** and just as malevolent, recorded in the Scottish Highlands. It has the ability to take the shape of a horse, bull or bird. There is a legend that places the monster in Loch Freisa on the Isle of Mull. A tenant farmer and his son were ploughing, but the ground was so hard that they had to use four horses. Then one of the horses cast a shoe and was unable to continue. As they were nine miles from the nearest blacksmith it seemed that their work would suffer a long interruption.

So it was fortunate that they saw a masterless horse grazing by the side of the loch. They caught it easily enough and attached it to the plough team. The horse seemed to know the work and pulled uphill and down, but as the team came to the end of the furrow and the farmer tried to turn them, the new horse proved difficult. The farmer gave it a light stroke with the whip whereupon the animal uttered an earth-shaking cry, changed into a huge bird and flew off, taking the horseteam and plough with it. It gained some height and then dived into the loch, horses, plough and all. (Campbell, *Pop. Tales*, IV, 307–8; Howey, *Horse Magic*, 145–6.)

BRAG, SEE PICKTREE BRAG

BRAN

The name given to a **Wurrum** said to live in Lough Brin, County Kerry, Ireland: 'Near our fishing quarters in Kerry there are two such lakes, one the beautiful lake at the head of the Blackwater River, called Lough Brin, or Bran as he is now called, the dreadful wurrum which inhabits it. The man who minds the boats there speaks with awe of Bran; he tells me he has never seen him and hopes he never may' (Le Fanu, *Sev. Yrs*, 107). Others have claimed to have seen it: a twelve-year-old boy saw it in 1940, along with two other sightings that year; local farmer, Timothy O'Sullivan, saw two hug fins rise out of the water on 24 December 1954. See also **Piast**.

BUCKLAND'S NONDESCRIPT

So-called 'nondescripts' were a strange species of curiosity formerly exhibited in Britain in the nineteenth century. Francis (Frank) Trevelyan Buckland, Her Majesty's Inpsector of Salmon Fisheries, among other things, described several, such as 'The Embalmed Nondescript', actually the preserved body of the hirsute Julia Pastrana. His most important find was made in the shop of Mr Wareham, 'china curiosity-dealer', on the corner of St Martha's Court, Leicester Square, London. He described it as 'the most extraordinary-looking thing I ever beheld'. All Buckland could learn of its history was that Wareham had bought it from 'an old gentleman'. He was unable to examine the creature in the shop as it was deemed too valuable to be removed from its glass case. Buckland bought it, nonetheless, and took it back with him to make a thorough exploration: 'The Nondescript is about as big as a baby three months old, and, as a crusty bachelor friend of mine once said, "really very much like one". He has wings on the top of his shoulder like the old army aiguilettes, and there are claws on the tips and on the extreme ends of each wing: these wings are so artfully contrived that one would believe they could be opened out and unfurled like a bat's wing at any moment the creature that carried it wished to take a fly either for business or amusement. The arms are amazingly human-like, and look as though the dried skin had shrunk fast on to the bone; the legs also represent a similar appearance. The hands and feet are demon-like, and of a long, scraggy, merciless appearance, and each finger and toe is armed with a formidable-looking claw. The ribs project frightfully, as though the nondescript had lately been in reduced circumstances, and had been living for some time *à la malcontent*. The head is about as big as a very large apple. The ears project outward and downward, like those of an African elephant. The face is wrinkled and deformed; the nose like a pig's snout; the eyes like those of a codfish; the teeth exactly the same as those in the mermaid above described [i.e., those of a catfish] double rows in each jaw, with protruding fangs in front; and surmounting this hideous countenance, a rough shock of fine wool like hair, presenting the true prison convict crop, as though the Nondescript had been in trouble and had had "the key turned upon him"; and this I should think more than likely, for a more villanous-looking rascal I never beheld; a policeman would be justified in taking him up on suspicion alone.' Using a surgical exploring needle, Buckland was able to ascertain that the creature had no bones, but was made of a soft wood (cedar, he thought) over which papier mâché had been 'most artfully put on in wrinkles, and admirably coloured and shaded to give the appearance of the dried body of some creature that had once existed'. See also P.T. Barnum's FeeJee Mermaid (see **Mermaid**) and **Waterton's Nondescript**. (Buckland, *Curiosities*, 139–42.)

BUNYIP

A water-dwelling monster of Australia known to the Aborigines. It is 15 m (50 ft) long and has a snake-like head. It has also been described as being covered in large scales that overlap like armour plating with the long neck and head of a giraffe adorned with a flowing mane, and two short legs sporting four great talons. Another account dated 1855 describes it as half-horse, half alligator; or in 1865 as being larger than an elephant, shaped like a bullock with eyes like burning coals and tusks like those of the walrus; or with countless eyes and ears. In 1849 it was reported that a bunyip skull was on display at the Colonial Museum of Sydney. In 1872, a story was published in the *Wagga Advertiser* in which the author claimed to have seen one: 'There really is a Bunyip or Waa-wee, actually existing not far from us […] in the Midgeon Lagoon, sixteen miles north of Naraudera. I saw a creature coming through the water with tremendous rapidity. The animal was about half as long again as an ordinary retriever dog, the hair all over its body was jet black and shining, its

Bunyip (1890)

coat was very long' (Morris, *Austral English*, 66–7). It is supposed that these legends are based upon the alligator, but in light of the last story the seal has also been proposed. It is similar to the *Bunnyar*, a more terrible relative of the bunyip. See also **Mindi**. (Calvert, *Aborigines*, 38–9; Lloyd, *Thirty-Seven Years*, 466–7.)

C

CAILLEACH-UISGE

The Scottish **Siren** or water-witch, from the Gaelic: 'The *cailliach* is old and clad in weeds, but her voice is young, and she always sits so that the light is in the eyes of the beholder. She seems to him young also, and fair. She has two familiars in the form of seals, one black as the grave, and the other white as the shroud that is in the grave; and these sometimes upset a boat, if the sailor laughs at the water-witch's song. A man netted one of those seals, more than a hundred years ago, with his herring-trawl, and dragged it into the boat; but the other seal tore at the net so savagely, with its head and paws over the bows, that it was clear no net would long avail. The man heard them crying and screaming, and then talking low and muttering, like women in a frenzy. In his fear he cast the nets adrift, all but a small portion that was caught in the thwarts. Afterwards, in the portion, he found a tress of woman's hair. And that is just so: to the Stones be it said'. (Macleod, *Wind and Wave*, 81–2.)

CAIT SITH

In Celtic folklore, the fairy cat, also *Cat Sith*; Irish, *Cat Sidhe*. Usually black, often of an unusually large size and sometimes endowed with the power of speech, the fairy cat finds itself mixed up with tales of witches and devils. A black fairy cat was said to guard a treasure hidden in a hillfort in County Louth, Ireland. It could be lured from its post by killing a lamb at midnight and letting its blood run down from the fort and across a plank bridge over a stream. The cat would follow the blood trail and once over the stream would lose its magic powers, and so could be killed. The entrance to the cave would then open, revealing the treasure within. Fairy cats were believed to have their stronghold at the ancient tumulus of Carnagat, County Tyrone, said to be from *Carraig na geat*, and would rove the surrounding countryside stealing corn. An old rhyme from Scotland runs: 'The Cats have come upon us, | The Cats have come upon us, | The Cats have come upon us, | They have come upon us! | To break in upon us, | To lift the spoil, | To steal the kine, | To strike the steeds, | To strip the meads, | They have come upon us!' (Carmichael, *Carm. Gad.*, II, 362). Cats in general were regarded with suspicion. Sometimes it is believed that it is the witches who take the form of cats to pester their neighbours. A story from Skye illustrates the point. For years, a dairymaid was troubled by a cat that would sneak in and drink enormous amounts of milk. Once when it had drunk so much that it could hardly move, the dairymaid chopped off one of its paws. Afterwards, a woman who lived nearby was discovered to have lost an ear. The cat is also connected to other powers of darkness. In a tale known as 'The Demon Cat' a fishwife of Connemara, Ireland, is plagued by a huge black cat who eats all her best fish until she uses holy water on it and it burns away to nothing in a thick cloud of black smoke. There is a gruesome ritual recorded in the West Highlands called *Taghairm*, or 'Giving his Supper to the Devil': by means of roasting cats alive, the Devil can be made to appear and grant a wish, or answer a question. Three instances of this spell have been recorded: by Allan the Cattle-Lifter at *Dail-a-chait* ('the Cats' Field'), Lochaber; by Dun Lachland at Pennygown on Mull; and by members of the clan Quithen at *an Eaglais Bhreige* ('The Make-Believe Cave') on the east side of Skye. (Campbell, *Sup. High.*, 5, 304–11; MacGregor, *Peat-Fire Flame*, 267; Morris, 'Feat. Com.', 172; Wilde, *Anc. Leg.*, n.p.; Wulff, 'Carnagat', 41.)

CALADRIUS

Also *charadrius*, a small bird formerly believed to be able to cure jaundice by prolonged eye-contact with the afflicted person. It was first described by Plutarch writing in the first century CE

Caladrius (Thirteenth Century)

(*Symp.* 5.7): 'we know how often those who suffer from jaundice are healed by looking at the bird charadrius. This small animal seems to be endowed with such a nature and character, that it violently attracts to itself the disease, which slips out of the body of the sick man into its own, and draws off from his eyes as it were a stream of moisture'. Pliny (*Nat. Hist.*, 30.28(11)) had also heard of it, but called it *icterus* ('jaundice') and wondered if it were the same bird called **Galgulus**. The legend was taken up by most of the medieval bestiaries, generally under the name *caladrius*, where the bird was further described as being like a white seagull, although in English translations of Plutarch his *charadrius* is often given as plover, or golden oriole. In modern scientific taxonomy, the plover belongs to the genus *Charadrius*. (Druce, 'Caladrius', 381–416.)

CALDELIA

Also *Caldelion*, a Mediterranean **Sea Monster**: 'On sailing along the coast of Corsica and Sardinia, June 9th, we saw a sea monster, which appeared several times the same day, spouting water from its nose to a great height. It is called Caldelia, and is said to appear frequently before a storm. A storm came on Monday, which lasted four days'. (Smith, *Travels* (1792), quoted in Brand, *Pop. Antiq.*, 536.)

CALYDONIAN BOAR

Also *Caledonian*, in Greek mythology, a boar of great size and strength. Born of the **Crommyonian Sow**, it was sent by Artemis to punish Oeneus and his kingdom of Calydon by attacking the cattle and preventing the fields from being sown. Oeneus promised the boar's skin to the one who could kill it, and the noblest Greeks set out to hunt it, including the heroes Jason and Theseus: Meleager was the one to deal the fatal blow, but on receiving the skin gave it to Atlanta who had drawn first blood. (Apollodorus, *Library*, 1.8.)

CAMBRIDGE CENTAUR

A **Jenny Haniver** made in 1962 by Geoffrey Hopkins of what was, up until 1993, the Sub-Department of Veterinary Anatomy at Cambridge University (now submerged within the new Department of Physiology, Development and Neuroscience). It was a skeleton about 60 cm (24 in) high and intended to be the mascot for the Cambridge University Veterinary Society. The head and torso are that of a macaque monkey fixed onto the body of a small dog. (Bailey, *Conn.* 108; Dance, *Animal Fakes*, 113–14.)

CAMELOPARD

Full name, *Camelopardalis*, also *Nabis*, the 'savage sheep' or camel-panther (pard) of Africa. Pliny (*Nat. Hist.*, 8.18): 'called of the Æthyopians, the Nabis, necked like an horse, for legge and foot not unlike the boeufe, headed for all the world as a camell, beset with white spots upon a red ground, whereupon it taketh the name of Camelopardalus [sic.]: & the first time that it was seen at Rome, was in the games Circenses set out by Cæsar Dictatour [Julius Caesar]: since which time, hee commeth now and then to Rome, to be looked upon more for sight than for any wild nature that he hath: whereupon some have given her the name of a Savage sheepe.' According to the ancient view, the beast was the offspring of the camel and panther – the panther was originally termed *pard* (Latin, *pardus*); the leopard (*Panthera pardus*) was itself believed to be the offspring of a lion and a pard. It was, of course, the giraffe, which today has the scientific name of *Giraffa camelopardalis* (Linnaeus, *Systema*).

CAMPE

Also *Kampe*, from Ancient Greek, *kampos*, 'crooked': the she-**Dragon** guardian of hell. The earliest surviving reference comes from the second century CE, where she is the appointed guardian of the hundred-handed giants and cyclops who are imprisoned in Tartarus (Apollodorus, *Library*, 1.6). The most detailed and graphic description dates from the fifth century CE: 'A thousand crawlers from her viperish feet, spitting poison afar, were fanning Enyo to a flame, a mass of misshapen coils. Round her neck flowered fifty various heads of wild beasts: some roared with lion's heads like the grim face of the riddling **Sphinx**; others were spluttering foam from the tusks of wild boars; her countenance was the very image of **Scylla** with a marshalled regiment of thronging dogs' heads. Doubleshaped, she appeared a woman to the middle of her body, with clusters of poison-spitting serpents for hair. Her giant form, from the chest to the parting-point of the thighs, was covered all over with a bastard shape of hard sea monsters' scales. The claws of her wide-scattered hands were curved like a crooktalon sickle. From her neck over her terrible shoulders, with tail raised high over her throat, a scorpion with an icy sting sharp-whetted crawled and coiled upon itself. Such was manifold-shaped Campe as she rose writhing, and flew roaming about earth and air and briny deep, and flapping a couple of dusky wings, rousing tempests and arming gales, that blackwinged nymph of Tartaros: from her eyelids a flickering flame belched out far-travelling sparks' (Nonnos, *Dion.*, II, 18.238ff). She is killed by Zeus, who frees the giants in order to aid him in his war against Cronos.

CAPELTHWAITE

A supernatural animal of the old county of Westmorland and neighbouring parts of Yorkshire: 'He had the power of appearing in the form of any quadruped, but usually chose that of a large **Black Dog**'. Capelthwaite Barn in the parish of Beetham near Milnthorpe was said to be the home of one such creature, who even helped the farmer drive the sheep home, although he disliked the vicar. Capelthwaite Farm near Sedbergh in Yorkshire was also haunted by one and the stuffed skins of five calves were said to be kept there as a memorial to their strange birth under the influence of the capelthwaite. (Henderson, *Notes*, 275–6.)

CAPRIMULGUS

Latin for 'goat-sucker' (plural *caprimulgi*) from the Greek. A bird first described by Aristotle (*Hist. Anim.*, c.xxx): 'Flying upon the goats, it sucks them, whence it has its name. They say that when it has sucked the teat it becomes dry, and that the goat becomes blind. It is not sharp-sighted by day: but it sees by night.' Pliny (*Nat. Hist.*, 9.40): 'Caprimulgi are nocturnal thieves; for they cannot see by day. They enter the folds, and fly to the udders of the goats in order to suck the milk, from which injury the udder dies away, and blindness falls upon the goats which have been so sucked.' In 1544, William Turner (*Turner*, 49–50) described his search for the bird: 'When I was in Switzerland I saw an aged man, who fed his goats upon the mountains […] I asked him whether he knew a bird the size of a Merula, blind in the day-time, keen of sight at night, which in the dark is wont to suck goats' udders, so that afterwards the animals go blind. Now he replied that he himself had seen many in the Swiss mountains fourteen years before, that he had suffered many losses from those very birds; so that he had once had six she-goats blinded by Caprimulgi, but that one and all they now had flown away from Switzerland to Lower Germany, where nowadays they did not only steal the milk of she-goats, making them go blind, but killed the sheep besides. And on my asking the bird's name, he said it was called the Paphus, otherwise the Priest. But possibly that aged man was jesting with me.' The bird was believed to be the nightjar, but of course, the nightjar does not suck goats. Linaeus, however, adopted the name in his scientific classification of animals and hence the nightjar is known as several species of the family *Caprimulgidae*. The nightjar has also been identified as the **Night-Raven**. For another 'goat-sucker', see **Chupacabra**.

CAT, WINGED

A single specimen known as 'Thomas Bessy', on account of its sex being unknown, was advertised for show in London in the early 1960s. According to the story, sometime in the nineteenth century this cat had developed wings when young and was spotted by a circus owner, who requisitioned the animal. When the original owner learned that it was being exhibited for money, he instigated legal proceedings to have it returned. The court found in his favour and the cat was sent back, packed in a box with some food. It was dead on arrival: poisoned by the food, some said. The owner had it stuffed. The author Peter Dance tried, unsuccessfully, to purchase the animal. (Dance, *Animal Fakes*, 113.)

CATOBLEPES

Also *Catoblepas*. Pliny the Elder says that among 'the Hesperian Æthyopians' at the source of the river Nile, a place he calls Nigris, 'there keepeth a wild beast called Catoblepes, little of bodie otherwise, heavie also and slow in his limmes besides, but his head onely is so great that his bodie is hardly able to beare it; hee alwaies carrieth it downe toward the earth, for if hee did not so, he were able to kill all mankind: for there is not one that looketh upon his eyes, but hee dyeth presently' (*Nat. Hist.*, 8.21). The Nile proper has two major tributaries that feed it – the Blue Nile and the White Nile – neither of which originate from a place called Nigris. This strange creature was described in bestiaries and books of natural history up until the seventeenth century. Edward Topsell's inclusion of it as the Gorgon or Catobleponta in his *Historie of Foure-Footed Beasts* of 1607 may be the last occasion on which it was seriously entertained as fact.

CATTLE OF GERYON,

SEE GERYON

CEFFYL DŴR

The Welsh **Water-Horse**: an evil spirit described as beautiful, grey, but small of stature, who would tempt lonely travellers to mount him and then, soaring over the rivers and mountains, disappear like the morning mist, leaving the rider to fall to his doom. Glyn-Neath and Flemingston in the Vale of Glamorgan were two such places where the creature might be found. At other times, by strange lights and unearthly noises, he might foretell a drowning. Equivalent to the Scottish **Kelpie**. (Owen, *Welsh Folk-Lore*, 138–9; Trevelyan, *Folk-Lore*, 58–61.)

CENTAUR

From the Greek κένταυρος, *centauros*, meaning 'bull killer': a monster, half man, half horse, of Ancient Greek mythology. First mentioned by Homer in both the *Iliad* and the *Odyssey*, they were initially a race of savage humans inhabiting the mountains and forests of Thessaly in Greece who were later imagined to be a combination of man and horse. They were depicted either as being whole humans with the hind body, legs and tail of a horse (Pausanius, *Desc. Gr.*, 5.19.7, describing a carved chest dating from the infancy of Cypselus, tyrant of Corinth, in the seventh century BCE), or, in the more familiar and probably later form, as having a human head and upper body mounted on the body and legs of a horse. Various fantastical stories are told of their origins. According to Pindar (*Pythian*, 2), writing in the fifth century BCE, the Lapith king Ixion mated with a cloud (the cloud nymph Nephele) that had been shaped by Zeus into the form of his wife, the goddess Hera, who gave birth to Centaurus – 'honoured neither by men nor by the laws of the gods' – who mated with the Magnesian mares to produce 'a marvellous horde, which resembled both its parents: like the mother below, the father above'. Diodorus (4.69) said that the centaurs

Centaur (Thirteenth Century)

were the sons of Ixion, who then mated with mares to produce the hippocentaurs. Others said that Ixion fathered the centuars directly on his mares (Serv., *Ad Aen.*, 8.293, in the fourth or fifth century CE); or that Zeus changed himself into a stallion and lay with Ixion's wife Dia (Nonnos, *Dion.*, 16.240, 14.193, also in the fourth or fifth century CE). The centaurs and hippocentuars (from *hippo-*, 'horse') appear at first as two disctinct races of beings, but in later writings merge into one and the same. The centaurs fought against the Lapithae tribe, the so-called *centauromachy*, 'battle of the centaurs', after a disagreement at the wedding feast of the Lapith king Peirithous (one of the centaurs tried to abduct the bride); the centaurs were defeated and expelled from their traditional lands. The centaur Cheiron was supposed to have taught the young Achilles. The myth of the horse-man centaurs probably derives from the fact that the early Thessalians were noted horsemen and bull-hunting on horseback was a national custom. (Smith, *Dict.*, 666.)

The theme of the attempted abduction was a popular one in Western art long after the passing of Ancient Greece. Examples include Rubens's *The Rape of Hippodame* (1636–8) and Albert-Ernest Carrier-Belleuse's dynamic statue *The Abduction of Hippodamia* (1877). For a modern 'specimen', see the **Cambridge Centaur**.

CENTICORE, SEE YALE

CEPHUS

Plural *Cephi*, also *Semivulpes*. According to Pliny the Elder, writing in the first century CE (*Nat. Hist.*, 8.19): 'Cn. Pompeius the Great [...] brought out of Æthyopia other beasts, named Cephi, whose fore-feet were like to mens hands, and the hinder feet and legges resembled those of a man. He was never seene afterwards at Rome.' Pliny did not describe what the rest of it looked like.

CERASTES

A horned **Serpent** described by Pliny the Elder in the first century CE (*Nat. Hist.*, 8.23): 'The Serpent Cerastes hath many times foure small hornes, standing out double, with moving whereof shee amuseth the birds, and traineth them unto her for to catch them, hiding all the rest of her bodie.' Writing in the seventh century CE, Isidore of Seville (*Etym.*, 12.4.18) added a few more fantastical elements: 'Cerastes is a serpent named because it has horns, similar to those of rams, on its head; the Greeks call horns κέρατα. It has four pairs of little horns.

Displaying the horns as if they were food, it kills animals tempted to approach. It hides its whole body in the sands, lest it show any sign of itself, except that part by which it captures the lured animals or birds. It is more flexible than other snakes; it seems not to have a spine.'

CERBERUS

The original hell-hound: a monstrous dog of Ancient Greek mythology that guards the entrance to Hades, the land of the dead. In the eighth century BCE, Homer mentions an unnamed dog with this function in both the *Iliad* and *Odyssey*. In his *Theogony* of *c.*700 BCE, Hesiod gave us both the name and a description: 'Cerberus who eats raw flesh, the brazen-voiced hound of Hades, fifty-headed, relentless and strong' (310ff). Cerberus was the offspring of the snake-woman **Echidna** and the **Dragon Typhon**. By the time of Euripedes in the fifth century BCE, his number of heads had reduced to three, but he had acquired a mane of snakes' heads and a dragon's tail, apparently also furnished with a biting head (Apollodorus, *Library*, 2.5). In the first century BCE, the Roman poet Horace increased the number of heads to a hundred (*Carm.* 2.13.34). To bring this monster up from the infernal regions was the last of Hercules' Twelve Labours: it echoes the first when Hercules used brute power to overcome Cerberus' half-brother, the **Nemean Lion**, although this time he spared the monster's life. In the first century CE, Pliny the Elder (*Nat. Hist.*, 27.2) referred to a fable

HERCVLES CERBERVM TRICIPITEM AD SVPEROS PERTRAXIT ·

IS ISB 45

Hercules and Cerberus (1545)

concerning the poisonous plant aconite, that it was produced from the foam dripping from Cerberus' mouth as Hercules dragged him up out of Hades: 'for which reason, it is said, it is still so remarkably abundant in the vicinity of Heraclea in Pontus, a spot where the entrance is still pointed out to the shades below'. For another multiple-headed dog of Greek mythology, see **Orthus**.

CERYNEIAN HIND

Also *Cerynitian*, in Greek mythology, a sacred hind of the goddess Artemis with golden horns. Euripides suggests a malevolent nature when he writes: 'that dappled deer with horns of gold, that preyed upon the country-folk' (*Her.* 375). Due to its fabled speed,

Ovid says that it 'did not run but fly' (*Met.* 9.188). Capturing the hind alive was the third labour given to Hercules by Eurystheus. He hunted it for a full year, going as far as 'the land at the back of the cold north wind' (Pindar, *Odes*, 3.28(50)ff), before finally wounding it with an arrow, but as he brought it back he was confronted by Artemis and Apollo, who demanded that they return it. Hercules convinced them of his need and successfully carried it back to Eurystheus at Mycenae (Apollodorus, *Library*, 2.5.3). Given the reference to the extreme north and the fact of its having horns (antlers), Ridgeway (*Early Age of Greece*, 360ff) proposed that the hind was in fact a reindeer, the female of which carries antlers like the male.

CHAMA

Pliny's *lupus cervarius*: a type of leopard-spotted wolf said to come from ancient Gaul (France), where it was called *rufius* (Pliny, *Nat. Hist.*, 8.28, 34). In older editions of Pliny, the terms *chaus* and *ruphius* were used, until a more authoritative MS in the Bibliothèque Nationale de France, Paris, was discovered with the current spellings; the first English translator, Philemon Holland, used the expressions 'hart-wolf' and 'hind-wolf', whilst Bostock preferred 'stag-wolf'. According to Pliny, Pompey exhibited the animal in Rome. They had strange feeding habits, in addition: 'This beast (they say) be he never so hungry when hee is eating, if he chaunce to looke backe, forgetteth his meat, slinketh away, and seeketh for some other prey.' It is generally supposed that some sort of lynx, as yet unidentified, is meant.

CHARYBDIS

A **Sea Monster** of Ancient Greek mythology, Charybdis is first mentioned in Homer's *Odyssey*, dating from the eighth century BCE, but undoubtedly based on an older oral tradition. The story relates Odysseus' adventures on his voyage home after the siege of Troy (recounted in the *Iliad*). With the aid of the god Hermes, he subdues the sorceress Circe, who then tells him, amongst other things, how to evade Charybdis and the equally fearful monster **Scylla**; hence the phrase 'between Scylla and Charybdis', meaning a forced choice between undesirable alternatives. As

Hercules and the Ceryneian Hind (1608)

Odysseus sails up a certain strait, Scylla lies on one side, Charybdis on the other: '[…] divine Charybdis fearfully sucked the sea-water down. Whenever she belched it forth, like a kettle in fierce flame, all would foam swirling up, and overhead spray fell upon the tops of both crags. But when she gulped the salt sea-water down, then all within seemed in a whirl; the rock around roared fearfully, and down below the bottom showed, dark with sand. Pale terror seized my men; on her we looked and feared to die' (*Odyssey*, 12.142–259). Modern attempts to identify Charybdis suggest that it was a whirlpool in the Straits of Messina. When we examine old sea charts showing monsters crashing through the waves, we might consider this personification of the natural hazards to be met in navigating the oceans as their prototype.

CHERSINA

A species of desert-dwelling tortoise said to live on nothing but dew. According to Pliny (*Nat. Hist.*, 9.10): 'There be also land Tortoises (called thereupon in the workes that are made of them in pannell wise, Chersinæ) found in the deserts and wildernesse of Affrick, and principally in that part which is drie and full of sands: and they are thought to live upon nothing els but the moist dew. And in very truth, no other living creature there breedeth besides them.' The name is given to the angulate tortoise (*Chersina angulata*) found in semi-arid, but not quite desert areas, of South Africa.

CHELYDROS

A type of fantastic **Serpent** described by Isidore of Seville (*Etym.*, 12.4.12): 'Chelydros is a serpent, also called chersydros, who dwells both in water and on land, for the Greeks call land χέρσος and water ὕδωρ. This snake causes the land it glides through to smoke, as Macer describes it: where the foul snake glides, the earth smokes, and their foaming back emit slime. […] It always moves straight: for if it twists itself while on course, it immediately snaps.'

CHIMÆRA

Also *Chimera*, a monster of Ancient Greek mythology. In the eighth century BCE, Homer described it as 'a thing of immortal make, not human, lion-fronted and snake behind, a goat in the middle, and snorting out the breath of the terrible flame of bright fire' (*Iliad*, 6.179–82). Hesiod (*Theog.*, 319): 'who breathed raging fire, a creature fearful, great, swift-footed and

Chimæra (Fourth Century BCE)

strong, who had three heads, one of a grim-eyed lion; in her hinderpart, a dragon; and in her middle, a goat, breathing forth a fearful blast of blazing fire'. According to Hesiod it was born of the union between **Typhon** and **Echidna**, and was slain by Bellerophon and **Pegasus**. The scientific name *Chimæra monstrosa* was given to the **Sea-Mouse**.

CHOL

From the Hebrew לוח, meaning 'sand', applied to the biblical and later rabbinical conception of the **Phoenix**. The word is used in Job 29:18: 'then I thought I shall die with my nest and shall multiply my days as the *chol*'. In rabbinical literature other words used are **Ziz** and *urshina*. According to tradition, the chol was in the Garden of Eden, but unlike the other birds and beasts, refused to eat the fruit of the tree of knowledge when offered by Eve. It was said to live for a thousand years when a fire erupts in its nest and burns it up, leaving only an egg from which it hatches again. The rabbis looked for an explanation as to why, like fallen man, the animals also died and so had Eve extend her temptation, and the obedience shown by the chol to God's command not to eat from the tree in turn explains its legendary longevity. In other stories, the chol is the guardian of the world, shielding mankind from the harmful rays of the sun with his outspread wings. He eats manna from heaven and drinks the dew of the earth from which he excretes a worm, which in turn excretes cinnamon. (Niehoff, 'Phoenix', 245–65.)

CHRYSAOR

Meaning 'golden blade'; in Greek mythology, a golden winged boar (usually depicted in human form), born of Poseidon and Medusa, brother of **Pegasus**. With the ocean-nymph Callirrhoë (**Nereid**), he fathered **Geryon** and **Echidna**. (Hesiod, *Theog.*, 280ff, 979.)

CHRYSOMALLUS

In Greek mythology, a flying golden-fleeced ram, born of Theophane and the sea-god Poseidon. An oracle decreed that if Phrixos, son of Nephele, were sacrificed to Zeus, prosperity would be returned to the people. Understandably, Nephele was not pleased with this and sent the golden ram to rescue Phrixos and her daughter Helle. The ram rode off through the skies with the children on its back, but Helle fell off and was drowned – the Hellespont is named after her – and only Phrixos made it to the safety of

Chrysomallus (Second Century CE)

Colchis. Here he sacrificed the ram to Zeus and gave the golden fleece to King Aeetes – he hung it on a tree in the sacred grove of Ares where Jason and his Argonauts would come looking for it. Chrysomallus was raised up to the heavens as the constellation of Aries. (Apollodorus, *Library*, 1.80; Smith, *Dict.*, I, 699.)

Chupacabra

Properly *Chupacabras*, Spanish, 'goat-sucker', a supposed animal of the Americas that feeds on the blood of livestock. It is described as being smaller than a human with short grey fur and an ability to change colour. The head is oversized and set with large red eyes. Spines run from the crown of the head down the back. Despite the mention of fur, popular depictions represent it as repitilian and standing on two legs. Its documented history is generally traced back to the so-called Moca Vampire, an animal or even alien said to be responsible for the mysterious deaths of livestock in Puerto Rico in 1974. Reports peaked in the 1990s and are today less common. (Eberhart, *Myst. Creat.*, I, 134–6.)

Church Grim

In parts of Yorkshire the term 'grim' was used for a ghost, or skeleton; and a grim's head meant a death's head. This is said to derive from the name 'church-grim': 'a custom prevailed with those engaged in the building of a church, to take the first living creature which crossed their path on a day approaching its completion, and build it alive in the wall. Thus it became the haunting inhabitant of the church, and it was the office of this sprite to give warning of approaching death. Accordingly, different animal forms pertained to the several kirke-grims of a district, as we hear of Barguests in the shape of a mastiff, a pig, a dog, a calf. Further, as kindly communicated by the Rev. J.O. Atkinson, author of the *Cleveland Glossary*, the Church-grim at times, "was visible to the priest while officiating at the grave, and to no one else. The priest was wont to cast his eyes towards the window of the church-tower where the apparition sat, and he could then tell by the creature's aspect whether the departed was saved or lost"' (Harland, *Gloss.*, 83). For the Scandinavian counterpart and probable source, see **Kirkegrim**.

Cinnamologus

The 'Cinnamon Bird', first mentioned by the Greek historian Herodotus, writing in the fifth century BCE, as a cinnamon-collecting bird of Arabia: 'Great birds, they say, bring the sticks which we Greeks, taking the word from the Phoenicians, call cinnamon, and carry them up into the air to make their nests. These are fastened with a sort of mud to a sheer face of rock, where no foot of man is able to climb. So the Arabians, to get the cinnamon, use the following artifice. They cut all the oxen and asses and beasts of burthen that die in their land into large pieces, which they carry with them into those regions, and place near the nests: then they withdraw to a distance, and the old birds, swooping

Cinnamologus (Thirteenth Century)

down, seize the pieces of meat and fly with them up to their nests; which, not being able to support the weight, break off and fall to the ground. Hereupon the Arabians return and collect the cinnamon, which is afterwards carried from Arabia into other countries' (*Hist.*, 3.111). In the fourth century BCE, Aristotle (*Hist. Anim.*, 14.2) added that the Arabs used lead-weighted arrows to knock the birds out of their nests; and Pliny the Elder (*Nat. Hist.*, 10.33) repeated it in the first century CE. The belief was a persistent one. Writing in the seventh century CE, Isidore of Seville (*Etym.*, 12.7.23) gave the same story, but used the name *cinnamologus*. And in the thirteenth century CE, we find Bartholomaeus Anglicus (*Prop. Rer.*, 17) repeating the tale, albeit with a heavy dash of salt: he thought the story was added 'to make things dear and of great price'.

CIREIN CRÒIN

The **Sea Serpent** of Scottish folklore, the largest animal in the world; also called *Mial mhòr a chuain*, 'great beast of the ocean', *cuartag mhòr a chuain*, 'great whirlpool of the ocean', and *uile-bhéis a chuain*, 'monster of the ocean'. A Caithness rhyme measures the beast: 'Seven herring are a salmon's fill, | Seven salmon are a seal's fill, | Seven seals are a whale's fill, | And seven whales the fill of a Cirein Cròin'; it was sometimes added that 'seven Cirein Cròin are the fill of the big Devil himself'. It derived from the Midgard Serpent **Jörmungandr** (Campbell, *Sup. High.*, 220). For the smallest animal, see **Gigelorum**.

COCK, TALKING

Pliny (*Nat. Hist.*, 10.21): 'We find in record among our Annales, that within the territorie of Ariminum, in that yeare when Marcus Lepidus and Quintus Catulus were Consuls, there was a dung-hill cocke did speake: and it was about a ferme-house in the countrey belonging to one Galerius. But this happened never but once, for ought that I could ever heare or learne.'

COCKATRICE

The word comes from a medieval attempt to translate the Greek *ichneumon*, meaning 'tracker', via Latin *calcatrix*, 'to tread', *calcatris* in French of the twelfth century, becoming first 'kokatrice' in Wyclif's English translation of the Bible in 1382, and, through variations, finally 'cockatrice' by the sixteenth century; an alternative derivation finds its source among various spellings intended to mean 'crocodile' (Breiner, 'Cockatrice', 32). Initially synonymous with **Basilisk**, 'cockatrice' is given in translation of the Latin *basiliscus*, as well as *regulus* and *aspis* used in the Vulgate (Latin version of the Bible). The cockatrice gradually developed its own peculiar shape and story. Its classic form is with a cock's head and wings (sometimes bat's wings) fixed to the hind legs and tail of a **Dragon**. The crest or crown of the basilisk bears resemblance to a cock's comb, hence through time the whole head and even wings appear. The cockatrice was believed to come from a cock's egg hatched by a toad or serpent. This birth, as well as creating a monster whose looks could kill, was also taken as an omen of impending doom. In heraldry, the idea arose that when the cockatrice's own egg is hatched, again by an obliging toad, a creature, known as the 'amphisian cockatrice', comes forth with a second dragon-like head on the end of its tail. According to Welsh folklore, Radnor Forest was home to a cockatrice that was supposed to suck blood from cows and fowls and had a particular fondness for eggs; and naughty children were told that it would come and suck their blood, too. It was said to have eyes in the back of its head as well as in the usual place. (Brand, *Pop. Antiq.*, 132; Trevelyan, *Folk-Lore*, 170.)

Cockatrice (1584)

COCKFISH

In heraldry, a cock with a fish's tail. It is found in the arms of the Geyss family of Bavaria, but is otherwise most rare (Fox-Davies, *Comp. Guide*, 231). Cockfish is also the name given to the South American fish *Callorhinchus callorynchus* (Linnaeus, 1758), or as 'cock fish' to male fish in general.

CRETAN BULL

In Greek mythology, a savage bull said to be either the one that carried the Phoenician princess Europa to Europe, or the bull sent by Poseidon out of the sea as a sacrificial animal for King Minos. Minos had pledged to sacrifice the first thing that should come out of the sea, but when he saw the beauty of this bull he sacrificed another in its stead. Poseidon was not fooled and as a punishment drove the bull mad and it went on a rampage across Crete. As his seventh labour, Eurystheus commanded Hercules to bring him this bull alive. Being Hercules he of course did so. Eurystheus then released the bull, which made its way to Marathon in Attica and there continued its nuisance (Apollodorus, *Library*, 2.5.7), becoming known as the Marathonian Bull. Medea, plotting against Theseus, had his father Aegeus, who did not recognise him, send Theseus after the bull expecting that he would be killed by it: she was disappointed, for Theseus was victorious against the monster (Apollodorus, *Epit.* E.1). The Cretan Bull fathered the **Minotaur** on Pasiphaë, wife of King Minos (Apollodorus, *Library*, 3.1).

Hercules and the Cretan Bull (1731)

CRO SITH

The sea-cow or fairy cow of Celtic folklore, from Socttish Gaelic; also *crodh-mara*. Usually dun-coloured, red and speckled versions have also been recorded. Said to have red ears, one or both being notched, it lives beneath the sea, but sometimes comes ashore. It can swim across the sea and feeds not on grass but on seaweed. Normal cows will attack it when it comes among them and it has no horns of its own to defend it. The 'hornless dun cows' were *bo adhaol odhar*. They can be prevented from returning to the sea if sand, or better yet earth from a graveyard, is scattered between them and the waves. Places mentioned in connection with it are Guershader near Portree, Luskentyre on South Harris, the Sound of Harris, Scorribreac on Skye, Tiree, and the Island of Berneray (Watson, 'High. Myth.', 54). The fairy herdswoman sings to them: 'Crooked one, dun one, | Little wing grizzled, | Black cow, white cow, | Little bull, black-headed, | My milch kine have come home, | O dear! That the herdsman would come!' At Struth, Obbe, on Harris, several sea-cows came ashore tended by a sea-maiden, singing a strange song: 'A low is heard in the sea of Canna. | A cow from Tiree, a cow from Barra, | A cow from Islay, a cow from Arran, | And from Green Kintyre of birches. | I will go, I will go, I will go to Mull, | I will go to Eirin of the bloody men, | I will go to little Man of the wherries, | And I will go to France and no mishap' (Campbell, *Sup. High.*, 29–30). MacGregor (*Peat-Fire*, 39) records that in 1854 a beast described as a 'water-cow' was observed in Loch Gairloch, or one of its neighbours, in Ross and Cromarty. See also the 'sea-bull', **Tarbh-Uisge**.

CROCODILE

The crocodile looks as though it should be impossible, but we well know that it is entirely possible. Here, in part, is the source of the **Dragon** legend, but the crocodile has its own fantastic history. Way back in the fifth century BCE, Herodotus (*Hist.* II.69) recorded some curious customs surrounding it: 'Now for some of the Egyptians the crocodiles are sacred animals, and for others not so, but they treat them on the contrary as enemies: those however who dwell about Thebes and about the lake of Moiris hold them to be most sacred, and each of these two peoples keeps one crocodile selected from the whole number, which has been trained to tameness, and they put hanging ornaments of molten stone and of gold into the ears of these and anklets round the front feet, and they give them food appointed and victims of sacrifices and treat them as well as possible while they live, and after they are dead they bury them in sacred tombs, embalming them: but those who dwell about the city of Elephantine even eat them, not holding them to be sacred. They are called not crocodiles but *champsai*, and the Ionians gave them the name of crocodile, comparing their form to that of the crocodiles (lizards) which appear in their country in the stone walls.' The crocodile was greatly valued for its supposed medicinal properties and Pliny lists nineteen different remedies derived from it, including an extract called 'crocodilea' (*Nat. Hist.*, 28.28), as well as the aphrodisiac properties of its eye-teeth (32.50). According to Pliny (8.40), the crocodile was first exhibited in Rome in the second century BCE by Marcus Aemilius Scaurus, during his term as aedile in charge of the public games. The crocodile has been worshipped by the Ancient Egyptians as Sobek – the goddess Taweret and the supernatural being **Ammut** also had crocodile characteristics – and by the Aztecs as Cipactli. See also the **Irish Crocodile**.

CROCOTTA

Also *corocotta*, *crocottas*, *crocutes*, *krokottas* or *kynolykos* (Greek, 'dog-wolf'), a monster of Africa: 'There is in Ethiopia an animal called properly the *Krokottas* but vulgarly the *Kynolykos*. It is of prodigious strength, and is said to imitate the human voice, and by night to call out men by their names, and when they come forth at their call, to fall upon them and devour them. This animal has the courage of the lion, the speed of the horse, and the strength of the bull, and cannot be encountered successfully with weapons of steel' (Ctesias, *Anc. Ind.*, 52–3). Pliny the Elder (*Nat. Hist.*, 8.30) described this beast as a species of mastif born of the union between a dog and a wolf: 'these are able to crash with their teeth whatsoever they can come by, and a thing is no sooner downe their swallow and got into their stomacke, but presently they digest it.' See also **Leucrocuta**.

CROMMYONIAN SOW

A monstrous sow of Greek mythology, said to be the offspring of **Echidna** and **Typhon**, or of an old woman called Phaea; named after the village Crommyon in Corinthia, or this woman Phaea. Plutarch said that it 'was no insignificant creature, but fierce and hard to master' (*Thes.*, 9). It was the mother of the **Caledonian Boar** before being slain by Theseus (Apollodorus, *Epit.* E.1; Strabo, *Geog.*, 8.6). Plutarch also offered the explanation that the sow was in fact 'a female robber, a woman of murderous and unbridled spirit, who dwelt in Crommyon, was called Sow because of her life and manners' (*Thes.*, 9).

CU SITH

Scottish Gaelic, 'the dog of the fairies', plural *Coin Sith*; Irish Gaelic *Cu Sidhe*: 'A creature of ill omen […] sometimes encountered on dark nights, moving swiftly and noiselessly from place to place' (MacGregor, *Peat-Fire*, 36). They are of huge size, as big as a two-year-old calf, and dark green in colour with lighter green about the feet. Their tails are either long and coiled over their backs, or flat and plaited 'like the straw rug of a pack-saddle'. Their bark is louder than an ordinary dog's, but sounds somewhat the same, although they bark three times only with a long pause between. When one bark is heard there is still time to escape; when two barks are heard, then it is sure to overtake the hearer. Pawprints have been found in sand, mud and snow as large as a human hand, or so they say. Also said to possess the power of the Evil Eye (Watson, 'High. Myth.', 68). On Tiree in the Inner Hebrides there is a cave near the shore known as the 'Lair of the Faery Dog' because the barking of a large dog has been heard to come from it. They run with the Sluagh, the Fairy Host or Wild Hunt, the spirits of the restless dead who ride through the air. The tooth of the Cu Sith is reputed to have magic powers: placed in a water trough it will heal sick cattle that drink from it; and it will also restore milk depleted by witches and evil spirits. Alasdair MacGregor had a friend whose grandfather, a Lewis man, claimed to have found such a tooth. Also of the supernatural kind is the talking white, red-eared hound (*Gadhar Cluas-dhearg Ban*) of the folktale 'The Knight of the Glens and Bens and Passes'; he is an enchanted fairy called Summer-under-dew (*Samhradh-ri-dealt*) who resumes his original form after marrying the knight's youngest daughter. It is said that Fionn's Hound, Bran, was his daughter by a woman who came to him in the form of an enchanted hound. The dog was held in high regard: the Celtic hero Cuchulain derives his name from *Cu* ('dog'); he was forbidden to eat the meat of the dog and breaking this taboo brought about his death. For supernatural canines in general, see **Black Dog**. (Henderson, *Survivals*, 173; MacDougall and Calder, *Folk Tales*, 6–7.)

Cutty Black Sow,

SEE Hwch Ddu Gwta

Cŵn Annwn

Welsh, the 'hounds of the underworld': spirit hounds that ran through the air comparable to the English **Gabriel's Hounds**; to hear their howling was an omen of death. They are variously described as: a) small and white with red-coloured ears and shining eyes; b) large and black with red spots, or red with black spots – the worst sort were blood-red in hue – with eyes like fireballs; c) grey with red spots; or d) again small but flame-coloured, a mixture of red and white, or the colour of liver. Their preferred nights for hunting were the eves of the Christian feast days of St John, St Martin, St Michael, All Saints, St Agnes, and St David, as well as Christmas, New Year and Good Friday. They met at crossroads; when their paws touched the earth the mandrake screamed aloud. They were encountered in packs, usually led by their master, Arawn, King of the Annwn, described as a gigantic, dark figure with horn and hunting pole. In Carmarthenshire, he goes on foot with two black hounds on a leash and a dog, half-wolf, following behind; he is welcomed by the Grey King, Brenin Llwd, in his Court of Mist and his hounds bed down with the *Cŵn Wybry*, the Dogs of the Sky, with whom they are sometimes confused (or perhaps the same). In Glamorgan, Brecon and Radnor, Arawn wears a grey cloak and rides a grey horse (cf. **Ceffyl Dŵr**). Throughout Wales he might be accompanied by the evil hag *Mallt y Nos*, or Matilda of the Night. See also **Gwyllgi**. (Trevelyan, *Folk-Lore*, 47–51.)

Cynocephalus

From the Greek κυνοκέφαλος, *kynokephalos*, via Latin, meaning 'dog-headed'; also called *Kynamolgoi*, meaning 'dog-milkers'. First mentioned by Herodotus in 440 BCE as inhabiting Libya (*Hist.*, IV.191). They were more fully described by Ctesias in the late fifth century BCE: 'In that part of India where the beetles (κανθάροι) are met with, live the *Kynokephaloi*, who are so called from their being like dogs in the shape of their head and in their general appearance. In other respects, however, they resemble mankind, and go about clad in the skins of wild beasts. They are moreover very just, and do no sort of injury to any man. They cannot speak, but utter a kind of howl. Notwithstanding this they comprehend the language of the Indians. They subsist upon wild animals, which their great fleetness of foot enables them

Cynocephalus (1642)

to capture with the utmost ease.' Pliny recounted Ctesias' earlier tale, but also added a new one: 'Apes that be headed and long snouted like dogs, and thereupon called Cynocephali, are of all other most curst, shrewd, & unhappie.' In the first or second century CE, Tertullian (*Apol.*, 6) used the term for **Anubis**. Where Ctesias' creature appears fantastical, Pliny's is evidently the baboon, genus *Papio*. These curious origins are reflected in the scientific naming of two species of baboon: *Papio anubis*, the olive baboon; and *Papio cynocephalus*, the yellow baboon. Shakespeare mentioned 'dog-apes' in *As You Like It* (2.26–7): 'that they call compliment | is like the encounter of two dog-apes'.

CYONOEIDES

A **Dragon** ('worm') or **Serpent** found in the river Ganges in India. According to Pliny (*Nat. Hist.*, 9.17): 'Statius Sibosus reporteth as strange a thing besides, namely, that in the said river there be certaine wormes or serpents with two finnes of a side, sixtie cubits long, of colour blew, and of that hew take their name [and be called Cyonoeides.] He saith moreover, that they be so strong, that when the Elephants come into the river for drinke, they catch fast hold with their teeth by their trunks or muzzles, and maugre their hearts force them downe under the water; of such power and force they are.' For another monster supposed to inhabit the Ganges, see **Odontotyrranos**.

D

DAGON

A water-god of the Philistines, Semitic *dag*, 'fish', derived from the Babylonian deity Dagan, or from another source meaning 'corn', considered to be half man, half fish. He is best known from the references found in the Bible: Beth-Dagon, the 'house or city of Dagon'; the temple of Dagon at Gaza destroyed by Samson; the temple of Dagon in Ashdod, where the image of the god was destroyed by the act of placing the captured Ark of the Covenant within it (Macalister, *Philistines*, 90ff; Mackenzie, *Myth. Bab.*, 31–2). See also **Oannes**.

DAMMHAST (DAM-HORSE), SEE BÄCKAHÄST

DANDY-DOG

In Cornwall, a spectral huntsman haunts the moors with his pack of baying hounds: the locals say it is 'the Devil and his Dandy-Dogs'. Wild nights and bleak moors are their preferred time and place, and disaster befalls those who meet them. The tale is told of a poor herdsman trudging home across the moor on just such a tempestuous night. Above the noise of the storm he hears the yelping of the dogs and cry of the huntsman. He hurries on, but the sounds grow louder, till, glancing back, he sees the hunter, burning eyes pierce the dark shape, a human silhouette spoilt by horns and swishing tail, and then the pack of dogs, fire snorting from their nostrils. As the priest would say, he fell on his knees, just as the pack were about to fall on him, and offered up a prayer that protected him from the snapping jaws and firey breath, and the Devil and his Dandy-Dogs ran on, looking for another victim. They are the same monsters known as Heath Hounds, **Yeth Hounds** and Wish Hounds. (Wright, *Rust. Sp.*, 196.)

DELPHINE, SEE PYTHON

DDRAIG GOCH

Welsh, meaning 'red dragon'; the national emblem of Wales. The familiar Welsh **Dragon** can be traced back to the Roman occupation of Britain when it was used as a military ensign. It was adopted by the inhabitants, e.g., it was flown by Harold at the Battle of Hastings, as can be seen on the Bayeux Tapestry. In the thirteenth century it was even borne on a banner by the English when fighting against the Welsh; and in the four-teenth century was born as a flag by the English at Crécy. However, the adoption of St George as the national saint of the English after the first crusade led to a necessary disuse of the dragon as a military and royal emblem, although Henry VII revived the dragon in the late fifteenth century (Tatlock, 'Dragons', 223–35). The earliest association of Wales with a red dragon is found in the *Historia Brittonum* attributed to Nennius written in the ninth century CE. After inviting the Saxons to aid him against the Picts and Scots, King Vortigern, a fifth-century king of the Britons (the early Celtic inhabitants of Britain), finds that his fierce guests turn on him and drive him to the western edge of his kingdom. Here in North Wales he decides to build a citadel to protect himself and his people at the place now called Dinas Emrys, but his coun-sellors, a group of twelve wise men, advised him that he could only successfully accomplish this by sanc-tifying the area with the blood of a boy born with no father. Vortigern sends out emmisaries to find such a youth and they duly return with one plucked from Bassalig in Monmouthshire. Finding out that he is about to be sacrificed, he challenges the wise men to interpret the strange scene that unfolds. Two serpents are discovered in a tent in a pool, one red, one white; they awaken and fight, the white is the stronger, but the red prevails, chasing the white away until both disappear from sight. The wise men are at a loss, but the boy turns to Vortigern: 'I will unfold to you the meaning of this mystery. The pool is the emblem of this world, and the tent that of your kingdom: the two serpents are two dragons; the red serpent is your dragon, but the white serpent is the dragon of the people who occupy several provinces and districts of Britain, even almost from sea to sea: at length, however, our people shall rise and drive away the Saxon race from beyond the sea, whence they originally came; but do you depart from this place, where you are not permitted to erect a citadel; I, to whom fate has allotted this mansion, shall remain here; whilst to you it is incumbent to seek other provinces, where you may build a fortress' (Giles, *Six Old Eng.*, 403). The boy gave his name as Ambrose (British, Embresguletic; also Emrys); Geoffrey of Monmouth in his twelfth-century *Historia Regum Britaniae* named him Merlin (also in Giles). In the late mabinogi folk tale of *Lludd and Llevelys* (twelfth or thirteenth century), two dragons, representing two unnamed tribes, fight and are imprisoned in Dinas Emrys. Other places in Wales are connected with dragon legends: at Llanrhaiadr-yn-Mochnant in North Wales a man-eating monster was tricked into killing itself upon a spiked pillar by its hatred of the colour red; the Vale of Neath in South Wales also had its dragon; the woods around Penllyne Castle, Glamorgan, were haunted by dragons that sparkled as though encrusted with jewels; and there are many other places besides (Trevelyan, *Folk-Lore*, 167–8).

Considering these origins, the red dragon is not so much Welsh as British, but Britain, so long subject to invasion, is no longer the land of the ancient Britons; and so it will be again.

DIOMEDEÆ

Also *cataractae*, the so-called Birds of Diomedes described by Pliny the Elder (*Nat. Hist.*, 10.61). They have teeth, red eyes 'bright as the fire' and white plumage; and are found on one island – San Nicola in the Isole Tremiti archipelago off the Italian coast – where the tomb and temple of Diomedes is. They squawk at everyone except Greeks being 'descended from the race of Diomedes'. They have a curious habit: 'Their manner is every day to charge their throat and wings full of water, and all to drench therewith the said temple of Diomedes, in signe of purification. And hereupon arose the fabulous tale, that the companions of Diomedes were turned into these birds.' Diomedes was one of the Greek heroes who fought in the Trojan War, as recounted in Homer's *Iliad*. According to two competing legends: a) on his death, Diomedes' men were transformed by the goddess Venus into birds when one of them spoke out irreverently against her; or b) the pitiful crying of Diomedes' men moved the goddess to transform them into birds. The name is given as a scientific classification of the albatross, family *Diomedeidae*, and the great albatross, genus *Diomedea* (Linnaeus). Adam (*Sum. Geo.*, 459) supposed that they were a species of heron and decided that Pliny had described them as coots; Bostock, in his edition of Pliny, suggested the petrel (*Procellaria*), as well as the white heron (*Ardea garzetta*).

DOBHAR-CHÚ

The Gaelic 'water-hound' of Irish and Scottish legend. In modern Irish the name *dobharchú* is given to the otter, more commonly called *mada-uisge;* but the original was more like the **Onchú**, also meaning 'water dog', and certainly connected with the mysterious **Irish Crocodile**. It is described as being half dog, half otter, sometimes with a single horn in the centre of its forehead. There is a grave in Congbháil (Conwall) Cemetery in Drumáin (Drummans), County Leitrim, known popularly as 'the Dobhar-Chú Tombstone'. It is a sandstone flag about 137 cm (4 ft 6 in) long by 56 cm (1 ft 10 in) wide with the carved figure of a mysterious creature: 'It shows a recumbent animal having body and legs like those of a dog with the characteristic depth of rib and strength of thigh. The tail, long and curved, shows a definite tuft. […] So far the description is canine. The paws, however, appear unusually large, while the long, heavy neck and the short head into which it shades off, together with the tiny ears are all like those of an Otter or such Mustelida' (Tohall, 'Dobhar-Chú', 127–9). A human hand is also shown, gripping a spear or harpoon with which it has run the animal through. The inscription, barely legible by the mid-twentieth century, reads something like '[Here lies the] body of Grace Connolly wife to Terence MacLoghlin who died

September the 24th Anno Domini 1722'. Another 'Dobhar-Chú Tombstone' was located at Cill Rúisc (Kilroosk) at the southern end of Glenade, but is now lost. In local folklore, a woman named Grainne (equivalent to Grace) went down to Loch Glenade to wash some clothes, but when she did not return, her husband, MacLoghlin, went in search of her and 'found her bloody body by the lakeside with the Dobhar-chú asleep on her breast' (Tohall, ibid.). MacLoghlin killed the beast with his dagger, but not before it was able to whistle to its mate. MacLoghlin ran for his life, but eventually was able to kill this one, too. A Dobhar-chú with a horn like a unicorn was said to have been killed in the stone circle of Caiseal-bán near Cashelgarron, County Sligo. The Dobhar-chú was also believed to be a type of King Otter, or Master Otter, and was said to be the seventh cub of an ordinary otter. In the Hebrides of Scotland it was once said that 'Where there are nine otters, there is the *dobhar chu*, the male otter. There is a spot under his breast, and he can be killed only by wounding this. The rest of his body is protected by enchantment. The smoke of him will fell a man sixty yards away' (Goodrich-Freer, 'More Folklore', 35). The white spot again links him with the Master Otter, see **Otter, Giant**. (Williams, 'Beasts and Banners', 62–78.)

DOG

The supernatural species of dog are often marked by colour: the dark green dog (**Cu Sith**); the white dog with red ears; the white **Gally-Trot**; the **Black Dog**. Other types are said to be found in water: **Dobhar-Chú**, **Sea Dog**. The dog could also be seen as an aspect of the soul: 'Sometimes the good and the bad angel of the person are seen contending in the shape of a white and a black dog' (Hazlitt, *Brand's*, 665). For dog-headed creatures, see **Cynocephalus**.

DOG-COLLARED SOMBRE BLACKBIRD

The *Clericus polydeniminata* identified by Frank A. Goodliffe and listed in the *Zoological Record* for 1964: 'Identification: similar to *common laity* but plumage and behaviour should serve to differentiate. Plumage black with narrow white collar – unbroken at throat. Feet black, of leathery appearance. Beak pink – often with blueish tint during winter months. [...] Nesting: this usually occurs close to old buildings with spires. They are usually very friendly and may be seen around nesting sites of *common laity* at tea-time'. Its distinctive call was 'Brrrrr—rethren' and 'usually sings in congregations'. (Dance, *Animal Fakes*, 82.)

DRAGON

As Isidore of Seville explains in his *Etymologies* written in the seventh century CE, 'the Greeks call it δράκων [*drakon*], whence it becomes *draco* in Latin' and via Old French, dragon in modern English; Greek δράκαινα (*drakaina*) was the she-dragon, used of the Erinyes (Furies), for example. As Isidore continues, it 'is larger than all serpents, as well as animals on earth'.

Dragons over Bavaria in 1533 (1540)

The original sense was of a serpent, but it acquired so many additional features that it came to be a separate class of beast by itself. The dragon features in several mythologies as a primordial creature, usually representing a state of chaos that must be conquered by a younger race of warrior gods or heroes: in Babylonian mythology, **Tiamat** is defeated by Marduk; in Ancient Greek mythology, **Typhon** is defeated by Zeus, **Python** by Apollo, **Ladon** and the **Lernæan Hydra** by Hercules; in Canaanite mythology, Lotan is defeated by Baal; in Jewish mythology, **Leviathan** is defeated by Yahweh; in Christian legend, the Archangel Michael and St George both defeat dragons representing Satan; in Norse and later Germanic mythology, Thor defeats the Midgard Serpent (**Jörmungandr**) and Sigurd/Siegfried defeats Fafnir; and in Old English literature Beowulf also kills an unnamed fire-breathing dragon, but is mortally wounded in the fight. The popular idea of a treasure-guarding, fire-breathing dragon is exemplified by the monster in *Beowulf*, where the poet speaks of the 'worm-infested fire' of 'that fire-fierce dragon'. We see that the connection with fire is a late addition; in the earliest myths of the Sumerian dragon **Kur** from the third millennium BCE, the dragon is a personfication of water, its serpentine shape is like the snaking river or the undulating waves.

However, the dragon was not confined to ancient mythologies, for in 792 CE, the *Anglo-Saxon Chronicle* (compiled about 890 CE) recorded: 'This year began with ominous signs over Northumbria, and these utterly panicked the people. Huge streaks of flame rushed across the full length of the sky, and flaming dragons as well were seen flying through the air, bringing fierce hunger with them.' (Plummer, *Sax. Chron.*) In 1864, more than a thousand years later, W. Winwood Reade (*Savage Africa*, 370) wrote: 'As for the winged dragons, it is not impossible that such an animal exists, as we have the type preserved in the draco volans, a little lizard with a membrane like a bat's wing; but it is, to say the least of it, very improbable.' For most of human history people have believed in dragons and, as the Chronicle records, apparently even seen them; and their possibility was seriously entertained even into Victorian times; although there were, of course, sceptics.

In the *Anglo-Saxon Chronicle*, the dragons can be interpreted as natural aerial phonemena. Indeed, this is the position taken by Albertus Magnus: 'I find it impossible to believe the anecdotes about dragons that fly through the air, breathing forth incandescent flames, unless they refer to certain vapours called "dragons"' (*An. Hist.*). His reference to vapours seems just as mysterious; he may have been referring to cloud formations tinged red by the sun, or shooting stars.

Dragons in the sky were generally interpreted as portents of disasters to come. When dragons were seen in England in 792 it seemed inevitable that 'And not long after that, on 8 June of this same year, ravaging heathens ruthlessly levelled God's Church in Lindisfarne with shameless robbing and butchering of men.' (Plummer, *Sax. Chron.*)

THE NATURAL HISTORY OF DRAGONS

The most influential early account of the dragon was written by the Roman author Pliny the Elder in the first century CE. He locates the monster firstly in India, specifically as the natural foe of the elephant: 'Elephants breed in that part of Affricke which lyeth beyond the deserts and wildernesse of the Syrtes: also in Mauritania: they are found also among the Æthiopians and Troglodites, as hath been said: but India bringeth forth the biggest: as also the dragons, that are continually at variance with them, and evermore fighting, and those of such greatnesse, that they can easily claspe and wind round about the Elephants, and withall tye them fast with a knot. In this conflict they die, both the one and the other: the Elephant hee falls downe dead as conquered, and with his heavie weight crusheth and squeaseth the dragon that is wound and wreathed about him […] The dragon therefore espying the Elephant when he goeth to releese, assaileth him from an high tree and launceth himself upon him; but the Elephant knowing well enough he is not able to withstand his windings and knittings about him, seeketh to come close to some trees or hard rockes, and so to crush & squise the dragon between him and them: the dragons ware hereof, entangle and snarle his feet and legges first with their taile: the

Elephants on the other side, undoe those knots with their trunke as with a hand: but to prevent that againe, the dragons put in their heads into their snout, and so stop their wind, and withall, fret and gnaw the tenderest parts that they find there. Now in case these two mortall enemies chaunce to reencounter upon the way, they bristle and bridle one against another, and addresse themselves to fight; but the principall thing the dragons make at, is the eye: whereby it commeth to passe, that many times the Elephants are found blind, pined for hunger, and worne away, and after much languishing, for very anguish & sorrow die of their venime. What reason should a man alleadge of this so mortall warre betweene them, if it be not a verie sport of Nature and pleasure that shee takes, in matching these two so great enemies togither, and so even and equall in every respect? But some report this mutuall war between them after another sort: and that the occasion thereof ariseth from a naturall cause. For (say they) the Elephants bloud is exceeding cold, and therefore the dragons be wonderfull desirous thereof to refresh and coole themselves therewith, during the parching and hote season of the yeere. And to this purpose they lie under the water, waiting their time to take the Elephants at a vantage when they are drinking. Where they catch fast hold first of their trunke: and they have not so soone clasped and entangled it with their taile, but they set their venomous teeth in the Elephants eare, (the onely part of all their bodie, which they

The Devil as a Dragon (1767–1768)

cannot reach unto with their trunke) and so bite it hard. Now these dragons are so big withall, that they be able to receive all the Elephants bloud. Thus are they sucked drie, untill they fall down dead: and the dragons again, drunken with their bloud, are squised under them, and die both together.' (*Nat. Hist.*, 8.11–12.)

Dragons, however, were not restricted to India. Pliny (*Nat. Hist.*, 8.13) tells us that 'In Æthyopia there be as great dragons bred, as in India, namely, twentie cubites long. But I marvell much at this one thing, why king Iuba should thinke that they were crested. They are bred most in a countrey of Æthyopia, where the Asachæi inhabite. It is reported, that upon their coasts they are enwrapped foure or five of them together, one within another, like to a hurdle or lattise worke, and thus passe the seas, for to find better pasturage in Arabia, cutting the waves, and bearing up their heads aloft, which serve them in steed of sailes.'

As well as being at constant war with the elephant, dragons had another intractable foe: the eagle, at least according to Pliny. As Pliny (*Nat. Hist.*, 10.4) argues, 'the Ægle hath not ynough of this one enemie, but she must warre with the Dragon also: howbeit the fight betweene them is more sharpe and eager: yea, and putteth her to much more daunger, albeit otherwhiles they combate in the aire. The Dragon of a naturall spight and greedie desire to doe mischeefe to the Ægle, watcheth evermore where the airie is, for to destroy the egges, and

so the race of the Ægles. The Ægle againe, wheresoever she can set an eie upon him, catcheth him up and carieth him away: but the serpent with his taile windeth about his wings, and so entangleth and tieth them fast, that downe they fall both of them together.' Pliny used the form *draco* in the original Latin.

THE DRAGON IN THE BESTIARIES

Pliny's theme of the war between the dragon and the elephant would feature in most, if not all, later works of natural history from Aelian's (Claudius Aelianus *c*.174–*c*.235 CE) *De Natura Animalium* (6.21) up to Bartholomaeus Anglicus in the thirteenth century. Notwithstanding Pliny's authority, later writers would add embellishments of their own, notably drawing increasingly from the Bible. In the twelfth century Hugo de Folieto brings in something from the **Basilisk**, saying that the dragon can kill by its breath as well as its tail, and that this, as well as its size, symbolically connects it with the Devil: 'The dragon, the greatest of all serpents, is the devil, the king of all evil. As it deals death with its poisonous breath and blow of its tail, so the devil destroys men's souls by thought, word and deed. He kills their thoughts by the breath of pride; he poisons their words with malice; he strangles them by the performance of evil deeds, as it were with his tail.' He also had a folk explanation for the tides: 'The Jews say that God made the great dragon which is called Leviathan, which is in the sea; and when folk say that the sea is ebbing it is the dragon going back'

(Hugo de Folieto, MS Sloane 278, in Druce, 'Elephant'). As yet there is no description of the dragon breathing fire: this undoubtedly emerges from the idea of its deadly breath. Another bestiary, this time from the thirteenth century (British Library Harley MS 4751), develops the idea 'this creature often stealing forth from its caverns mounts into the air, and the air is violently set in motion and glows around it'. This brings us back to the idea of 'flaming dragons' in the sky found in the *Anglo-Saxon Chronicle*.

THE EVIDENCE FOR DRAGONS

In the late thirteenth century, the great traveller Marco Polo described the province of Carajan (Yun-Nan, China) where 'snakes and great serpents of such vast size as to strike fear into those who see them, and so hideous that the very account of them must excite the wonder of those to hear it'. He said that they they were ten paces long with only two front legs ending in claws like those of an eagle or lion, huge heads set with eyes 'bigger than a great loaf of bread'. Their mouths were filled with pointed teeth and large enough to swallow a man whole. When an illustrated version of his *Travels* was published in 1403 as the *Livre des Merveilles*, his serpents had sprouted wings and looked every part the dragon, although with only two legs they must be considered to be technically species of **Wyvern**. The first English printer, William Caxton, published his *Mirrour of the World* in 1481 – it was the first illustrated book to be printed in England and one of

the earliest encyclopedias; it, of course, included dragons, confidently asserting that they lived on an Indian island called Probane, along with the **Griffin** and **Manticore**. Edward Topsell still counted the dragon among the rest of creation in his *Historie of Foure-Footed Beastes* published in London in 1607, with full use of Pliny's many fantasies. A late as 1614, there appeared a pamphlet by 'A.R.' called *True and Wonderfull: A Discourse Relating a Strange and Monstrous Serpent, or Dragon*, detailing the ravages of a dragon in Sussex: it was nine feet or more in length, with large feet, its scales were black on top and red underneath, and it could spit venom to the distance of four rods. Then there were those who even claimed to have actual specimens. In the seventeenth century, Jacob Bobart, professor of botany at Oxford University, had a small dried 'dragon' in his possession, or at least that is what he said it was. From clouds like 'flaming dragons flying through the air' to the ebb and flow of the tides, there had always been apparent evidence for the dragon. Combined with the authority of antiquity, such reports as Marco Polo's coming back to Europe from newly explored regions of the world could only affirm the existence of dragons. The discovery of fossilised remains of the dinosaurs had always been a source of wonder and speculation concerning races of giants and monsters. Widespread ignorance of their true nature allowed unscrupulous individuals to concoct monstrous fantasies out of their bones and exhibit them to the public. Combined with the ready supply of various examples of **Jenny Haniver**, like Bobart's dragon, the credulous could be easily convinced. And then there was always the confusion between the dragon of the imagination and the real reptiles provided by nature; as Winwood Reade noted, we have even scientifically and popularly classified some of them as dragons, from the *Draco* genus of gliding lizards to the 'river-dragon' (crocodile) of Milton to the Komodo Dragon (*Varanus komodoensis*). Other important dragons not already mentioned include the Welsh Dragon (**Ddraig Goch**), the Scottish Dragon (**Beithir**) and the **Chinese Dragon**. See also **Worm** and specific cases, such as the **Laidley Worm**, **Lambton Worm**, **Linton Worm** and **Stoorworm**.

DRAGON, CHINESE

Ancient authorities, such as Wang Fu, relate that the Chinese variety of dragon has 'the head of a camel, the horns of a stag, the eyes of a demon, the ears of a cow, the neck of a snake, the belly of a clam, the scales of a carp, the claws of an eagle, and the soles of a tiger'; it has a sort of air bag on its head that enables it to fly, it is jointed in three parts and has a specific number of scales, some of which are counted good and the rest bad. There are any number of variations: cow-dragons, dog-dragons, fish-dragons, horse-dragons, snake-dragons, toad-dragons and so on. Its mortal enemy is the tiger; even so, there are tiger-headed dragons. It may in addition take any shape, human, animal, even inanimate. They are gods of wind and water. (Mackenzie, *Myths China*, 46–7.)

DRANGUE

Also *Drangoni* (plural *Drangonis*), *Dragu* (plural *Dragona*), from Latin *draco(nem)*, Italian *dragone*: in the folklore of the *Shcypetaar* tribesmen of Albania, a dragon who battles the storm-bringer Kulshedra, who is intent on the destruction of humankind. Drangue is considered to be a beneficent male spirit, Kulshedra a malevolent female one. After death, a man or a male animal can become a Drangue – if his body is cut open and found to contain a heart of gold with a precious stone embedded in it, then it is so – whilst women may become serpents and other harmful creatures. The tribesmen say that during heavy thunderstorms, Drangue and Kulshedra are fighting. (Durham, 'High Alb', 453–72; Haussig, *Götter*, 473.)

DUDLEY LOCUST

Also known as a Dudley Insect; an impossible fossil named after the town of Dudley in the West Midlands. Dudley was at one time known for its limestone quarries and many trilobite fossils from the Palaeozoic age were discovered there. However, they were mostly incomplete and as only complete specimens achieved the highest prices, enterprising quarrymen would doctor whole fossils out of bits and pieces, often creating new and unknown species of trilobite in the process. The National Museum of Wales has a fine collection of them. Similarly doctored ammonites are known as **Snakestones**. (Dance, *Animal Fakes*, 104.)

DUNNIE

Sometimes a horse, sometimes a dead man, the Dunnie was known in Haselrigg, Northumberland, for its unwelcome pranks. His favourite mischiefs are as follows: 'When the midwife is wanted in a farmer's family, and the master goes out to saddle his horse that he may fetch her, the Dunnie will take its form. The false creature carries him safely, receives the midwife also on his back behind the farmer; but on their return, in the muddiest part of the road, he will suddenly vanish, and leave the unhappy pair floundering in the mud. Or, again, when the ploughman has (as he believes) caught his horse in the field, brought him home, and harnessed him, he will, to his dismay, see the harness come "slap to the ground", while the steed kicks up his heels and starts across the country like the wind.' But he was also seen, apparently in human form, wandering the Cheviots and lamenting having 'lost the key o' the Bounders' for which he was 'ruined for evermair', and from this is supposed to have been one of those reivers who formerly raided the border country and having lost his treasure among the crags died forlorn and certainly poor. See also the **Hedley Kow** and **Picktree Brag**. (Henderson, *Notes*, 270.)

E

EACH-SITH

The Scottish fairy horse, from the Gaelic. Often given as an alternative term for the **Kelpie**, although the **Each-Uisge** might also be implied.

EACH-UISGE

The Celtic **Water-Horse**, from the Scottish Gaelic for 'water horse'; Irish, *Aughisky*: 'the most terrible and the most feared of all the supernatural beings which the Gael has to contend with' (Kennedy-Fraser, *Songs*, 94). In contrast to the white or grey colour of water-horses of continental Europe, the Each-Uisge is nearly always pitch black. Not to be confused with the similar **Kelpie**, he often appears in a shape suited to the viewer: 'To men he appears as a huge black hairy monster whose snort and gnash haunt them ever after like a nightmare; to women, especially the young and fair, he appears as a handsome youth' (Kennedy-Fraser). Locations reputed to be haunted by such creatures include: the river Spey, the Island of Raasay, the Isle of Lewis, Eigg, and the Monach Islands. On his tour of the Scottish Highlands and Islands with Samuel Johnson in 1773, James Boswell (*Journal*, 195–6) recorded that Malcolm M'Cleod, his guide (Boswell went without Johnson), 'told me a strange fabulous tradition'. They were on their way to the mountain of Dùn Caan on the Island of Raasay and had passed two lochs; it was the first one (Loch na Mna, rather than Loch na Meilich) that brought the tale to Malcolm's mind: 'He said, there was a wild beast in it, a sea-horse, which came and devoured a man's daughter; upon which the man lighted a great fire, and had a sow roasted at it, the smell of which attracted the monster. In the fire was put a spit. The man lay concealed behind a low wall of loose stones, and he had an avenue formed for the monster, with two rows of large flat stones, which extended from the fire over the summit of the hill, till it reached the side of the loch. The monster came, and the man with the red-hot spit destroyed it. Malcolm shewed me the little hiding-place, and the rows of stones. He did not laugh when he told this story.' See also **Kelpie**, **Tarbh-Uisge** ('water-bull'). (Campbell, *Pop. Tales*, IV, 307–8; Henderson, *Survivals*, 116; MacDougall and Calder, *Folk Tales*, 307–319.)

EALE, SEE YALE

ECHENEÏS

From the Greek ἔχειν (*echein*), 'to hold' and ναυς (*naus*), 'boat'; in Latin *remora*, 'delay': a small fish given supernormal powers by Pliny the Elder: 'a single fish, and that of a very diminutive size – the fish known as the "echeneïs" – possesses the power of counteracting [sea storms]. Winds may blow and storms may rage, and yet the echeneïs controls their fury, restrains their mighty force, and bids ships stand still in their career; a result which no cables, no anchors, from their ponderousness quite incapable of being weighed, could ever have produced! A fish bridles the impetuous violence of the deep, and subdues the frantic rage of the universe – and all this by no effort of its own, no act of resistance on its part, no act at all, in fact, but that of adhering to the bark! Trifling as this object would appear, it suffices to counteract all these forces combined, and to forbid the ship to pass onward in its way! Fleets, armed for war, pile up towers and bulwarks on their decks, in order that, upon the deep even, men may fight from behind ramparts as it were. But alas for human vanity! – when their prows, beaked as they are with brass and with iron, and armed for the onset, can thus be arrested and rivetted to the spot by a little fish, no more than some half foot in length! At the battle of Actium, it is said, a fish of this kind stopped the prætorian ship of Antonius in its course, at the moment that he was hastening from ship to ship to encourage and exhort his men, and so compelled him to leave it and go on board another. Hence it was, that the fleet of Cæsar gained the advantage in the onset, and charged with a redoubled impetuosity. In our own time, too, one of these fish arrested the ship of the Emperor Caius in its course, when he was returning from Astura to Antium: and thus, as the result proved, did an insignificant fish give presage of great events; for no sooner had the emperor returned to Rome than he was pierced by the weapons of his own soldiers. Nor did this sudden stoppage of the ship long remain a mystery, the cause being perceived upon finding that, out of the whole fleet, the emperor's five-banked galley was the only one that was making no way. The moment this was discovered, some of the sailors plunged into the sea, and, on making search about the ship's sides, they found an echeneïs adhering to the rudder. Upon its being shown to the emperor, he strongly expressed his indignation that such an obstacle as this should have impeded his progress, and have rendered powerless the hearty endeavours of some four hundred men. One thing, too, it is well known, more particularly surprised him, how it was possible that the fish, while adhering to the ship, should arrest its progress, and yet should have no such power when brought on board. According to the persons who examined it on that occasion, and who have seen it since, the echeneïs bears a strong resemblance to a large slug'

(*Nat. Hist.* 32.1, Bostock's trans.). Pliny adds that the Greeks believed that it had magical powers and worn as an amulet could prevent miscarriage or, if preserved in salt, encourage giving birth. Linnaeus used the word to name the genus *Echeneis* and classify the species *Echeneis naucrates*, the live sharksucker, in 1758; the Russian naturalist Zuiew added the *Echeneis necratoides*, whitefin sharksucker, in 1789 – the genus is distinctive for having a suction pad on its head with which it can attach to a host fish.

ECHIDNA

A nymph or lesser goddess of Ancient Greek mythology, the daughter of Ceto and **Phorcys**; she was half woman, half snake. Hesiod described her in his *Theogony* of *c.*700 BCE: 'fierce Echidna who is half a nymph with

Echidna, Mother of the Colchian Dragon (c.1663)

glancing eyes and fair cheeks, and half again a huge snake, great and awful, with speckled skin, eating raw flesh beneath the secret parts of the holy earth. And there she has a cave deep down under a hollow rock far from the deathless gods and mortal men. There, then, did the gods appoint her a glorious house to dwell in: and she keeps guard in Arima beneath the earth, grim Echidna, a nymph who dies not nor grows old all her days' (Hesiod, *Theog.*, 307). According to Hesiod, she bore several monstrous children to the dragon **Typhon**, namely the two-headed dog **Orthus**, the multi-headed **Cerberus**, the **Lernæan Hydra**, **Chimæra**, **Ladon** and the Colchian Dragon; and to Orthus she bore the **Sphinx** and the **Nemean Lion**. Apollodorus also added the **Crommyonian Sow** to her brood. According to Herodotus, Hercules also stayed with her in return for his horses, which she had spirited away, and fathered Agathyrsus, Gelonus and Scythes, the future king of the Scythians (*Hist.*, 4.8–10). According to Apollodorus, she was slain in her sleep by Argus, who 'had eyes in the whole of his body' (*Library*, 2.1.2).

ELEPHANT

Various impossible species of the elephant are recorded, such as the sea-elephant and the winged elephant. The winged elephant, like an Indian Pegasus, is met with in Hindu mythology and art; and the *Matangalila*, a book on elephants, depicts several winged specimens. Also from Hindu mythology, Mahapudma is the giant elephant that holds up the world. (Murthy, *Myth. An. Ind.*, 13.)

EMMET

The heraldic ant, also called a **Pismire**, used to symbolise industry and understanding. John Guillim wrote in *A Display of Heraldrie* (1610): 'By the Emmet or Pismire may be signified a Man of great Labour, Wisdom, and Providence in all his Affairs, and of a pregnant and ready Memory'. In Milton's *Paradise Lost* we read: 'The parsimonious Emmet, provident | Of future, in small room large heart enclosed— | Pattern of just equality perhaps'. Along with the bee, it is the only insect found in heraldry. In Scotland a rough form of weather divinitation was performed by cupping the emmet (*Caora-Chòsag*) in the hands and shaking it like a die before rolling it out on the table: whether it lay on its back or belly, and how fast it tried to escape indicated, in some now forgotten manner, the next day's weather (Campbell, *Sup. High.*, 228).

ENBARR

In Irish mythology, the white horse of Manannán mac Ler. His name means 'splendid mane'. He was 'swifter than the wind of spring' over both land and sea, and his bridle had been taken from a **Water-Horse**. (Eiichirô, '"Kappa" Legend', 35; Howey, *Horse Magic*, 142–3.)

ENFIELD

A composite animal found in Heraldry having a fox's head, a greyhound's chest, an eagle's talons, a lion's body

Hercules and the Erymanthian Boar (1608)

and the hind legs and tail of a wolf; or sometimes the hind legs of a greyhound and tail of a lion. Used in the coat of arms of the London Borough of Enfield, the enfield is nevertheless most closely associated with the Irish Kelly or O'Kelly family. According to family legend: 'There is a tradition among the O'Kellys of Hy-Many, that they have borne as their crest an enfield, since the time of this Tadhg Mor, from a belief that this fabulous animal issued from the sea at the battle of Clontarf, to protect the body of O'Kelly from the Danes, till rescued by his followers' (O'Donovan, *Tribes*, 99). Williams ('Beasts', 62–78) believes that the origin of this beast is in the Irish **Onchú**.

ERCINEE, SEE HERCYNIA

ERYMANTHIAN BOAR

In Greek mythology, a giant boar from mount Erymanthus that terrorised the countryside round the city of Psophis in northern Arcadia. Capturing the animal alive was the fourth task given to Hercules. After fighting a **Centaur** band on the way, Hercules finally ran the animal down in deep snow and having tired it out was able to bring it back to Mycenae. (Apollodorus, *Library*, 2.5.4.)

EXOCOETUS

A sort of amphibian supposedly found in the Greek Peloponnese peninsula. According to Pliny (*Nat. Hist.*, 9.19): 'The Arcadians make wonderous great account of their Exocoetus; so called, for that he goeth abroad, and taketh up his lodging on the drie land for to sleepe. This fish (by report) about the coast Clitorius, hath a kind of voice, and yet is without guils. And of some hee is named Adonis.' The name comes from the Ancient Greek, meaning literally 'sleeping outside'. Today, the name *Exocoetus* is given to a genus of flying fish.

EXTRAORDINARY FISH

The 'Extraordinary Fish' was a Victorian 'Wonder of the Deep'. It was said to have been caught in 1861 off Port Talbot Bar. It was described as being between four and five feet in length and 'amongst other peculiarities is possessed of two legs, with hoofs similar to a calf's, four rows of teeth, &c., &c., and is well worthy of Inspection'. It was exhibited at the Golden Lion Inn, Commercial Place, Aberdare: entrance tuppence, half-price for children. The handbill for this exhibition is now preserved in the Museum of Wales, Cardiff.

F

FAUN

In Roman mythology, a creature half human and half goat, like the Greek **Satyr**. There was also a supposed god called Faunus, who had much the same nature as the Greek **Pan**, with whom he was later identified. Fauna was his sister and later wife; according to legend, he beat her to death with myrtle boughs after she became intoxicated on wine, but, being struck with remorse, made her divine. The fauns (*fauni*) were seen as his attendants and believed to have frivolous and sometimes mischievous natures (they were blamed for causing nightmares). In Rome, two festivals of the Faunalia were celebrated in his honour, one on 13 February, the other on 5 December. (Peck, *Harper's Dict.*, 662–3.)

FEARSOME CRITTERS

The term for a broad menagerie of fabulous beasts invented by the lumberjacks of North America. Somewhere in-between folklore, tall tales and outright jokes, the critters include: the Argopelter who lives in hollow trees and throws sticks at passersby; the Axehandle Hound, a dog that looks like an axe and eats unattended axes; the Ball-Tailed Cat and subspecies Digmaul and Silvercat; the leaping Billdad of Boundary Pond in the Hurrican Township; the Cactus Cat, covered in spines and noted for getting drunk and shrieking all night long; the camp Chipmunk that subsists on discarded prune stones; the Central American Whintosser; the alligator-like, mouthless Dungavenhooter that inhales its prey; the Fish Hound, bred from a 'hell diver' and a mink; Flittericks, dangerous high-speed flying

A Fearsome Critter: The Splintercat (1910)

squirrels; the Funeral Mountain Terrashot; the **Fur-Bearing Trout** or Furry Trout; the Gillygaloo bird that lays square eggs to stop them rolling down the hillside; the Goofang fish that swims backwards to keep the water out of its eyes; the backwards flying Goofus Bird; the Gumberoo, with a round leathery body larger than a bear's and apt to explode at night; the Gyascutus with telescopic legs that subsists on rocks and lichen; the Hangdown, which likes to swing from branches; the Hide-Behind, a tall, thin creature that hides behind trees and likes to dine on the bowels of human beings; the swamp-dwelling Hodag; the Hoop Snake that can put its tail in its mouth and roll like a wheel; the thirteen-foot-high Hugag who ruins loggers' huts by leaning up against them; the Hyampom Hog Bear; the blue-striped, triple-jointed Luferlang that could run in every direction (there was a surprise); the featherless Phillyloo bird that flies upside down; the one-winged Pinnacle Grouse that is forced to fly round and round any suitable peak; the Roperite that uses its rope-like beak to lasso sprinting rabbits; the blanket-like Rumtifusel that throws itself over the unwary and sucks the flesh off their bones; the Sidehill Dodger, specially adapted to running on hillsides with two long legs on one side and two short legs on the other, uphill, side; the Slide-Rock Bolter of the Colorado mountains; the propeller driven Snoligoster of Florida; the Splintercat that breaks trees with its head; the unhappy Squonk of the Pennsylvanian hemlock forests; the whistling, steam-snorting Teakettler; the Tote-Road Shagamaw that eats items of clothing unwisely left by lumberjacks hanging on trees or logs; the tripod-legged Tripodero that can shoot clay pellets out of its gun-like beak; the Upland Trout that nests in trees (although it was recently discovered that the mangrove rivulus or killifish does just that); the Wapaloosie; the Whiffenpoof, a fish with a taste for cheese; the Whirling Whimpus that spins so fast on its one hoof that it is practically invisible. If it were not for the decline in the lumberjack trade, the list would no doubt be considerably longer; the diligent will discover that the list is, indeed, longer. Critters like the Gumberoo and Splintercat were clearly invented to humourously explain the features and oddities of the forest, such as otherwise inexplicable night noises, which can often be surprisingly loud, and storm-shattered trees. Some of these, such as the Furry Trout, were supported by spurious **Jenny Haniver** creations. The **Jackalope** is sometimes included in this category. The first published collection was William T. Cox's *Fearsome Creatures of the Lumberwoods* of 1910, with George B. Sudworth adding fanciful Latin classifications. Henry Harrington Triton popularised the term 'fearsome critters' in his 1939 book of the same name. It was dedicated 'To those who have held the bag on a Snipe hunt, who have jumped sideways at the call of the Treesqueak' and so on. Both books were illustrated. Other important collections are two short books on the legendary lumberjack Paul Bunyan by the former head of the State Historical Museum in Madison, Wisconsin, Charles Edward Brown (1872–1946), and *The Hodag* by Luke Sylvester 'Lake Shore' Kearney.

FENGHUANG

Also *Fung-Whang*, the Chinese **Phoenix**, one of four supernatural creatures symbolising the four quarters of the heavens, in this case fire. It is shown as crested and with long tail feathers, looking somewhat like the peacock. It is brightly coloured with feathers of red, azure, yellow, white and black – the colours of the five virtues – and the Chinese ideograms for uprightness, humanity, virtue, honesty and sincerity are stamped upon it. The name is composed of the male *Feng* and female *Huang*. The same creature is known in Japan as the *Ho-Ho*. (Ingersoll, *Birds*, 207–8.)

FENRIR

Also *Fenris*, *Fenris-ulfr*, a giant wolf of Norse mythology. He is born of Loki and the witch Angerboda; his siblings are the Midgard Serpent, **Jörmungandr**, and the death-goddess Hel. The gods took him in, thinking to tame him, but he became so large and unruly (and prophecy warned that he would be their doom) that they decided to bind him; in the process he bit off the hand of the war-god Tyr. A sword was thrust into his mouth to prop it open and the slather running out created the river called Van. The giant hound **Garmr** watched over him. At the final battle of Ragnarok, Fenrir kills Odin and is killed in turn by Odin's son Vithar. (Rydberg, *Teut. Myth*, I, 215;

Sturluson, 'The Beguiling of Gylfi', §34, *Prose Edda*, V, 42–3.)

FIRE BIRD

Pliny's *incendiaria avis*: 'This fire-bird Incendiaria is likewise unluckie, and as our Chonicles and Annales do witnesse, in regard of her the citie of Rome many a time hath made solemne supplications to pacifie the gods, and to avert their displeasure, by her portended: as for example, when L. Cassius and C. Marius were Consuls: in that very yeere when by occasion of a Scritch-owle seene, the citie likewise was purged by sacrifice, as is abovesaid, and the people fell to their prayers and devotions. But what bird this should be, neither doe I know, nor yet finde in any writer. Some give this interpretation of Incendiaria, to be any bird whatsoever, which hath been seene carrying fire either from altar or chappell of the gods. Others call this bird Spinturnix. But hitherto I have not met with any man who would say directly unto me, That he knew what bird this should be' (*Nat. Hist.*, 10.13). Pliny also reported that 'In Hercinia, a forrest in Germanie, wee have heard that there bee strange kinds of birds, with feathers shining like fire in the night season' (10.47); he thought the story far-fetched, but see **Hercynia**. Other fire-birds include the Persian Huma, the Greek and Roman **Phoenix**, the Slavic Zhar-ptitsa, and the Chinese Zhū Què (Vermillion Bird).

FIRE-DRAKE

Various forms of light phenomena, previously believed to be endowed

Odin and Fenrir (1909)

with life. In Bullokar's 1616 *Expositor* we read: 'There is a fire sometimes seen flying in the night, like a dragon: it is called a fire-drake. Common people think it a spirit that keeps some treasure hid' (quoted in Brand, *Pop. Antiq.*, 235). According to Burton in his *Anatomy of Melancholy* of 1621: a will-o'-the-wisp, 'Fiery spirits or devils are such as commonly work by fire-drakes, or *ignes fatui*, which lead men often *in flumina et praecipitia*' (120–1); or St Elmo's Fire, 'spirits or fire in the form of fire-drakes and blazing stars, sit on the ship masts' (121). (Dyer, *Folk-Lore*, 80.)

FORMICOLEON

The ant-lion, according to Isidore of Seville (*Etym.*, 12.3.10): '*Formicoleon* is named, either because he is the lion of ants or because he is equally lion and ant. It is a small animal, very hostile to ants. It hides in the dust and kills ants while they are carrying grain. Thus it is called both lion and ant since, to other animals, it is an ant, but to the ants it is a lion'. In the nineteenth century, George F. Moore (*Desc. Voc.*, 54, 58) translated the Australian Aboriginal name for the bull ant, *kallili* or *killal*, as 'lion-ant'.

FUWCH FRECH

Welsh, also *Fuwch Fraith*, the 'particoloured or freckled cow'; a fabulous cow of Welsh folklore that gave milk to all who wanted it and it could never be milked dry. The tale is told that 'To that cow there came a witch to get milk, just after the cow had supplied the whole neighbourhood. So the witch could not get any milk, and to avenge her disappointment she made the cow mad. The result was that the cow ran wild over the mountains, inflicting immense harm on the country; but at last she was killed by Hu near Hiraethog, in the county of Denbigh.' There was at one time an enormous bone in the inner court of a house at Llanrwst and the people of the area said that it was the rib of the *Fuwch Frech*: it seems to have been a whale bone. It was said to be the mother of the *Ychain Banawg*, or large-horned oxen. Equivalent to the English Dun Cow; and other tales are told of a similar white cow. Another Welsh supernatural cow was the *Fuwch Gyfeiliorn*, the 'stray cow', said to have come from a fairy herd and likewise to give abundantly until some imprudent action of humans. (Owen, *Welsh Folk-Lore*, 130–7; Rhys, *Celtic Folklore*, vol. 2.)

FUR-BEARING TROUT

The Fur-Bearing or Furry Trout is, as its named suggests, a supposedly fur covered fish. There is a specimen in the Royal Scottish Museum in Edinburgh with the description: 'Caught while trolling in Lake Superior off Gros Cap, near Sault Ste. Marie, district of

Fur-Bearing Trout (2009)

Algoma. It is believed that the great depth and the extreme penetrating coldness of the water in which these fish live has caused them to grow their dense coat of (usually) white fur. Mounted by Ross C. Jobe, Taxidermist of Sault Ste. Marie Ont.' The fish was brought to the museum by a woman who had bought it and wanted to find out more about it: Museum staff kindly explained that it was a trout covered in rabbit fur. She left it with them (Dance, *Animal Fakes*, 115). It is a more fully coated cousin of the Icelandic **Lod-Silungur**, or 'shaggy trout', a fish said to have reddish hair on its lower jaw and around the neck with additional hairy patches here and there along its body (Davidson, 'Folk-Lore', 331).

G

GABRIEL'S HOUNDS

Also *Gabriel Ratchets*, Gabble Ratchets, Gabble Raches, from Old English, *ræcc*, meaning a dog that hunts by scent, *gabble* meaning to talk quickly and unintelligibly. They are supernatural dogs of Northern England, particularly Yorkshire and Lancashire, whose yelping carries across the lonely landscape in the dead of night, or in the wee small hours of morning. To hear them is a portent of death, either of the listener or one to whom he is related or acquainted. Undoubtedly a survival of the Wild Hunt, a widespread motif in European mythology, they have been Christianised as representing the wailing souls of children who have died without baptism. Gabriel must lead them till doomsday as a punishment for having hunted on a Sunday. Wordsworth alludes to this superstition in one of his Sonnets: 'For overhead are sweeping Gabriel's Hounds, | Doomed, with their impious lord, the flying hart | To chase for ever on aerial grounds'. A certain Mr Holland of Sheffield, writing in 1861, claimed to have heard them: 'I can never forget the impression made upon my own mind when once arrested by the cry of these Gabriel hounds as I passed the parish church of Sheffield, one densely dark and very still night. The sound was exactly like the greeting of a dozen beagles on the foot of a race, but not so loud, and highly suggestive of ideas of the supernatural (quoted in Hardwick, *Traditions*, 153–4). The term was recorded in the *Catholicon Anglicum* as early as 1483: 'Gabrielle rache, camalion'. It is supposed that the sound attributed to this spectral chase is actually that of geese or other wild fowl as they make their way south at the onset of winter. (Wright, *Rust. Sp.*, 195; Swainson, *Prov. Names*, 98.) See also **Dandy-Dog** and **Yeth Hound**.

GALGULUS

The Latin name, meaning 'small bird', plural *galguli*, hardly describes this strange bird. According to Pliny (*Nat. Hist.*, 10.50): 'the birds called Galguli, men say for a truth, that they take their sleepe hanging all by their legges to some braunch, thinking by that meanes they are in more safetie.' He said nothing more about it, although a certain incredulity might be discerned, but from this description of its chief pecularity, Linnaeus gave the name to what was earlier called the sapphire-crowned parrakeet (*Psittacus galgulus*), now the blue-crowned hanging parrot (*Loriculus galgulus*). Travellers' tales from Sumatra and the Philippines documented similar behaviour in this bird. The Swedish explorer Peter Osbeck encountered the bird near Java in 1751: 'it hangs itself with its feet so, that the back is turned towards the earth, and seldom changes this situation' (*Voyage*, I, 151). Whether this was Pliny's bird, or not, it turns out that there was such a creature; although translators often give 'witwall' for *galgulus*, another name for the golden oriole.

GALLY-TROT

Also *galley trot*; a British monstrous dog. In the North Country and Suffolk, a gally-trot is a bullock-sized white dog – perhaps an albino version of the more common **Black Dog**, although other accounts have given its colour as black. Its territory covers the area of Woodbridge and Bath-slough in particular. A famous incident was described in a 'A Strange and Terrible Wonder' of 1577, detailing an attack carried out at that time in the vicinity of 'Bongay' (Bungay in Suffolk): during a wild storm, a giant black dog burst into the parish church and throttled two parishoners at their prayers. The word is said to be from *gaily*, meaning to frighten, scare, in the local dialect; it can also be used as a general term for supernatural phenomena. Compare the Gallitrap ('Gallows-trap') of Devonshire, an enchanted piece of ground that catches people destined to be hung. (Gurdon, *Suffolk*, 85–6; Henderson, *Notes*, 278; Wright, *Rust. Sp.*, 194.)

GARGOUILLE

French, 'waterspout', the name of a **Dragon** that once lived in the river Seine in the seventh century CE. According to legend he terrorised the city of Rouen until slain by St Romanus, Bishop of Rouen, who was undoubtedly filling the boots of some earlier pagan hero. The name, if not the memory, survives in the word 'gargoyle' used for the grotesque water spouts on medieval churches. (Vinycomb, *Fict. Sym.*, 81.)

GARMR

Also *Garm*, a giant dog in Norse mythology. It is described as foremost among dogs, as Odin is foremost among gods and **Sleipnir** foremost among horses. It functions as a guard dog: its barking heralds Ragnarok when the chains of Loki and **Fenrir** burst asunder. But we also read that he, too, is bound and, like Fenrir, frees himself at the end to attack the war-god Tyr. (Rydberg, *Teut. Myth.*, II, 564; Sturluson, 'The Beguiling of Gylfi', §51, in *Prose Edda*, V, 79.)

GARUDA

Also *Superna*, in Hindu mythology, a half giant, half eagle, the king of the birds. Representations vary: sometimes he has a human body with the head and wings of a bird; sometimes he has only bird's claws; other times he has a human head on a bird's body. He was the offspring of Kasyapa the sage and Vinatā, or, according to another legend, of Kasyapa and Diti. His mother's sister, Kadru, was the mother of serpents and, due to a quarrel between the sisters, Garuda was the mortal enemy of serpents. Garuda steals the ambrosia, called *amrita*, of the gods, the magical substance that gives them their power and immortality. Indra, the thunderer, assaults it with his thunder bolts, but succeeds in dislodging only a single feather. Garuda gave the amrita to the serpents in return for his mother, whom they had kept captive; and Indra steals it back. In the *Mahàbhàrata* Garuda was the mount (Vāhan) of the god Vishnu and 'mocked the wind with his fleetness'. He can be equated with the Sumerian **Zu Bird** (Mackenzie, *Myth. Bab.*, 74–5). The *Garuda Purana* (Wood and Subrahmanyam), composed sometime in the Middles Ages, is a dialogue between Garuda and Vishnu that concerns death, funeral observances and reincarnation; it is read during Hindu funeral ceremonies. The name of Garuda, repeated three times, is also used as a charm against snakes. (Wilkins, *Hindu Myth.*, 450–6.)

GERYON

Geryon was originally a giant with three heads; later three torsos and six arms were added and (in some sources) six legs (see, e.g., Hesiod, *Theog.*, 287). He was the progeny of **Chrysaor**, the brother of **Pegasus**, and Callirrhoë, daughter of Ocean. By the time Dante had finished with him, however, he

had the upper body of a man and the long tail of a giant serpent, ending in a scorpion's sting (*Inferno*, C, xvii). He lived on the fabulous island of Erytheia where he was served by **Orthus**, a two-headed dog, who, with the giant Eurytion, guarded his herd of red oxen. He was slain by Hercules in accomplishment of his Tenth Labour (Apollodorus, *Library*, 2.5.10).

GIGELORUM

Also *Giolcam-daoram*, in Scottish folklore it is the smallest of animals, making its nest in the ear of a mite. (Campbell, *Sup. High.*, 220.)

GIRTABLILU

Also *girtablullû*, the Babylonian 'scorpion-man': a monster created by the sea-dragon **Tiamat**. In the *Enuma Elish*, the Babylonian Creation Myth, Tiamat creates the scorpion-man as part of her army of eleven evil monsters whom she fields against Marduk. After Tiamat's defeat, Marduk subjugates the eleven. The scorpion-man subsequently became a beneficent demon, warding off evil demons and illness. The figure is depicted as a man, usually wearing a horned cap, either with or without wings, his feet are the talons of some bird of prey and his penis terminates in a snake's head; he holds his hands up with palms outwards to ward off evil. He is of considerable antiquity: the *Enuma Elish* is derived from stories as old as 2000 BCE; and depictions survive from the twelfth century BCE, for example. The *kudurru* of Nebuchadnezzar I, a boundary stone from *c.*1125–1104 BCE, shows a scorpion-man in an aggressive posture with bent bow (BM 90858). A Late Assyrian cylinder seal that belonged to Remani-ilu, a eunuch official of the governor of Kalhu at the end of the ninth century or beginning of the eighth century BCE, is shown being protected by a scorpion-man (Florence 14385). Although originally created by Tiamat, the scorpion-man is also shown fighting Tiamat (or the **Zu Bird**), apparently as a representation of Marduk (Langdon, 'Six Bab.', 46). In the Gilgamesh Epic, a male and female girtablilu guard the gate of mount *Māšu* (Mashu), the place of terrors, through which the sun rises and sets. Girtablilu can be identified with the constellation of Sagittarius. He is sometimes seen as a prototype of the later Pazuzu. (Green, 'Scorpion-Man', 75–82; Jastrow, *Rel. Bab.*, 488–9; Wiggerman, *Mes. Prot. Sp.*, 180–1.)

GLAISTIG

A Scottish water creature, sometimes described as half woman, half goat, sometimes as a thin grey woman with yellow hair growing down to her feet and a fondness for green clothes; her face was once described as being like 'a grey stone overgrown with lichen' (MacGregor, *Peat-Fire*, 58–65). Her nature is changeable, sometimes benign, sometimes malevolent and 'harmless and loveable as a rule' in the old tales, but now 'she has degenerated into a kind of female ruffian' (Watson, 'High. Myth.', 54). From the Gaelic *glas*, *glaise*, 'grey-green', taken to mean water. The forms *glastic*, *glaisnig*, *glaisric* and *glaislid* are all recorded; on the Isle of Man they say *glashtin*. The Highland region of Lochaber is a favoured haunt of the Glaistig. Places with Glaistig legends include: Carn-na-Caillich by the Sound of Mull; Glenborrodale, Lochaber; Achantore, Lochaber; Ardtornish Bay, Lochaber; Ruighe-na-cloiche beside Ciaran Water on Ben Breck, Lochaber; Ardnadrochaid, Isle of Mull; Ach-na-Creige, Isle of Mull; Morven peninsula, Lochaber; the Isle of Colonsay, Inner Hebrides; Castle Camus, Sleat of Skye; Inveraw House, Loch Etive, Argyll and Bute; the Island House, Isle of Tiree; Breachacha Castle, Island of Coll; Dunstaffnage Castle, Loch Etive, Argyll and Bute; Dunollie Castle, Argyll and Bute; there is a Glaistig's Stone at Staonnaig on Iona. A frequent motif is that a small voice is heard as if far off, but grows louder and louder as the Glaistig approaches at great speed. She was also reputed to have an unnatural ability to shout loudly. She frequently preys on cattle and supplication was made to appease her. On Colonsay in 1880 a woman told of her ritual of leaving milk in a bowl for the Glaistig. It was also a tradition on Colonsay that on the first night of the year on which the cattle could be left out all night, each crofter gave all of the night's milk from one of his cows to the Glaistig by pouring it into a cavity in a stone near the farmhouse of Balnahard, recorded as recently as 1910. In an old folktale, a Glaistig of Glenhurich takes a new-born foal from a grey mare and drowns it in a hole above an underground stream. The Glaistig herded deer, normally something only to be seen by those who had the Second Sight. A Glaistig that was well looked after could also help in the household, always at night, in the manner of the Brownie; but also had quite a mind for mischief. People who had a Glaistig always knew when guests were coming, as the Glaistig would work extra hard in tidying up and making things ready; she would also mislead those self-same guests if they left their rooms in the night, and leave them wandering and lost in the unfamiliar surroundings. Lazy servants and those who did not take her seriously were often subject to nocturnal assaults. A man who went out to fish and came back empty-handed might say that the Glaistig had taken them from him. In most stories the Glaistig is particularly averse to dogs, but in one variation she takes the form of a dog herself. One should never give her anything from one's hand as she will seize it and drag you off. A sprig of holly above the door, or a Bible on the lintel, was said to keep her at bay, not always successfully. (MacDougall and Calder, *Folk Tales*, 233–69.)

GLASHTYN

A malevolent **Water-Horse** in the folklore of the Isle of Man, somewhat indistinguishable from the *fenodyree*, meaning one who has hair for stockings or hose. It takes the form of a grey colt and has a liking for Manx womenfolk. (Rhys, *Celtic Folklore*, 288–9.)

GLYCON

A snake with a human face revealed as a new god by a certain Alexander, called 'the Paphlagonian' or 'of Abonoteichos' (his birthplace), in the second century CE. Abonoteichos (later called Ionopolis, apparently after Alexander's suggestion) was a coastal town in Paphlagonia, which was an ancient region in Anatolia on the southern shores of the Black Sea. The story is told by the Roman satirist Lucian (*Alex.*, 6). Glycon was apparently found by Alexander among the foundations of a new temple then being constructed. He inserted a newly born snake into a goose egg and hid it in the mud. He then announced the coming of the god in the market-place and led the people to marvel at his discovery as he found the egg and re-opened it. Lucian thought Alexander an outright fraud who had 'prepared and fitted up a serpent's head of linen, which had something of a human look, was all painted up, and appeared very lifelike. It would open and close its mouth by means of horsehairs, and a forked black tongue like a snake's, also controlled by horsehairs, would dart out'. With this ingenious contraption he received countless visitors in a dimly lit room and so convinced them of all that he said. 'Next,' said Lucian, 'came paintings and statues and cult-images, some made of bronze, some of silver, and naturally a name was bestowed upon the god. He was called Glycon in consequence of a divine behest in metre; for Alexander proclaimed: "Glycon am I, the grandson of Zeus, bright beacon to mortals!"' He later produced a talking version: 'It was no difficult matter for him to fasten

Glycon (Possibly Second Century BCE)

cranes' windpipes together and pass them through the head, which he had so fashioned as to be lifelike. Then he answered the questions through someone else, who spoke into the tube from the outside'. Alexander proceeded to propound prophecies and oracles from this Glycon (for a fee) until his death in 170 CE. An apparently mysterious 'Glycon' had been earlier mentioned by Horace (*Epistles*, Bk I) in 20 BCE: 'you despair of the muscles of the invincible Glycon' – it is supposed that a statue of Hercules made by the very human sculptor Glycon, which was known as 'The Glycon', is meant.

GOAT-SUCKER,

SEE CAPRIMULGUS AND CHUPACABRA

GOLDEN LIMPET

In Paris in 1776 there was a craze for 'golden limpets'. These rare and wondrous shells were, in fact, only the limpet *Patinigera deaurata* commonly found on the Falkland Islands, roasted in hot ashes or gently pan-fried to turn their russet colour into shining gold. Other fake shells have been known, including a heat-treated Lurid Cowry (*Cypraea lurida*), Chinese rice-paste forgeries of the Precious Wentletrap (*Epitonium scalare*), and the rare Tapa Cowry, a rubbed-down Arabic Cowry (*Cypraea arabica*), offered in quantity to tourists on the Fiji Islands. (Dance, *Animal Fakes*, 90.)

GOOMCHER

A rodent of the Himalayas with a reputation for the impossible. Major Lawrence Austine Waddell of the British Indian Army documented these and local folk-beliefs concerning them while exploring the Kanchen-Junga region in the 1890s: 'I also saw some tail-less rats or marmots. These small mammals called Goomcher by the Bhotiyas, are credited with supernatural powers, in that, if they are harmed in any way, they produce fearful and disastrous storms. This belief is evidently due. I think, to the habits of these animals burrowing into the bowels of the earth, where live, according to the Tibetans, the dragon-spirits or Nagas that cause thunder-storms. Owing to this superstition few natives will assist you in catching the animal, yet they do not scruple to rob it of its hoards of stored grass and grain whenever they are in need of fuel or fodder.' (Waddell, *Am. Him.*, 219.)

GOOSEBERRY-WIFE

On the Isle of Wight, the Gooseberry-Wife is a large furry caterpillar that guards the gooseberries, particularly from naughty children. (Wright, *Rust. Sp.*, 198.)

GRAVE-SOW, SEE KIRKEGRIM

GRIFFIN

Also *griffon*, *gryphon*, etc., from the Greek γρύψ, 'gryps', meaning 'hooked'; in Latin *gryphus*; first described as a wolf-sized bird with lion's legs and claws. In heraldry, the male griffin is called **Alce**; the winged variety **Opinicus**. The griffin had been a popular theme in Greek art since the seventh century BCE, but Herodotus, writing in the fifth century BCE, was the first to document these creatures in a tale involving gold and a race of one-eyed humans: 'The northern parts of Europe are very much richer in gold than any other region: but how it is procured I have no certain knowledge. The story runs, that the one-eyed Arimaspi purloin it from the griffins; but here too I am incredulous, and cannot persuade myself that there is a race of men born with only one eye, who in all else resemble the rest of mankind. Nevertheless it seems to be true that the extreme regions of the earth, which surround and shut up within themselves all other countries, produce the things which are the rarest, and which men reckon the most beautiful. Aristeas also, son of Caystrobius, a native of Proconnesus, says in the course of his poem, that rapt in bacchic fury, he went as far as the Issedones. Above them dwelt the Arimaspi, men with one eye; still further, the gold-guarding Griffins; and beyond these, the Hyperboreans, who extend to the sea [...].' Later in the same century, the physician and historian Ctesias also wrote about

Griffin (Medieval)

gold-guarding griffins, but placed them in India: 'those many high-towering mountains which are inhabited by the Griffons, a race of four-footed birds, about as large as wolves, having legs and claws like those of the lion, and covered all over the body with black feathers except only on the breast where they are red'.

Pliny the Elder had heard of them in the first century CE and noted their 'long eares, and a hooked bill', but thought them merely fabulous (*Nat. Hist.*, 10.70). Writing in the seventh century CE, Isidore of Seville (*Etym.*, 12.2.17) expressed no doubts when he stated that the 'Griffin is named *grypes* because it is a four-footed, winged animal. This wild animal is born in the Hyperborean mountains. They are lions in their body; similar to eagles in their wings and faces; very dangerous to horses. They tear apart any human they see'. Bartholomaeus Anglicus (*Med. Lore*) largley repeated this in the thirteenth century CE, but added the curious piece of information that the griffin 'layeth in his nest a stone that hight Smaragdus against venomous beasts of the mountain' – the smaragdus is more commonly known today as the emerald. In the fourteenth century, Sir John Mandeville (*Travels*, 177) described a land he called Bacharia (possibly Bactria, now divided between Afghanistan and Tajikistan) – full of evil, cruel people, bitter waters, trees that bear wool, **Hippotayne**s and griffins: 'In that country be many griffins, more plenty than in any other country. Some men say that they have the body upward as

an eagle and beneath as a lion; and truly they say sooth, that they be of that shape. But one griffin hath the body more great and is more strong than eight lions, of such lions as be on this half, and more great and stronger than an hundred eagles such as we have amongst us. For one griffin there will bear, flying to his nest, a great horse, if he may find him at the point, or two oxen yoked together as they go at the plough. For he hath his talons so long and so large and great upon his feet, as though they were horns of great oxen or of bugles or of kine, so that men make cups of them to drink of. And of their ribs and of the pens of their wings, men make bows, full strong, to shoot with arrows and quarrels.' The Zoological Museum in Copenhagen has a stuffed 'griffin' in its collection.

GRIM, SEE CHURCH GRIM

GRUCK

From 'grouse' and 'duck'. A single specimen of this bird exists, preserved in the collection of the Royal Scottish Museum, Edinburgh. It is unlikely that there will be any further discoveries of this unusual species: former museum taxidermist Ian Lyster concocted it from the head of a tufted duck and the body of a red grouse, with sundry additional feathers from an unidentified duck species added for emphasis. (Dance, *Animal Fakes*, 80.)

GRYLLUS

Plural *grylli*, meaning 'crickets', a name given by Pliny the Elder to a popular fantastical animal motif in Roman art comprising two sorts: combinations of animal and human heads, occasionally with the addition of birds; or the bodies of birds (usually cocks) with different heads and masks, such as those having horse's heads, being reminiscent of the Ancient Greek **Hippalectryon**. They were believed to have magical properties and were used as charms up until the Middle Ages and possibly beyond. Similar combinatory creatures have been found in the necropolis of Tharros in Sardinia (dating from the fourth century BCE), in Scythia – a gold plaque design of a human and lion head – and in the Ancient city of Ur in Mesopotamia. (Blanchet, 'Recherches', 43–51; Roes, 'New Light', 232–5.)

GULLFAXI

In Norse Mythology, Gullfaxi (Old Norse, 'golden mane') first belonged to the giant Hrungnir. When Odin rode **Sleipnir** to the land of the giants, Jötunheimr, he came to the dwelling of Hrungnir. The giant complimented him on his horse and Odin bet his head that there was none better. Incensed, Hrungnir produced his own horse, Gullfaxi, and took up the challenge. Hrungnir rode after Odin, Sleipnir was faster. However, Hrungnir's fury drove him on till he had ridden into Asgard, home of the gods. Here the gods invited him to drink, but he drank too much and threatened to destroy Valhalla and kill the gods, save Freyja and Sif, whom he would carry off. For his insolence, Thor challenged him to single combat.

They met later as arranged and after a great battle, Thor smashed Hrungnir's head with his mighty hammer Mjöllnir. Hrungnir fell dead to the ground, but in doing so trapped Thor with his foot across his neck. Thor's son Magni was the only one able to move this great weight. As a reward for saving his life, Thor gave him Gullfaxi. Odin was not pleased; he had wanted Gullfaxi for himself (Sturluson, 'Skáldskaparmál', §36, in *Prose Edda*, 28). Another story of Gullfaxi was recorded as the Icelandic fairy tale 'The Horse Gullfaxi and the Sword Gunnföder' and included by Andrew Lang in *The Crimson Fairy Book* (1903).

GUYTRASH

Also written *gytrash*: an evil spirit in the north of England encountered in the shape of a cow or dog and believed to portend death. In the nineteenth century the area around what were Horton Lane, Legrams Lane and Bowling Lane, now Manchester Road, were haunted by the 'The Horton Guytrash', described by one who recalled the stories from childhood as 'a great black dog with horrid eyes', sometimes dragging clanking chains, sometimes not. A certain Edmund Riley of Horton Green is remembered for his account of a Horton resident who 'was going home one night, about the "witching hour," when, as he was passing the gates of Horton Hall, he was startled in his meditations by something jumping at his heels. He looked round, and, sure enough, there was the "great black dog." He made his way home as fast as he could, and when he got there either fainted or was near doing so. The next morning he was told that Mr Sharp, who inhabited Horton Hall, had died just about the time he was passing and saw the "Guytrash"' (Peacock, 'Ghostly Hounds', 266–7). Charlotte Brontë painted her own picture of the animal: 'I remembered certain of Bessie's tales, wherein figured a North-of-England spirit called a "Gytrash," which, in the form of horse, mule, or large dog, haunted solitary ways, and sometimes came upon belated travellers, as this horse was now coming upon me. It was very near, but not yet in sight; when, in addition to the tramp, tramp, I heard a rush under the hedge, and close down by the hazel stems glided a great dog, whose black and white colour made him a distinct object against the trees. It was exactly one form of Bessie's Gytrash – a lion-like creature with long hair and a huge head: it passed me, however, quietly enough; not staying to look up, with strange pretercanine eyes, in my face, as I half expected it would' (*Jane Eyre*, 124). (Wright, *Rust. Sp.*, 194.) For a creature that is surely related, see also **Trash**.

GWYLLGI

Welsh, 'dog of darkness', a supernatural **Black Dog**, from *gwyll*, 'darkness' and also 'fairy, goblin, witch', and *ci*, 'dog' (Richards, *Antiquæ*, 92, 256). It was said to be the size and shape of a large mastiff with a spotted coat; its enormous burning eyes might first be seen in the dark. A tale is told of Nansi Llwyd, who, finding herself on the road after nightfall near Aberystruth, Monmouthshire, once kicked it and lost the use of her foot. Usually encountered as a solitary animal, it is sometimes considered a member of the **Cŵn Annwn** pack. (Thomas, *Welsh Fairy*, 167; Trevelyan, *Folk-Lore*, 52.)

HAEMORRHOIS

Also *emorrosis*: a type of fabulous **Serpent** that causes its victims to bleed to death. We first read of it in Lucan's *Pharsalia* (9.821–39): 'Haemorrhois huge spreads out his scaly coils, | Who suffers not his hapless victims' blood | To stay within their veins'. Isidore of Seville perpetuated the tale in the seventh century CE, adding that the victim 'sweats blood' (*Etym.*, 12.4:12–16); and the story again appears in the twelfth century 'Aberdeen Bestiary' under the name 'emorrosis'.

HAFGUFA

A **Sea Monster** of great proportions reputed to haunt the seas about Greenland: 'Its Shape, Length and Bulk seems to exceed all Size […] more like a Land than a Fish, or Sea Animal'; 'its body reaches several Miles in Length […] when it comes out of the water, it seems to cover the whole Surface of the Sea, having many Heads and a Number of Claws' (Egede, *Nat. Desc. Green.*, 86, 87). There are only two at any time, or else they would consume all that was edible in the sea. It eats once a year, opening its jaws wide and emitting such a pleasant scent that all sorts of fish and even whales are drawn to it and sucked down into its belly; and it eats so much at one meal that it must devote itself to digestion for the remainder of the year. First mentioned in the thirteenth-century Orvar-Odds Saga (Boer, *Orvar-Odds Saga*, 132), the Danish missionary Hans Egede later equated it with the **Kraken**. Similar, if not identical, to the 'heather-back' (*lýngbakur*), see **Island Fish**.

HAI HO SHANG

The 'sea Buddhist priest', also known as the 'sea bonze' ('bonze' comes from the Sanskrit word *bhiksu*, meaing an ordained Buddhist monk); the Chinese variety of **Sea Monk**, known in Japan as the Umibozu. Depicted as a dark figure with bulbous head, as in Utagawa Kuniyoshi's print of the sailor Tokuzo outwitting the Umibozu (*c.*1845). It raises storms and sinks boats. Rituals to ward off this monster include waving a stick with red streamers attached to it whilst beating a gong, and burning feathers. It has been suggested that the legend originates with real squid or cuttlefish, or perhaps with skates and rays. The world's largest species of ray, the great devil fish (*Manta birostris*), for example, is of huge size and has a most uncanny representation of a human-like face on its underside. It can grow to 7 m (23 ft) across and has been known to leap above the waves, producing a thunderous clap when it hits the water again. Over-fishing due to demand from the Traditional Chinese Medicine market has seriously threatened this species. (Carrington, *Mer. Mast.*, 59–62.)

HALCYON

From Greek ἀλκυών, 'halcyon', also *Alcyon*, *Alcyone*, from the Latin *alcedo*: 'The halcyon-bird of many sorrows' is first mentioned by Homer (*Iliad*, 9.560). The myth is explained by Apollodorus (*Library*, 1.7, Frazer's ed.): 'Alcyone was married by Ceyx, son of Lucifer. These perished by reason of their pride; for he said that his wife was Hera, and she said that her husband was Zeus. But Zeus turned them into birds; her he made a kingfisher (alcyon) and him a gannet (ceyx)'. The name *Alcedo* is given to the genus of kingfishers. According to Pliny: 'They hatch their young at the time of the winter solstice, from which circumstance those days are known as the "halcyon days": during this period the sea is calm and navigable'.

HALSYDRUS PONTOPPIDANI

At a meeting of the Wernerian Natural History Society on 19 November 1808, the horticulturalist Patrick Neill informed the audience that 'a great Sea-Snake' had been washed ashore at Rothiesholm Bay on the Island of Stronsay, Orkneys. It was 16.75 m (55 ft) long, having 'the girth of an Orkney pony', the head about the size of a seal's; filaments hung down from its back like a mane and on each side it had three large paw-like fins. The body had been broken up in a tempest, but what was left was to be collected and sent to the University Museum in Edinburgh. Neill was later able to produce signed affidavits of eye-witnesses. He proposed the name *Halsydrus pontoppidani*, in honour of Erich Pontoppidan (see **Kraken**), to describe what was apparently a new species. It was later found to be the decomposing remains of a basking shark (*Cetorhinus maximus*); the adult typically reaches a length of 8 m (26 ft), so it was, at any rate, an exceptionally large specimen. It was the subject of huge debate at the time, with discussions lasting until the 1850s. (Oudemans, *Grt. Sea-Serp.*, 61–88.)

HARPY

'Bird-bodied, girl-faced things they are; abominable their droppings, their hands are talons, their faces haggard with hunger insatiable' (Virgil, *Aeneid*, 3.209ff). The harpy, usually encountered in the plural harpies, from the Greek Ἅρπυιαι ('Harpyiae'), meaning 'the swift robbers', were personifications of the storm winds, dating back to Homer in the eighth century BCE. The sudden disappearances of people were attributed to their malevolence, as, for example, when they kidnapped the daughters of King Pandareus and gave them to the Erinnyes (Furies). Two or three are usually referred to, but in all we find nine different names for them among the ancient authors: Aëllo ('storm-wind, whirlwind'); Aëllopos ('storm-footed'); Acholoë; Celaeno ('black one'); Nicothoë ('running victor'); Ocythoë, Ocypetes ('swift flier'), and Ocypode, which seem to be variations of the same; and Podarge ('flashing-footed'), the harpy first mentioned by Homer. Some said they lived on the islands of Strophades, near the entrance to the underworld, or in a cave on Crete (Virgil, *Aen.* Iii. 210, vi. 289; Apollon. *Rhod.* ii. 298). In the story of Jason and the Argonauts, we find them harassing the blind Phineus by stealing or despoiling his food. He promises to help the Argonauts if they can rid him of these monsters. Although usually depicted as having human heads and often with the bodies to match, we also read that 'They are said to have been feathered, with cocks' heads, wings, and human arms, with great claws; breasts, bellies, and female parts human' (Pseudo-Hyginus, Fabulae 14), and Aeschylus called them 'the eager hounds that range the air' (Fragment 155); Hesiod (*Theog.*, 267, &c.) called them 'of the lovely hair' (although some translators simply gave 'long-haired'). Because of their swiftness, several mythical horses were said to have been born of harpy mothers: the two immortal horses (**Hippoi Athanatoi**) Xanthos and Balio who drew Achilles' chariot during the Trojan War; Phlogeus and Harpagos, another pair of immortal horses, who, together with Xanthos and Cyllaros, drew the chariot of the Dioskouroi twins, Castor and Pollux; and Areion (or Arion), again an immortal horse, once owned by Hercules. Their role as personifications may explain why, even to this day, cyclonic storms, such as Hurricane Katrina, are given female, rather than male names. (Smith, *Dict.*, II, 352 –3.)

HAVESTRAMB

The merman of Greenland, described by the Danish missionary Egede in the eighteenth century: 'the Likeness of a Man, as to the Head, Face, Nose and Mouth; save that its Head was oblong and pointed like a Sugar-Loaf. It has broad Shoulders, and two Arms without Hands. The Body downwards is slanting and thin. The rest below the Middle, being hid in the Water, could not be observed' (*Nat. Descr. Green.*, 86). For the female, see **Margya** and **Mermaid**.

HEDLEY KOW

A bale of straw that could run, a cow that could laugh, a horse that could slip the limmers, such was the Hedley Kow, a mischievous spirit of the village of Hedley near Ebchester, County Durham. A favourite trick was to disguise itself as a truss of straw and lie in the path of some elderly person out gathering sticks for the fire. The straw would be gratefully hoisted onto the back, but gradually grow so heavy as to become unbearable; on being taken off, it would run away, laughing. It would take the appearance of a favourite cow to lead the milkmaid a merry dance round the field before kicking over the pail during milking, slipping its tie and disappearing with its characteristic laugh. It was considered to be the source of general confusion and annoyance about the household and farmyard. (Henderson, *Notes*, 270–1.)

HELHEST

Danish for 'Hel-horse', a three-legged harbinger of Death. According to folklore, 'he goes round the churchyard, he fetches Death'; and it was once said that a live horse was buried in every graveyard, before it was used to bury the human dead, to become the 'walking dead-horse', or **Kirkegrim**. It is sometimes also described as headless. In Schleswig, Germany, they once said that, in times of plague, it is the goddess of death, Hel, riding on her three-legged horse (Grimm, *Teut. Myth.*, 2.844). Thorpe relates a story of Aarhus Cathedral (Århus Domkirke) in Denmark: 'A man, whose windows looked into the cathdral yard, exclaimed one evening as he sat in his apartment: 'What horse is that outside?' 'It is perhaps the Hel-horse,' answered one sitting by him. 'Then I will see it!' said the man. While looking out of the window he grew as pale as a corpse; but he never mentioned afterwards what he had seen. Shortly after he fell sick and died' (*North. Myth.*, 209). (Schütte, 'Dan. Pag.', 360–71.)

HEPTET

A **Serpent**-headed goddess of Ancient Egypt. She is depicted with the head of a bearded snake, having horns surmounted by a solar disc, Atef Crown and uraei; in each hand she holds a knife. She was involved in the

resurrection of the god Osiris. (Budge, *Gods*, 131.)

HERCYNIA

Plural *Hercyniae*, 'are birds named from the Hercynian forest in Germany, where they are born. Their feathers shine in the dark so much that, although the night is spread over with dense shadows, they are seen clearly. With them placed in front of the arranged route as a convoy, the course of the road is clear, disclosed by their shining feathers', according to Isidore of Seville in the seventh century CE (*Etym.*, 12.7.31). He was drawing on an older description by Pliny the Elder (*Nat. Hist.*, 10.67) in the first century CE, but added the additional detail of their practical applications. Pliny gave no name to the birds and dismissed the story, but Isidore is quite credulous.

Hercynia (Thirteenth Century)

HEREN-SUGE

Also *Serpent d'Isabit*, a seven-headed **Dragon** of Basque folklore. According to an oral folk tradition recorded in the nineteenth century: 'The serpent lay with his head resting on the summit of the Pic du Midi de Bigorre, his neck stretched down towards Barèges, while his body filled the whole valley of Luz, St. Sauveur, and Gédres, and his tail was coiled in the hollow below the cirque of Gavarnie. He fed but once in three months, or the whole country would have been desolate. With a strong inspiration of his breath, he drew into his capacious maw, across the valleys, whole flocks of sheep and goats, herds of oxen, men, women, children, the population of whole villages at once. He was now asleep, and inert, after such a repast. The whole male population of several valleys assembled to consult on what should be done. After long and fruitless debate an old man arose and spoke: "We have nearly three months yet before he will wake; let us cut down all the forests on the opposite hills; then let us bring all our forges and all the iron we possess, and with the wood thus cut down let us melt it all into the red-hot fiery mass; then we will hide ourselves behind the rocks, and make all the noise we can to try and awaken the monster." So said, so done. The serpent awoke in a rage at having his slumbers broken, he saw something bright on the opposite side of the valley, and drew in a long breath, and the fiery mass, with a roar like a thunderbolt, flew across the valley, right down the monster's throat. Then, what convulsions ensued; rocks were uptorn or split open, the mountains were shattered, the glaciers beaten into dust as the serpent twisted and lashed about

in his agony. To quench his agony of thirst he descended to the valley, and drank up all the streams from Gavarnie to Pierrefitte. Then, in his last convulsion, he threw himself back upon the mountain side and expired; his head rested in a deep hollow; as the fire within him slowly cooled, the water he had swallowed poured out of his mouth, and formed the present Lac d'Isabit.' (Webster, *Basque*, 21–2.)

HIPPALECTRYON

The horse-cock; from the Greek Ἱππαλεκτρυων, *hippalektryôn*, usually Latinised as *hippalectryon*, composed of *hippo-*, 'horse', and *alectryon*, 'cock, cockerel'. It appears in early Athenian vase painting from the sixth century BCE and in literature from fifth to fourth centuries BCE, but not later. If Aristophanes is correct, the design may be traceable to Ancient Mesopotamia where the solar cock is associated with a horse in a form known as a *parodash*. (Roes, 'New Light', 232-5.)

HIPPOCAMPUS

From the Greek Ἱπποκαμπος, 'Hippokampos', plural *Hippokampoi*, usually Latinised as *Hippocampus*, plural *Hippocampi*: the sea-horse of Greek and Roman mythology. The name means, literally, 'crooked horse'. In the eighth century BCE, Homer described them as having brass hooves, but did not say anything about fish-tails. One of the earliest descriptions comes from the third century BCE: 'A great horse came bounding out of the sea, a monstrous animal, with his golden mane waving in the air. He

Hippocampus (*c*.1910)

shook himself, tossing off the spray in showers. Then, fast as the wind, he galloped away' (Apollonius Rhodius, *Argonautica*, 4.1533ff). In the second century CE, Pausanias described an image in the temple of Poseidon in Korinthos (Corinth) that depicted 'a horse like a *ketos* [sea monster, whale] from the breast downwards' (Pausanias, *Desc. Gr.*, 2.1.7–9). In the third century CE, Philostratus the Elder described an ancient Greek painting in Neapolis (Naples) showing Poseidon in a chariot drawn by hippocampi: 'creatures with web-footed hoofs, good swimmers, blue-eyed, and, by Zeus, in all respects like dolphins' (Philostratus the Elder, *Imagines*, 1.8). As well as pulling Poseidon's chariot, hippocampi were often depicted being ridden by Nereids (sea nymphs), with fine examples in art surviving from the fifth century BCE. They were believed to be full-grown adult versions of those well-known small fish with horse-like heads, also called the sea-horse: the species is known by the scientific classification *Hippocampus*, and from the similarity of shape has also lent its name to a region of the human brain.

HIPPOCENTAUR, SEE CENTAUR

HIPPOGRIFF

Also *hippogryph*, *hippogrif*, a monster born of a **Griffin** and a mare, from Greek *hippos*, 'horse', and *gryps*, 'griffin'. The creature appears most famously in Ludovico Ariosto's sixteenth century poem 'Orlando Furioso', where it is ridden by the hero Ruggiero. Similar to the **Simurgh**. (Vinycomb, *Fict. Sym.*, 161.)

HIPPOI ATHANATOI

Literally, the 'immortal horses' of the gods in Greek mythology, sometimes depicted as having the wings of birds: 'they winged their way unreluctant through the space between the earth and the starry heaven' (Homer, *Iliad*, 5.711ff). They were mostly the offspring of the male wind-gods, the Anemoi, and female storm-demons, the Harpies (see **Harpy**), and also of the sea-god Poseidon. The Anemoi, the gods of the four winds – Boreas, Zephyros, Notos and Euros – sometimes took the form of horses to pull the chariot of Zeus. Ares had four fire-breathing specimens: Aithon, Phlogios (or Phlogeus), Konabos and Phobos: 'Murderous Ares came, unmarked of other Gods, down from the heavens, eager to help the warrior sons of Troy. Aithon (Red-fire) and Phlogeus (Flame), Konabos (Tumult) and Phobos (Panic-fear), his car-steeds, bare him down into the fight, the coursers which to roaring Boreas grim-eyed Erinnys bare, coursers that breathed life-blasting flame: groaned all the shivering air, as battleward they sped. Swiftly he came to Troy: loud rang the earth beneath the feet of that wild team' (Q. Smyrnaeus, *Fall of Troy*, 8.239 ff). Poseidon, of course, had sea-horses, the Hippokampoi (see **Hippocampus**).

HIPPOTAYNE

In the fourteenth century Sir John Mandeville described a country he called Bacharia which lay somewhere beyond the Caspian Sea: it is probable that he meant Bactria, a region now divided between Afghanistan and Tajikistan. It was a land of cruel people, of trees that bore wool like sheep, of rivers with bitter water, of the **Griffin** and of the hippotayne: 'In that country be many hippotaynes that dwell sometime in the water and sometime on the land. And they be half man and half horse, as I have said before. And they eat men when they may take them.' (*Travels*, 177.)

HNIKUR

The Icelandic **Water-Horse**: 'he appears like a handsome grey horse, though with his hoofs turned backwards, and strives to tempt people to mount him, when he will gallop off with them into the water. Some efforts to tame him have been partially successful, and he has been made to work, though for a short time only'. (Thorpe, *North. Myth*, 22.) See also **Nicker**.

HODGSON'S ANTELOPE,

SEE ANTELOPE HODGSONII

HÓFVARPNIR

'Gná: her Frigg sends into divers lands on her errands; she has that horse which runs over sky and sea and is called Hófvarpnir', so we read in the thirteenth century *Prose Edda*. From the Old Norse, meaning 'hoof-thrower',

Hófvarpnir is the flying, water-walking horse ridden by the goddess Gná, messenger of Frigg, wife of Odin. When once seen flying, Gna answered 'I fly not, | Though I fare | And glide through the air | On Hófvarpnir.' Hófvarpnir is not described as having eight legs like **Sleipnir**, or wings like **Pegasus**, but shares their ability to move between the worlds of gods and men. (Sturluson, 'Gylfaginning', §35, in *Prose Edda*, 47.)

HOODEN HORSE

Possibly from 'wooden', pronounced 'ooden', or 'hooden'; or the name of the god Odin or Woden. The Hooden Horse is the centrepiece of the custom of Hoodening, once widespread in the county of Kent. It is a horse's head made from wood with movable jaws into which rows of hob-nails are hammered for teeth. It is worn on the head of a ploughman, called the 'Hoodener', and he is covered with sacking to disguise him; he is led by the 'Waggoner', who makes use of a long whip to drive his charge. A 'Rider' or 'Jockey' attempts all the while to mount the horse; 'Molly' follows, a man dressed up as a woman, with a birch broom to sweep as she goes. The procession tours the villages on Christmas Eve and is rewarded with money. (Ditchfield, *Old Eng. Cust.*, 26; Maylam, *Hooden Horse, passim*.)

HOODWINK

Two species of Hoodwink are known: Meiklejohn's Hoodwink (*Dissimulatrix spuria*); and the Bare-Fronted Hoodwink. Both are twentieth-century varieties of **Jenny Haniver** in the collection of the Royal Scottish Museum in Edinburgh. Meiklejohn's Hoodwink was described by M.F. Meiklejohn supposedly in a 1950 article in *Bird Notes*. The museum was fortunate to be able to acquire a study skin made up of bits of rather shabby and unexceptional birds together with a text that is wholly unable to identify them. Museum taxidermist Ian Lyster, the man responsible for the **Gruck**, made the discovery in time for an exhibition on 1 April 1975; say no more. The Bare-Fronted Hoodwink was constructed by another former museum taxidermist Willie Sterling using the head of a carrion crow, the body of a plover, the wings and tail feathers of a duck and the feet of a wading bird of some description. The 'bare-fronted' effect was achieved with the use of red wax. (Dance, *Animal Fakes*, 80-1.)

HORSE

Among the tribes of ancient Europe, the horse was widely revered and involved in many myths and legends, and is still the subject of folk customs surviving in some parts to this day. Several fabulous horses feature in Norse mythology: 'These are the names of the Æsir's steeds: **Sleipnir** ['The Slipper'] is best, which Odin has; he has eight feet. The second is Gladr ['Glad'], the third Gyllir ['Golden'], the fourth Glenr ['The Starer'], the fifth Skeidbrimir ['Fleet Courser'], the sixth Silfrintoppr ['Silver-Top], the seventh Sinir ['Sinewy'], the eighth Gisl ['Beam', 'Ray'], the ninth Falhófnir ['Hairy-Hoof'], the tenth Gulltoppr ['Gold-Top'], the eleventh

Léttfeti ['Light-Stepper']. Baldr's horse was burnt with him; and Thor walks to the judgment' (Sturluson, 'Gylfaginning', §15, in *Prose Edda*, 28). In addition: **Gullfaxi**, **Hófvarpnir**. See also **Helhest**. Around Europe old traditions featuring horses include 'Old Hob' of Cheshire folk custom, the **Hooden Horse** of Kent, the *Penglas* (or *Penglaz*) of Cornwall, the **Mari Llwyd** of Wales, and the *Laare Vane* of the Isle of Man; and further afield, the *Schimmel* (and *Schimmelreiter*) in various parts of Germany. And in similar animal-related customs of the **Klapperbock** of Usedom, an island in northern Germany, the *Habersack* in the Harz mountains, also in Germany, and the *Habergaiss* in what was once Upper Styria. All are vestiges of ancient European cult practices. Forming a separate species is the **Water-Horse**. We see among all these sorts a rough division between the sky-horses, such as **Pegasus**, and water-horses, such as the **Kelpie**; the former are the steeds of the gods and heroes, the latter malevolent spirits preying on humankind. See also **Unicorn**.

HORSE-EEL

The name given to a supposed type of eel, larger than the ordinary, with a mane like a horse's. The upper lake of Glendalough, Ireland, is said to be inhabited by them. Once, one of them left the water and ate a cow grazing nearby, so it is said. (Lover, *Legends*, 235.)

HORUS

Falcon-headed god of Ancient Egypt, the son of Isis and Osiris, mysteriously conceived after **Set** had dismembered Osiris; seen as the avenger of Osiris and hence the eternal enemy of Set. In general, a god of the sky and kingship. He is first mentioned around 3000 BCE. One of his primary symbols is 'The Eye of Horus' (*udjat*-eye). The eye he lost in one of his many battles with Set, it represents the moon. (Shaw and Nicholson, *Dict. Anc. Eg.*, 133–4.)

HOUNDS OF ANNWN,

SEE CŴN ANNWN

HRAE-SVELGR

Also *Hraesvelg*, 'corpse-swallower'; a giant eagle in Norse mythology, the origin of the wind: 'Tell me ninthly, | Since thou art called wise, | Whence the wind comes, | That over ocean passes, | Itself invisible to man. | Hraesvelg he is called | Who at the end of heaven sits, | A Jötun (giant) in eagle's plumage: | From his wings comes, | It is said, the wind | That over all men passes' ('The Lay of Vafthrudnir', *The Edda*, trans. Thorpe). It is not clear why this wind should swallow corpses, but *svelgr* can also mean 'whirlpool, vortex' (Arnoldson, *Body*, 49), hence the wind in question is one that raises storms at sea, storms that drown sailors. (Schütte, 'Dan. Pag.', 365.)

HRŌKK-ÁLL

The Icleandic 'coil-eel', said to be about 60 cm (2 ft) long and fond of ditches and stagnant pools. According to Davidson: 'If any animal or human being puts foot into the water where it is, the eel coils itself round their leg and cuts into the bone, or even takes it right off. This frequently happens with horses, but sheep escape because their legs are too slender for the eel to work upon. How the cutting is done is a point on which opinions differ. Some say that the venom in the eel is so strong that it corrodes the flesh and bone; others say that the eel has fins as sharp as the teeth of a saw, and does the work with these. It is also said to have thin scales as hard as iron, and its flesh is poisonous. One time some of these eels, which had been taken in a net, were thrown out on hard ground at some distance from a brook. They immediately wriggled into the ground, and so made their way to the water. As to the origin of the *Hrökk-áll*, the story is that a wizard put life into a dead and half-rotten eel, and so made it into this poisonous creature' (Davidson, 'Folk-Lore', 330–1.).

HUMBABA

An ancient Mespotamian monster – Assyrian *Humbaba*; Sumerian *Huwawa* – defeated by the hero Gilgamesh and his companion Enkidu. The encounter is described in the *Epic of Gilgamesh* (Thompson, Third Tablet): 'Humbaba the Fierce [...] his roar was a whirlwind, Flame (in) his jaws, and his very breath Death!' He guarded a forest of cedars; some have located this in the forest of Lebanon. He is depicted with a grimacing mouth set with rows of teeth and was used as an apotropaic charm as, for example, in ancient Babylon where Humbaba masks were discovered fixed to tombs. Similarities between the slaying and the use of the head, both in mythology and art, have suggested an ancient link to the Greek Perseus and his slaying of the Gorgon Medusa. (Hopkins, 'Ass. Elem.', 341–58.)

HYDRA

In the first edition of his *Systema Naturae* published in 1735, Carolus Linnaeus included a number of creatures under the heading of **Animalia Paradoxa**; the Hydra was one of them. He described it as having the 'body of a snake, with two feet, seven necks and the same number of heads, lacking wings' from a specimen exhibited in Hamburg and compared it to the description of the Beast of the Apocalypse, what he called *Hydrae Apocalyptica*, given in the Bible. He rejected this, however, arguing that multiple heads never occur naturally on one body; from his own observations of the Hamburg Hydra he had identified its teeth as normally belonging to the weasel and so concluded that the whole thing was a fraud. For the monster of Greek mythology, see the **Lernæan Hydra**.

HYDRARCHOS SILLIMANNII

In 1845, the inhabitants of New York were given the unique opportunity to examine for themselves the skeleton of a 35 m (113 ft) long **Sea Serpent** in the Apollo Saloon on Broadway. A contemporary illustration shows the snaking spine and gigantic jaws of a truly fearsome monster towering above the groups of genteel onlookers. It was named after Prof. Benjamin Silliman and for 25 cents, visitors could see it for themselves. Whilst the majority were suitably impressed by the

Hydra (*c.*1560)

supposed fossil of 'an extinct marine serpent', Prof. Jeffries Wyman was not: 'these remains never belonged to one and the same individual, and that the anatomical characters of the teeth indicate that they are not those of a reptile, but of a warm blooded mammal'. When news of the serpent reached London, the geologist and paleontologist Gideon Algernon Mantell quickly exposed the fraud: 'the so-called Sea-Serpent, as having been exhibited in America under the name of *Hydrarchos Sillimannii*, was constructed by the exhibitor Koch, from bones collected in various parts of Alabama, and which belonged to several individual skeletons of an extinct marine cetacean, termed Basilosaurus by the American naturalists, and better known in this country by that of Zeuglodon, a term signifying yoked teeth'. Albert C. Koch had gone to the USA following the scandal of another faked fossil, the **Missourium**. After Wyman's revelations, he left New York for Dresden in Germany and exhibited his creation there. (Mantell, *Illus. Lon.*; Oudemans, *Grt. Sea-Serp.*, 30–4; Wyman, *Proc.*, 65.)

HYENA

In Pliny's *Natural History* (8.44), the hyena is a marvellous and impossible thing: 'as touching Hyænes, it is commonly beleeved, that they have two natures, and that every second yeere they chaunge their sexe, being this yeere males, and the next yeere females. Howbeit, Aristotle denieth it. Their necke and the mane therewith, together with the backe, are one entire bone without any joynt at all, so as they cannot bend their necke without turning the whole bodie about. Many strange matters are reported of this beast, and above all other, that hee will counterfet mans speech, and comming to the sheepheards cottages, will call one of them forth, whose name he hath learned, and when he hath him without, all to worrie and teare him in peeces. Also it is said, that hee will vomit like a man, thereby to traine dogs to come unto him, and then will devour them. Also, this beast alone of all others, will search for mens bodies within their graves and sepulchres, and rake them forth. The female is sildome taken. Hee chaungeth his eies into a thousand diverse colours. Moreover, if a dog come within his shadow, he presently looseth his barking, and is quite dumbe. Againe, by a kind of magicall charme or enchantment, if he goe round about ay other living creature but three times, it shall not have the power to stirre a foot, and remoove out of the place.' When they mate with lionesses, and they do, says Pliny, they bring forth the **Leucrocuta**.

HWCH DDU GWTA

Welsh, a tailless black sow, or 'cutty black sow', a spirit associated with *Nos Galan Gaeof* (Hallowe'en). An old rhyme goes '*Hwch ddu gwta | Ar bob camfa | Yn nyddu a chardio | Bob nos G'langaea* ('A cutty black sow | On every stile, | Spinning and carding | Every Allhallows' Eve'. (Rhys, *Celtic Folklore*, 226.)

I

ICHNEUMON

In the first English translation of Pliny (*Nat. Hist.*, 8.36) this creature was called an *Icheneumon*: 'the Ichenumones [sic] or rats of India. A beast this is, well knowne to the **Aspis**, in this regard especially, that it is bred likewise in the same Ægypt. The manner of this Icheneumon is, to wallow oftentimes within the mud, and then to drie it selfe against the Sunne: and when hee hath thus armed himselfe as it were with many coats hardened in this manner, he goeth forth to combat with the Aspis. In fight he sets up his taile, & whips about, turning his taile to the enemie, & therin latcheth and receiveth all the strokes of the Aspis, and taketh no harm thereby: and so long maintaineth he a defensive battell, until he spie a time, turning his head ato-side, that he may catch the Aspis by the throat, & throttle it. And not content thus to have vanquished this enemie, he addresseth himselfe to a conflict with another, as hurtfull every way and dangerous as the former.' Pliny also credited this creature with

Ichneumon (*c*.600–500 BCE)

attacking crocodiles: 'Now when he is lulled as it were fast asleepe with this pleasure and contentment of his: the rat of India, or Ichneumon abovesaid, spieth his vantage, and seeing him lie thus broad gaping, whippeth into his mouth, and shooteth himselfe downe his throat as quicke as an arrow, and then gnaweth his bowels, eateth an hole through his bellie, and so killeth him' (*Nat. Hist.*, 8.37). The fantastical *Ichneumon* is generally taken to be the widespread Egyptian mongoose, whose scientific name is *Herpestes ichneumon*, less scientifically it is known as the 'rat of the pharaohs'.

ICHTHYOCENTAUR

The **Triton** was sometimes represented as having two horse's feet in place of arms, hence being called **Centaur**-Triton or Ichthyocentaur, from the Greek meaning 'fish-centaur'. (Smith, *Dict.*, III, 1116; Tzetz, *ad Lyc.*, 34, 886, 892.)

ILLHVEL

The 'wicked whales' of Icelandic folklore. More creatures of the imagination than of the seas, they were great monsters who delighted in smashing boats and devouring fishermen. Luckily, the 'harmless whales' would often swim protectively alongside the boats, keeping the wicked whales at bay. There were several specific types. The *stökkull*, 'jumper', was considered the most deadly on account of its high-leaping habit that often brought it crashing down on a boat: 'it always wants to sink everything that it sees floating, and its constant springing into the air is done so that it may look about and see whether there is anything near that it may fall upon – a boat or anything else'. Fishermen would throw an empty cask or buoy over the side as a decoy and escape whilst the jumper tired itself leaping and crashing on the object. The *hross-hvalur*, 'horse-whale', had something like a horse's head and mane, and even neighed like a horse; its appearance always foretold bad weather. It was about 15 or 18 m (50 or 60 ft) in length and smelt terribly. One of the largest of the wicked whales was the *naut-hveli*, 'ox-whale', so named on account of its bellowing like an ox, loud enough to knock the oars out of fishermens' hands. The *svín-hvalur*, 'swine-whale', was 'very fierce and dangerous to small boats'. It is especially fatty and the fat is of such a strength as to immediately ooze out of the pours of anyone eating the meat. The *raud-bingur*, 'red-crest', or *raud-kinnúng*, 'red-cheek', gets its name either from the crest of red hair down its back, or its red cheeks, and is 'so insanely fond of destroying boats, that if one escapes him, and he does not find another the same day, he will kill himself out of pure chagrin'. Eighteen metres (60 ft) long and swift, the red-crest is a formidable monster. One champion of this evil breed once destroyed eighteen boats in succession and the nineteenth only escaped by the cunning of its captain. He dressed a log in some clothes and threw it overboard. Every time the red-crest tried to drown it, it bobbed up again, and so pre-occupied allowed the captain and his crew to make good their escape. The red-crest and the narwhal are great companions on the seas: the red-crest smashes the boats and the narwhal eats the drowning sailors. Others of this species are the *brúnn-fiskur*, 'brown-fish', said to have some sort of tusk; *tauma-fiskur*, 'bridle-fish', so named from the white stripes on its black skin; the *skeljúngur* or *svarf-hvalur*, 'shell-whale', that cannot bear to hear iron being filed; the *mjaldur*, 'snow-whale', that never forgets an injury; and the mighty *lýngbakur*, 'heather-back', or *hólma-fiskur*, **Island Fish**, so large that it is mistaken for an island when at the surface, complete with vegetation growing on it. (Davidson, 'Folk-Lore', 315–21.)

IRISH CROCODILE

They say Ireland had its crocodiles in the seventeenth century: 'Here is one rarity more, which we may terme the Irish crocodil [sic], whereof one as yet living, about ten years ago, had sad experience. The man was passing the shore just by the waterside, and spyed far off the head of a beast swimming, which he tooke to have been an otter, and tooke no more notice of it; but the beast it seems there lifted up his head, to discern whereabouts the man was; then diving, swom under water till he struck ground; whereupon he runned out of the water suddenly, and tooke the man by the elbow, whereby the man stooped down, and the beast fastened his teeth in his pate, and dragged him into the water; where the man tooke hold on a stone by chance in his way, and calling to minde he had a knife in his pocket, tooke it out and gave a thrust of it to the beast, which thereupon got away from him into the lake. The water about him was all bloody, whether from the beast's bloud, or his own, or from both, he knows not. It was of the pitch of an ordinary greyhound, of a black slimy skin, without hair, as he immagined. Old men acquainted with the lake do tell there is such a beast in it, and that a stout fellow with a wolf dog along with him met the like there once; which after a long strugling went away in spite of the man and dog, and was a long time after found rotten in a rocky cave of the lake, as the water decreased. The like, they say, is seen in other lakes of Ireland; they call it *Dovarchu*, i.e. a water dog, or *Anchu*, which is the same' (Hardiman, *Chor. Desc.*, 19-20). Hardiman connected it with the **Each-Uisge** and said the story was still told in the locality of Lough Mask (Loch Measca), County Mayo, Ireland. For Dovarchu and Anchu, see **Dobhar-Chú** and **Onchú**.

ISLAND FISH

In Icelandic folklore, a whale of such proportion that it is taken for an island and even has heather growing on it: 'The "heather-back" (*lýngbakur*) is mentioned even in the sagas, and is said to be the biggest whale of all. When it lies on the surface of the water it has the appearance of an island overgrown with heather; hence its name. The heather-back does not require to eat oftener than every third year; then it simply swallows everything that comes between its jaws, fish or birds, or other sea-creatures, without distinction. There is only one of the species, so that it does not multiply its kind, but on the other hand it will continue to live till the end of the world. It is said that St Brandan celebrated mass on a heather-grown island out in the main ocean, and all at once the island sank; this was the heather-back. It is still seen occasionally, and is now known as the "island-fish" (*hólma-fiskur*)' (Davidson, 'Folk-Lore', 323). For other named varieties, see **Aspidochelone**, **Hafgufa** and **Jasconius**.

J

JACKALOPE

The antlered jackrabbit (hare) of North America; the name is composed of 'jackrabbit' and 'antelope'. Every year, the Chamber of Commerce in Douglas, Wyoming, issues thousands of hunting permits for jackalope. Road signs warn motorists to 'Watch Out for the Jackalope'. A local taxidermist, Douglas 'Doug' Herrick (1920–2003), with his brother Ralph, invented the creature on a whim in 1932, although depictions of the **Lepus Cornutus** date back to the sixteenth century. Ralph's son Jim carries on the trade. The Smithsonian's National Museum of Natural History in Washington, DC, holds an example of this spurious species. The brothers also created the Wyoming Catfish. The jackalope is similar to the German **Wolpertinger**. (Martin, 'Douglas Herrick', n.p.)

JACULUS

Greek, ἀκοντίας, Latin *jaculus*, the flying javelin-snake first described by Lucan: 'Behold! afar, around the trunk of a barren tree, a fierce serpent – Africa calls it the jaculus – wreathes itself, and then darts forth, and through the head and pierced temples of Paulus it takes its flight: nothing does venom there affect, death seizes him through the wound. It was then understood how slowly fly the stones which the sling hurls, how sluggishly whizzes the flight of the Scythian arrow' (*Phar.*, 9.962–6). From there it found itself taken up by Pliny (*Nat. Hist.*, 8.35): 'The jaculus darts from the branches of trees; and it is not only to our feet that the serpent is formidable, for these fly through the air even, just as though they were hurled from an engine'. Galen (*Ther. Pis.*, c.8) in the second century CE and Ælian (*Anim. Nat.*, vi.c.18) after him both included this beast in their works, as, much later, did Isidore of Seville (*Etym.*, 12.4.28): 'They leap into trees, and, when an animal is at hand, they throw (*jactant*) themselves on it and kill it, whence their name.' In Lucan the comparison with slings and arrows is a metaphor for the speed of this snake; in later writers it is taken literally. Modern zoology knows no such snake-spear.

JALEBHA

The mythical sea-elephant, known in Indian art as a type of *makara*, or composite creature. (Murthy, *Myth. An. Ind.*, 48.)

JALA-TURANGA

The Indian sea-horse, a version of the Greek **Hippocampus**. It is depicted with the fore-parts and head of a horse and the tail of a fish. In the *Mahabharata*, the reverse, a fish with a horse's head, the *Minavajis*, is mentioned. (Murthy, *Myth. An. Ind.*, 48.)

JASCONIUS

In medieval Irish legend, a huge fish mistaken for an island, from the 'Voyage of Saint Brendan', the earliest manuscript version of which dates from around 900 CE. Brendan builds a currach and sets sail with a band of fellow monks in search of the Island of Paradise. On their journey they come to a strange island: 'there was no grass on the island, very little wood, and no sand on the shore'. The monks spend the night on it in prayer, although Brendan, knowing it for a fish, stays in the boat. In the morning they celebrate Mass and afterwards set a fire so that they can cook their breakfast. Of course, the 'island' does not take kindly to this: 'after they had placed more fuel on the fire, and the caldron began to boil, the island moved about like a wave'. The monks run back to their boat in panic and sail off as fast as they can: 'Afterwards they could see the fire they had kindled still burning more than two miles off'. Brendan explains the mystery to them: 'it was not an island you were upon, but a fish, the largest of all that swim in the ocean, which is ever trying to make its head and tail meet, but cannot succeed, because of its great length'. (O'Donoghue, *Brendaniana*, 126–7.) See also **Island Fish**.

JENNY HANIVER

A fantastic beast artificially constructed from an actual animal or animals. The term is most often applied to creations from the skate and ray family of fish, having a human-like 'face' on the underside and a pliable skin that can be shaped and dried in extraordinary shapes. The word is of uncertain origin and absent from the *Oxford English Dictionary*. The term Jenny is often used to denote the female of the species as jenny-howlet or Jenny Wren (the wife of Robin Redbreast). It is conjectured that Haniver may be from Anvers, the French name for Antwerp, where a certain trade in these monsters is assumed. Marco Polo first documented the production of artifical monsters when he visited Sumatra in the twelfth century; these were pygmies supposed to come from India: 'there is on the Island a kind of monkey which is very small, and has a face just like a man's. They take these, and pluck out all the hair except the hair of the beard and on the breast, and then they dry them and stuff them and daub them with saffron and other things until they look like men' (*Travels*, vol. II, 3.9). The first published example, the *piscis monachi* or **Sea Monk**, appeared in Pierre Belon's *De Aquatilibus* published in 1553. In 1554 Guillaume Rondelet, regius professor of medicine at the university of Montpellier, published a depiction of *de pisce Episcopi habitu*, the **Sea Bishop**, in his *Libri de Piscibus Marinis*. Belon appeared to be taken in by the dupe, but Rondelet was more doubtful. Conrad Gessner also published an

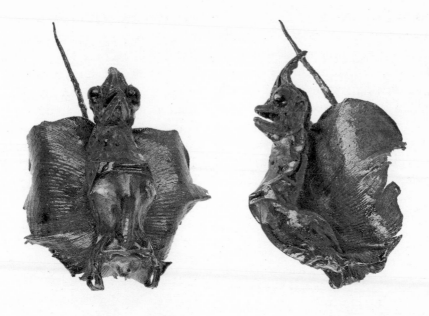

Jenny Haniver

illustration of a 'flying dragon' that he had seen in his 1558 book *Historia Animalium*, specifically as a warning to others not to be fooled, and he revealed their procedure: 'The vendors of [quack] medicines and certain others [of that ilk] are accustomed to dry rays and fashion their skeletons in varied and wonderful shapes for [exhibition to] the multitude. They also exhibit others which resemble the serpent or the winged dragon. [To make these] they bend the body [of a ray], distort the head and mouth, and cut away other parts. They take away the forward parts of the sides [the fins or wings] and raise up the remainders that they may simulate wings, and other parts they modify as they wish' (trans. Gudger, 'Jenny Hanivers'). Two

such concoctions were described as being types of **Basilisk** in Aldrovandi's *Serpentum et Draconum Historiae* ('History of Serpents and Dragons') of 1640: one of them is a typical manipulated ray; the other is more unusual in having a crown and eight legs. We can see, then, that a roaring trade was being done in these bizarre creations and, if not every naturalist was able to see the imposture, what would the uneducated have made of these marvels? Jenny Hanivers certainly aided and abetted the legends of **Mermaid**s, sea monks and sea bishops, **Dragon**s, basilisks and **Cockatrice**s, and many more besides; and as such have played an important and often overlooked role in the development and maintenance of these legends.

They were commonly found in the private museums of the wealthy in the eighteenth and nineteenth centuries. Today, the Rijksmuseum, Leiden, has an interesting example that closely matches that depicted by Aldrovandi in 1613 as a '*Draco effictus ex raia*', a 'dragon made out of a ray'. Regional specialities include the **Cambridge Centaur**, German Elwetritsch, Rasselbock and **Wolpertinger**, the Swedish Skvader and **Vitrysk Strandmuddlare**, and the American **Jackalope**. Several such creations have been publicly exhibited, notably the FeeJee Mermaid (see **Mermaid**) and **Hydrarchos Sillimannii**. There are many other lesser known specimens such as the **Pig-Faced Lady** and **Buckland's Nondescript**. The Royal Scottish Museum in Edinburgh has a nice selection of Bare-Fronted **Hoodwink**, **Fur-Bearing Trout** and **Gruck**. Jenny Hanivers are still being sold, although they are often termed 'alien creature' or similar. (Carrington, *Mer. Mast.*, 62–3, 69–71; Dance, *Animal Fakes*, 17ff.)

JÖRMUNGANDR

In Norse mythology, the Midgard Serpent, an enormous **Serpent** that encircles the world so that it bites its own tail; born of Loki and Angrboda, its siblings are the giant wolf Fenrir and the death-goddess Hel. The gods captured the serpent and threw it into the deep sea, but it did not die; instead it grew until it encompassed all the land. Thor later tried to kill it; not every version of the tale says that he was successful. See also **Níðhöggr**. ('Gylfaginning', §48, in Sturluson, *Prose Edda*, 42, 70.)

Thor and Jörmundgandr (1906)

K

KAPPA

A Japanese river monster. It is described as having an ape-like head, the body of a tortoise and scaly limbs. There is a hollow in the crown of its head that is filled with a magical fluid, which is the source of the monster's power. It challenges humans to single combat; they cannot refuse, but if one is polite and accepts with a bow, then the Kappa bows also and the magic fluid runs out of the top of its head and enfeebles it. Those who defeat it in combat, however, are still fated to mysteriously waste away. At other times it preys on people bathing or swimming in the water and is said to suck their blood. (Davis, *Myths*, 350; Eiichirô, 'Kappa', 1–152.)

KATZENKNÄUEL

German, a ball or knot of cats. A version of the **Rat King** involving cats,

The Katzenknäuel of 1683

Zu finden bey JS. Felsecker.

or kittens, knotted at the tails. Felsecker published a depiction of one in 1683 (*Aber. Wund.*) after the sensation of the Strassburg rat king of 1682; it was probably a **Jenny Haniver**.

KELPIE

'When thowes dissolve the snawy hoord, | An' float the jinglin' icy-boord, | Then water-kelpies haunt the foord | By your direction | And 'nighted trav'llers are allur'd | To their destruction' (Burns, 'Address to the Deil', *Works*, 73). The belief in the kelpie is widespread in Scotland, but the exact origins of the word are unknown. Jameison proposed that it derived from 'calf', but this has not been universally accepted (Mackay, *Dict. Low. Scot.*, 105). It may come from 'kelp', the name for several types of seaweed, the collection of which was a major occupation in the Hebrides and Orkneys: 'the kelpie was a creature supposed or alleged to lurk among the kelp or sea-weed, which in some coasts not only grows to an incredible height and size, but disposes itself in all sorts of fantastic and weird forms' (Brand, *Pop. Antiq.*, II, 352). It was usually black in colour, although a white variety has been recorded; and there are several cases in which it could assume human form and almost always had the power of speech. Although cursed with a dark reputation, the kelpie could also be helpful to humans. The Kelpie of Braemar was particularly fond of the womenfolk of the region and one especially, a miller's wife, he helped get for milling when her supply ran out; but the miller would have none of it and

broke the kelpie's leg with a stone whorl and so he fell into the mill pond and was himself drowned. At Strichen Burn, Aberdeenshire, the kelpie could assume human form, usually that of an old man. Near the Bridge of Luib on the River Don by the place called the Kelpie's Stane, the monster there could also take human shape. (Blind, 'Scottish', 186–207; MacGregor, *Peat-Fire Flame*, 69–70; Mackinlay, *Folklore*, 155ff.) Other local varieties include the Black Steed of Loch Pityoulish with its silver harness and the **White Horse of Spey**. There was a noted kelpie in the environs of Loch Ness that undoubtedly fed the rumours of their being a **Loch Ness Monster**. The usual view in folklore is to see the kelpie as a personification of the dangerous power of water (Anon., 'Tales', 511). For the other Scottish **Water-Horse**, see **Each-Uisge**.

KINNARA

In Hindu and Buddhist mythology the *kinnara* (male), *kinnari* (female), is part human, part horse and part bird; although other versions say half human, half horse, or half human, half bird. For the most part, according to the Buddhists, they seem to have been harmless creatures who enjoyed hopping to the sound of cymbals and are often depicted carrying garlands and even wearing flowers. They were believed to dwell in the Himalayas and live on pollen. They might be caught and displayed in cages for the pleasure of kings. In Hindu myth they were not so pleasant, but retained a love of music. (Murthy, *Myth. An. Ind.*, 13–16.)

KING CHARLES I'S PARROT

In the early years of the nineteenth century, workmen conducting repairs to Windsor Castle discovered a skeleton bricked up in an old and disused chimney in one of Queen Victoria's apartments. The opinion of the most senior servants of the Castle was that it was the remains of King Charles I's favourite parrot. That was the story told to Frank Buckland when presented with a box during his time as assistant surgeon with the 2nd Life Guards: 'The box was opened with great solemnity, and I beheld the strange looking and weird skeleton now presented in the portrait. Its bird-like attitude, I confess, deceived me for a moment, but I quickly discovered that a trap had been laid by some of the troopers to catch "the Doctor".' Buckland examined the thing more closely and concluded that 'this curious object is simply the skeleton of a rabbit, put up in a bird-like attitude; the rabbit has been cut into two, and the flesh taken off the bones, which are coloured brown to give an appearance of antiquity'. (Buckland, *Log-Book*, 28–31.)

King Charles I's Parrot (1875)

KIRKEGRIM

An animal buried alive in a graveyard to act as its guardian. In Sweden the **Helhest** ('Hel-horse') and grave-sow were said to perform this function.

Thorpe (*North. Myth.*, 210) recorded the following legend: 'In the streets of Æröskiobing [Ærøskøbing] there is often seen a Grave-sow, or, as it is also called, a Gray sow. This is said to be the apparition of a sow formerly buried alive, and when it appears, to forebode death and calamity.' Elsewhere, 'Many places and churches have, according to tradition, got their names from these spectres, such as "Hestveda" town and church in Skaane, which is said formerly to have been called "Hest-hvita", because a white horse was "Kirkegrim" there. When such spectres are seen, they are warnings of important events, lucky or unlucky' (Craigie, *Scan. Folk.*, 402). See also **Church Grim**. (Schütte, 'Dan. Pag.', 365.)

KIRKELAM

The 'church-lamb', similar to the **Kirkegrim**. According to Scandinavian legend, an animal is buried under or within the church itself, usually the altar: 'When any one enters a church alone and when there is no service, it often happens that he sees the Church-lamb running about; for the church is built over a lamb, that it may not sink. Formerly, when a church was being built, it was customary to bury a living lamb under the altar, that the building might stand immoveable. This lamb's apparition is known by the name of the Church-lamb'. (Thorpe, *North. Myth.*, 210.)

KLAPPERBOCK

The Yuletide spirit of the island of Usedom in north-eastern Germany. It was a goat's head and skin on a pole with moveable jaws operated by the carrier, and so was made to snap at the children and terrify them. It was carried as part of a procession comprising three persons: one carrying a rod and a bag of ashes, another the *Klapperbock*, and a third riding on a white horse. (Thorpe, *North. Myth.*, 146–7.)

KLUDDE

A protean creature met with in Brabant and Flanders: 'Kludde often transforms himself into a tree, small and delicate at first, but rapidly shooting into the clouds, while everything it shadows is thrown into confusion. Again, he presents himself as a black dog, running on its hind-legs, with a chain round its throat; and will spring at the throat of the first person he meets, fling him to the ground, and vanish. Occasionally Kludde will assume the form of a cat, frog, or bat, in which disguises he may always be known by two little blue flames fluttering or dancing before him; but most commonly he appears as an old half-starved horse, and so presents himself to stable-boys and grooms, who mount on it by mistake, instead of on their own horse or mare. Kludde sets off at full speed, the frightened lad clinging on as best he may, till they reach water, into which he rushes and laughs wildly, till his victim, sullen and angry, has worked his way to dry land again.' The Kludde wonderfully combines all that is most feared of the **Black Dog** and **Water-Horse**, and should be compared to other shape-shifting bogies, such as the **Picktree Brag** and the **Hedley Kow**. (Henderson, *Notes*, 272–3.)

KNUCKER

The Sussex **Dragon**, reputed to live in the Knucker Hole, a lake or spring near Lyminster: 'a foul Monster which ravaged the country for miles round, flying with inconceivable rapidity through the air, and seizing men, women, and children, with sheep and oxen, it carried them off to its home in the swamps of the Arun, and there devoured them'. As it should be, the king (nameless) offers his beautiful daughter in marriage to the fearless knight who should defeat the monster. Many try, many are slain; at last a young hero is triumphant and all live happily ever after. At Lyminster church there is, so the author has been informed, the 'Grave-Stone of the Man that killed the Dragon'. (Evershed, 'Legend', 181–2.)

KRAKEN

Also *Kraxen, Krabben, Horven*, or *Anker-trold*, a species of Scandinavian **Sea Monster**. The most authoritative source for the monster was Erich Pontoppidan, Bishop of Bergen and member of the Danish Royal Academy of Science. In his *Natural History of Norway* he claimed that the Kraken

The Kraken may have been a Giant Squid (1867)

was the largest sea monster of the world, in shape 'round, flat, and full of arms, or branches'. He reported what he believed were eye-witness accounts, most dramatic of which was the manner of the monster's appearance: 'Our fishermen unanimously affirm, and without the least variation in their accounts, that when they row out several miles to sea, particularly in the hot Summer days, and by their Situation (which they know by taking a view of certain points of land) expect to find 80 or 100 fathoms water, it often happens that they do not find above 20 or 30, and some times less. At these places they generally find the greatest plenty of Fish, especially Cod and Ling. Their lines they say are no sooner out than they may draw them up with the hooks all full of Fish; by this they judge that the Kraken is at the bottom. They say this creature causes those unnatural Shallows mentioned above, and prevents their sounding. These the fishermen are always glad to find, looking upon them as a means of their taking abundance of Fish. There are sometimes twenty boats or more got together, and throwing out their lines at a moderate distance from each other; and the only thing they then have to observe is, whether the depth continues the same, which they know by their lines, or whether it grows Shallower by their seeming to have less water. If this last be the case, they find that the Kraken is raising himself nearer the surface, and then it is not time for them to stay any longer; they immediately leave off fishing, take to their oars and get away as fast as they can. When they have reached the usual depth of the place, and find themselves out of danger, they lie upon their oars, and in a few minutes after they see this enormous monster come up to the surface of the water; he there shows himself sufficiently, though his whole body does not appear which in all likelihood no human eye ever beheld (excepting the young of this species, which shall afterwards be spoken of) its back or upper part, which seems to be in appearance about an English mile and an half in circumference, (some say more, but I choose the least for greater certainty) looks at first like a number of small islands, surrounded with something that floats and fluctuates like sea-weeds. Here and there a larger rising is observed like sandbanks, on which various kinds of small Fishes are seen continually leaping about till they roll off into the water from the sides of it; at last several bright points or horns appear, which grow thicker and thicker the higher they rise above the surface of the water, and sometimes they stand up as high and as large as the masts of middle-siz'd vessels' (211–2, spelling modernised). Pontoppidan claimed that it could drag down into the depths the largest man-of-war with its many strong arms; but this was not the least of it, for as it sinks it creates a whirlpool that pulls down with it anything that strays too close. It could emit a strong smell that drew fish into its clutches and as it feasted it excreted all the while, turning the seas brown and turbid; yet more

fish came to feast on this appetising muck and so became the Kraken's dinner in turn 'and converts them, after the due time, by digestion, into bait for other Fish of the same kind' (212). This 'excrement' was probably plankton, a major source of food for many large sea creatures, which would account for the feeding behaviour; or an algal bloom. Contrary to rumour, Carolus Linnaeus did not include the Kraken in the first edition of his *System Naturae* of 1735 as a cephalopod with the scientific name of *Microcosmus marinus* – that was his term for plankton. However, writing in 1818 a certain 'W.' set forth a long argument in support of the existence of the monster, citing Linnaeus as one of his authorities and stating that the great taxonomist had included 'the great Polypus or Cuttle Fish' under the heading *Microcosmus*, but in such a way that later readers thought that it was the Kraken that was so listed ('Remarks', 646); otherwise, W.'s giant squid theory is still accepted in some circles today. The Victorian poet Alfred, Lord Tennyson, immortalised the monster in his famous poem 'The Kraken' (*Poems*, 1830): 'Below the thunders of the upper deep; | Far, far beneath in the abysmal sea, | His ancient, dreamless, uninvaded sleep | The Kraken sleepeth [...]' (*Poems*, 154). See also **Hafgufa**, **Halsydrus Pontoppidani**, **Illhvel**.

KRAMPUS

A German Yuletide monster with shaggy bear-like coat, horns, and a long red tongue. He typically wears a bell around his neck and clanks chains as part of a Yule procession on 6 December, frightening naughty children. The Christians have imposed the person of St Nicholas as the leader of this procession, but older forms of the name survive, such as Pelzmärte, or when equipped with a bag of ashes, Aschenklas. The Krampus figure is widespread in the German-speaking alpine region, although other names, such as Klaubauf, Bartel or **Rawuzel**, might be used; variants of the female name Berchta are also met with, such as Budelfrau, Berchtel and Buzebergt. For the meaning of St Nicholas, see **Nicker**. For similar British customs, see **Hooden Horse** and **Mari Llwyd**. (Miles, *Christmas*, 219.)

KULULLU

The 'fish-man' created by the sea-dragon **Tiamat** as part of her army of eleven evil monsters whom she fields against the god Marduk, as told in the Babylonian Creation Myth, the *Enuma Elish*. After Tiamat's defeat, Marduk subjugates the eleven and the fish-man became an apotropaic symbol, warding off the powers of evil. It was used as a foundation figurine and in monumental sculpture. It was often found paired with a 'goat-fish', the **Suhurmasu**. A rarer female counterpart, the *kuliltu*, 'fish-woman', has also been recorded. A human figure in a 'fish cloak' is known as a fish-*apkallu*; one named example was **Oannes**, but they seem to have been quite different. Other recorded forms are *ha-galu-gal-lu* and *nun-ameli*. It is equated with the zodiacal constellation we know as Aquarius. (Green, 'Note Ass. "Goat-Fish"', 25–30.)

KUR

The Sumerian **Dragon** or **Serpent** of primordial chaos and prototype of the Babylonian **Tiamat**. *Kur* can mean 'mountain' and 'land' – Sumer itself was called *kur-gal*, 'great land' – but it is also related to *ki-gal*, 'great below', the Sumerian hell or nether world, which could be simply called *kur*. The story of Kur, dating from the third millennium BCE, is known only through fragments of three or four myths. The exact appearance of Kur is uncertain, but the underlying concept is of a huge serpent living at the bottom of the lowest depths, the well-spring of the primeval waters. When slain, these waters gush forth and flood the earth. It is conjectured that Kur abducts the goddess Ereshkigal and takes her down into the abyss, whereupon the water-god Enki battles the monster and saves her; or, in another version, is destroyed by the god Ninurta (son of serpent goddess **Nintu**), inadvertently unleashing the flood, which after devasting the land, Ninurta is able to control; a third myth has Kur defeated by Inanna, the goddess of love, one of whose epithets is 'destroyer of Kur', although Kur in this case is said to be the 'moutain Ebih' in northeast Sumer (Kramer, *Sum. Myth.*, 76–83). The myth thus comprises elements of a creation epic and the familiar flood narrative, as well as the control and use of water to cultivate the land, just like Hercules and the **Lernæan Hydra**.

KUSARIKKU

Akkadian 'bull-man', or more literally 'bison-man', from the original Sumerian *gud-alim*, *gud-dumu-an-na*: a monster named in the Babylonian Creation Epic, *Enuma Elish*, as one of the spawn of the sea-dragon **Tiamat**. Like Tiamat's other monstrous brood, once subjugated by Marduk, Kusarikku became a beneficent demon used to protect entrances. Esarhaddon had two representations of the kusarikku made from 'shining bronze'; they had heads looking front and back, and were large enough to support the rafters of the roof of the entrance porch to the temple of Ashur. The image of a composite monster with the top half of a man and the lower part of a bull appears on seals from the Akkadian period as far back as the third millennium BCE. As a pair, kusarikku are associated with the sun-god as his guardians. (Gadd, 'Some Contrib.', 105–21; Huxley, 'Gates and Guard.', 109–37.)

L

LADON

In Greek mythology, the **Dragon** borne to **Typhon** and **Echidna**, or, in an older account, **Phorcys** and Ceto. The goddess Juno appointed him guardian of the golden apples growing in the garden of the Hesperides, the four daughters of Night (Erebus). He had a hundred heads, each of which spoke with its own voice, and curled himself around the tree to keep his sleepless watch. He was slain by Hercules, who, commanded by Eurystheus, came to pluck the apples as his Eleventh Labour. (Apollodorus, *Library*, 2.5; Hesiod, *Theog.*, 304; Smith, *Dict.*, II, 705.)

LAHMU

The 'hairy one': a diety begotten by **Tiamat** and Apsu; the counterpart of Lahamu. The generation of Lahmu and Lahamu is told in the Babylonian Creation Myth, the *Enuma Elish*. From a single entity he seems to have become a class of monster. In 'The Description of the Gods', known from texts dating to the 1st millennium BCE found in Nineveh, Assur and Uruk, several lahmu variations are recorded: *Lahmu ippiru*, the *lahmu* of struggle, is described as a **Sea Monster** with lion characteristics; other accounts describe the *lahmu* type as having a horned snake's head, a bearded human face, a dog's head and wings. Lahma and Lahamu functioned as the gate-posts of the heavens holding apart the two parts of Tiamat's sundered body, and Mesopotamian temple design reflected this cosmology in stone. In addition, clay models and plaques of Lahmu (or *lahmus*) holding a pole were buried close to doorways to prevent evil gaining entrance, as their inscriptions confirm: one reads 'Come in, good spirit! Go out, evil spirit!' (Ellis, 'Trouble', 159–65; Lambert, 'Pair Lahmu', 189–202; Thompson, *Devils*, 155–7.)

LAIDLEY WORM

'She's witched her body to a laidley worm, | A laidley worm to be [...] It has the tongue of a maid-woman, | And a worm's foul body' (Swinburne, *Border Ballads*, 46–7). The term *laidley* means loathly or loathsome, and *worm*, **Dragon**: hence, the 'loathsome dragon', but as such is entirely restricted to one specimen said to haunt Spindleston Heugh near Bamburgh Castle in Northumberland. According to the story, a wicked stepmother being jealous of her step-daughter's beauty, and also being a witch, put a spell on her, transforming her into the worm. On finding herself so, the stepdaughter, once the Princess Margaret, fled to this place, Spindleston Heugh and took refuge in a cave. Her brother, Childe Wynd, finally returned from adventures in foreign lands and rescued her: by kissing the worm three times she was restored to her former state. Of course, the wicked stepmother met a bad end: she was turned into a toad (Jacobs, *Eng. Fairy*, 214–19). The 'Cheviot Bard', Duncan Frasier, who flourished about 1270 CE, wrote a popular ballad on the subject (Crawhall, *History*).

LALAGE MELANOTHORAX

In his catalogue of birds in the collection of the British Musem, R. Bowdler Sharpe described the subspecies of *Lalage melanothorax* from Madras: 'Similar to *L. sikesi*, but with a very much larger bill; the whole head and neck and the throat and chest glossy steel-black, extending much further down than in *L. sykesi*.' Seven years later he realised his mistake. The specimen of the bird owned by the museum was in fact a **Jenny Haniver**: the head of a drongo had been stuck expertly on the body of a cuckoo-shrike. (Sharpe, *Catalogue*, 91; and 'Notes', 354.)

LAMASSU

A Babylonian winged bull with human head. It was the protector of palaces. Its name may mean 'divine guardian'. Counterpart to the **Shedu**. (Langdon, *Bab. Lit.*, 137; Mackenzie, *Myth. Bab.*, 65.)

A Lamassu at the Palace of Sargon II
(Eighth Century BCE)

LAMBTON WORM

A **Dragon** of old County Durham, named after the Lambton family who in turn take their name from Lambton (now in Tyne and Wear) in North East England. According to the legend, an unnamed 'heir of Lambton' caught a small worm whilst fishing and, carelessly throwing it into a well (the Worm Well), thought no more of it. The worm grew to a great size and left the well for the river Wear and a certain green mound, now known as the Worm Hill, where it would coil itself – the signs of which may be seen today. The heir, returning from some other adventures, was aghast at this development and undertook to slay the monster. With the advice of a witch or wise woman he fixed razor blades to his mail coat and allowed the worm to wrap itself round him and, in its attempts to crush him to death, sliced itself to pieces. The tale has much in common with that of the **Linton Worm**, except that as a finale the heir was required by the witch to slay the first living thing he met after performing the deed. He had arranged that, on hearing him blow his hunting horn, his father would release his faithful hunting dog, but his father, so overjoyed was he that his son had survived the combat, rushed out to greet him and forgot about the dog. His son could not slay the unfortunate man and so a curse descended upon the house of Lambton: that no head of the family should die easy in his bed. The story was, in part, the basis for Bram Stoker's *The Lair of the White Worm* (1911). (Surtees in Crawhall, *History*, 13ff.)

LAMIA

Lamia was a daughter of Poseidon, who by Zeus became the mother of the Sibyl Herophile; or a beautiful Libyan queen, again loved by Zeus. Zeus' jealous wife Hera robbed Lamia of her children; Lamia, in her turn, sought revenge on others by destroying their children also. Her terrible occupation rendered her ugly and Zeus added the ability of being able to remove her eyes and put them back in again. She was sometimes named as the mother of **Scylla**. In time, the *lamiae* were thought of as a class of seductive female ghosts who drained the blood of young men (Smith, *Dict.*, 713). In the first English translation of the Bible, she is a woman with horses' hooves: 'Ther shal lyn lamya, that is a thirs [thurse] or a beast hauende the bodi lie a woman and horse feet' (Wyclif, Isaiah 34:15, *c.* 1380). In later English translations of the Bible, lamia was translated as screech owl (see **Strix**)

and night-monster; in German with *Kobold*; in Danish with *Vætte* (see **Wight**). In the seventeenth century, Edward Topsell (*Historie*, 352ff) added 'the members of a Goat' to the horse's feet and gave her 'the eyes of a Kite'; the illustration in his book showed a four-legged beast with a woman's head and breasts, a scaly body, lion-like front paws, cloven hooves on the rear legs, a horse's tale and a male generative organ. The monster was still being found in scientific works even into the eighteenth century: Carolus Linnaeus included it as one of the **Animalia Paradoxa** in the 1740 edition of his *Systema Naturae*, describing it as having 'a human face, virgin's breasts, a quadroped's body, scaled, forefeet of a wild animal, rear, of cattle' (66). However, the Romantic poets would lose all the unattractive embellishments of the bestiaries and develop her seductive qualities. In John Keats' poem *Lamia*, written in 1819, she was a fantastic serpent woman: 'a gordian shape of dazzling hue, | Vermilion-spotted, golden, green, and blue; |

Lamia (1658)

Striped like a zebra, freckled like a pard, | Eyed like a peacock, and all crimson barr'd; | And full of silver moons […] Her head was serpent, but ah, bitter-sweet! | She had a woman's mouth with all its pearls complete […] Her throat was serpent, but the words she spake | Came, as through bubbling honey, for Love's sake'.

LAVELLAN

A small furry animal with the power of inflicting harm on cattle from a distance of forty yards, according to Scottish folklore. It terrorised Caithness in particular. The skin was preserved and, filled with water, was given to sick cattle to drink from as a cure. Folklorists have suggested that the animal is the 'water shrew mouse' or 'water mole'; its supernatural powers surely come from the holes it leaves as a trap for cows' legs. It was once the habit of Jacobites to toast 'the little gentleman in the black velvet waistcoat' because William of Orange's horse stumbled over a mole hill, throwing the king and causing his death. (Campbell, *Sup. High.*, 220–1.)

LEGLESS BIRD OF PARADISE

Around 1420, the Italian merchant Niccolo de Conti was in Java and described seeing a 'remarkable bird resembling a wood pigeon without feet and with an oblong tail'. The naturalist Conrad Gessner described the bird in his *Icones Animalium* of 1560 with appropriate illustration, although it looks like a somewhat unravelled vulture *sans* legs, of course, and additionally lacking wings. In 1758 Carolus Linnaeus classified it as *Paradisaea apoda*, literally, 'footless bird of paradise'. It has since been found to have both legs and feet, and wings. It took some time to discover that it was the habit of the natives to prepare the birds by removing their legs and wings, either to sell to travellers or for their own use. This led to the belief that these birds were forever in flight and subsisted on dew and the nectar of spice trees. Although the scientific name has stuck, it is now called the greater bird of paradise. (Dance, *Animal Fakes*, 75–6.)

LEOCAMPUS

The rare sea-lion of Ancient Greek and Roman mythology: from the Greek, *leo-*, 'lion', and *kampos*, 'crooked', usually Latinised as *leocampus*. An example in art is found on an undated mosaic in a villa in the Roman city of Volubilis in Morocco: a triton has a sea-lion on a lead and seems to pull it after him. The city was overrun by hostile tribes *c*.285 CE, so the mosaic must predate this.

LEONTOPHONUS

Also *Leontophone, Leontophonos*: Pliny (*Nat. Hist.*, 8.57) praised it for its 'urine worketh straunge and wonderfull effects'. It is described as small and deadly to lions: 'he breedeth in no countrey but where there be lions: a little creature it is, but so venimous, that the lyon (king of beasts, before whome all others tremble) for all his might and puissance, dieth presently if hee tast never so little thereof. And therefore they that chase the lion, get all the

Leontophones that they can come by, burne their bodies, and with the pouder of them bestrew and season as it were the pieces of other flesh they lay for a bait in the forrest, and thus with the verie ashes (I say) of his enemie, kill him; and deadly and pernicious it is to the lion. No marveile therefore if the lion abhorre and hate him, for so soon as he espieth him, he crusheth him with his pawes, and so killeth him without setting tooth to his bodie. The Leontophone for his part againe, is as readie to bedrench him with his urine, knowing right well that his pisse is a verie poison to the Lion.'

LEPUS CORNUTUS

The 'horned hare' was first described in Conrad Gessner's *Historiae Animalium* ('History of the Animals'), his monumetal work of natural history published in Zurich in five volumes from 1551 to 1558 and 1587. This led to the animal being included in many other important early works of natural history – including Hoefnagel's *Animalia Quadrupedia et Reptilia* (1580), Collaert's *Animalium Quadrupedum* (1612) and Bonnaterre's *Tableau Encyclopedique et Methodique* (1789) – until it was finally rejected as a fantasy. The misconception was confounded by the existence

Lepus Cornutus (1789)

INDEFESSA GERENS REDIVIVIS BELLA COLVBRIS   ARGOLIS AD LERNÆ TVNDITVR HYDRA VADVM

Hercules and the Lernæan Hydra (*c.*1565)

of several supposed specimens of the creature. However, it is known that certain types of virus, e.g., *Shope papilloma virus* first identified by Richard E. Shope in 1933 ('Inf. Pap. Rab.', 607–24), can cause hares and rabbits to develop tumorous protrusions (papillomas) around the head that can, in extreme cases, resemble horns. See also **Jackalope** and **Wolpertinger**.

LERNÆAN HYDRA

In Greek mythology, a monster first mentioned by Hesiod as the progeny of **Typhon** and **Echidna** (Hesiod, *Theog.*, 313); Apollodorus says only that it was bred in the swamp of Lerna (Apollodorus, *Library*, 2.5.2). It had a gigantic body and nine heads, eight of which were mortal, except that in the middle, which was immortal, and held the surrounding countryside in a state of terror. Conquest of this monster was the second task given to Hercules by Eurystheus. Hercules tracked it to its lair beside the spring of Amymone and rained flaming arrows on the place, driving it out from hiding. He then attempted to wrestle the monster, but it wound itself around him. Hercules smashed its heads with his club, but as soon as one was destroyed, two more grew up to replace it. An enormous crab scuttled out to aid the Hydra, seizing Hercules' foot in its claws. Hercules was able to kill it, but called to Iolaus, his charioteer, to help him. Iolaus set light to a piece of wood and burned the stumps to prevent new heads from sprouting. Finally, only the immortal head remained: Hercules cut it off and hid it under a heavy rock. He cut up the rest of the body and dipped his arrow heads in its poisonous gall. Hera, Hercules' arch-enemy, took the crab and set it in the sky as the constellation of Cancer. The number of heads varied: Diodorus and Ovid said one hundred; Pausanius only one (Paus. *Desc. Gr.*, 2.37.4). Isidore of Seville (*Etym.*, XII.4.23) classed this monster among the serpents: 'The hydra is a many-headed snake, such as existed in the marsh Lerna, in the province of Arcadia. This is called *excetra* in Latin, because three heads grew, *excrescebant*, from one cut. But this is legend, for Hydra was a place where waters were driven, destroying the nearby town. When one channel closed, many broke out. When Hercules saw it, he drained the area, and so closed the channels of water.'

LEUCROCUTA

Also *leucrocotta*, *leocrocuta*: a deer-lion with cloven hooves, a badger's head and a huge mouth filled, not with teeth, but with bone, said by Pliny the Elder to be found in Africa. He described it as 'a most swift beast, as big almost as an hee-asse, legged like an Hart, with a neck, taile, and breast of a Lion, headed like these grayes or badgers, with a cloven foot in twaine: the slit of his mouth reacheth to his eares: instead of teeth, an entire whol bone. They report, that this beast counterfeiteth a mans voice' (*Nat.*

Hist., 8.30). On the amazing jaws, Pliny later adds, 'hee hath one entire bone in steed of teeth in either jaw (and no gombs at all) wherewith he cutteth, as with a knife. Now these bones, because they should not waxe dull and blunt with continuall grating one against the other, they are enclosed each of them within a case or sheath' (8.45). The leucrocuta is the product of a mating between the male hyena and female lion, according to Pliny. Edward Topsell included it in his *Historie of Foure-Footed Beasts* in 1607. See also **Crocotta**, with which it seems to be somewhat confused.

Leucrocuta (Medieval)

LEVIATHAN

'Canst thou draw out leviathan with an hook?': we first meet Leviathan in the Book of Job (41) where this rhetorical question is answered with 'no one is fierce enough to rouse it'. A full description of the monster is given: 'I will not conceal his parts, nor his power, nor his comely proportion. Who can discover the face of his garment? Or who can come to him with his double bridle? Who can open the doors of his face? His teeth are terrible round about. His scales are his

Leviathan (1866)

pride, shut up together as with a close seal. One is so near to another, that no air can come between them. They are joined one to another, they stick together, that they cannot be sundered. By his neesings a light doth shine, and his eyes are like the eyelids of the morning. Out of his mouth go burning lamps, and sparks of fire leap out. Out of his nostrils goeth smoke, as out of a seething pot or caldron. His breath kindleth coals, and a flame goeth out of his mouth. In his neck remaineth strength, and sorrow is turned into joy before him. The flakes of his flesh are joined together: they are firm in themselves; they cannot be moved. His heart is as firm as a stone; yea, as hard as a piece of the nether millstone. When he raiseth up himself, the mighty are afraid: by reason of breakings they purify themselves. The sword of him that layeth at him cannot hold: the spear, the dart, nor the habergeon. He esteemeth iron as straw, and brass as rotten wood. The arrow cannot make him flee: slingstones are turned with him into stubble. Darts are counted as stubble: he laugheth at the shaking of a spear. Sharp stones are under him: he spreadeth sharp pointed things upon the mire. He maketh the deep to boil like a pot: he maketh the sea like a pot of ointment. He maketh a path to shine after him; one would think the deep to be hoary. Upon earth there is not his like, who is made without fear. He beholdeth all high things: he is a king over all the children of pride.' Leviathan is also mentioned in Psalms (74:14, 104:26) and Isaiah (27:1); in the latter the monster is described as 'Leviathan

the piercing **Serpent**, even Leviathan that crooked serpent' and 'the **Dragon** that is in the sea'. In the Apocryphal Book of Enoch (sec. X, ch. lx. 7, 8), Leviathan is described as being female: her male counterpart is **Behemoth**. In the bestiary of Hugo de Folieto (MS Sloane 278 in Druce, 'Elephant') Leviathan is involved in a folk explanation of the tides: 'The Jews say that God made the great dragon which is called Leviathan, which is in the sea; and when folk say that the sea is ebbing it is the dragon going back. Some say that it is the first fish created by God and that it still lives.' Leviathan is generally interpreted as a Jewish version of the Babylonian **Tiamat** (Barton, 'Tiamat', 22). Milton, however, moves the monster northwards, where it meets the folklore of the **Illhvel** and the Midgard Serpent (**Jörmungandr**) of the Sagas: 'that sea-beast | Leviathan, which God of all his works | Created hugest that swim th' ocean-stream. | Him, haply slumbering on the Norway foam' (*Paradise Lost*, 1.192–282).

LICH-FOWL

The 'corpse-fowl': a bird portending death, like the **Night-Raven**. The name is recorded as having been used in Shropshire for the nightjar. The German equivalent is the *Leichhuhn* ('corpsehen'). (Swainson, *Prov. Names*, 98.)

LICORNE

Pliny the Elder described an Indian creature that was like a zoologically deranged **Unicorn**. It had the head of a stag with a single huge horn, the body of a horse, elephant's feet and a boar's tail: 'the most fell and furious beast of all other, is the Licorne or Monoceros: his bodie resembleth an horse, his head a stagge, his feet an Elephant, his taile a bore; he loweth after an hideous manner; one blacke horn he hath in the mids of his forehead, bearing out two cubits in length: by report, this wild beast cannot possibly be caught alive'. (*Nat. Hist.*, 8.31; Bostock omits the name from his translation.)

LIMGRIM

A giant boar in Scandinavian legend. According to the story, a woman wished to have a child that would be greater than the creator of the world: she gave birth to Limgrim, whose bristles stand taller than the trees in the forest and whose rooting created a huge furrow in the ground that became the firth of Limfjord. When someone is destined to drown, he is heard shouting 'The time has come, but the man has not yet come!' (Schütte, 'Dan. Pag.', 365).

LINDWORM

Also *Lindwurm*, *Lintwurm*, a type of wingless **Dragon**, possibly meaning 'beautiful' or 'shining worm' from Old High German *Lint* (Grimm, *Teut. Myth*, II, 688), or 'lithe' (Grimm's translator), but there is also a poetic connection with the dragon Fafnir whom Siegfried finds under the Linden tree. Several towns in Germany called Limburg derive their name from this beast. In heraldry, a dragon or **Wyvern** without wings is still called a lindworm. (Gould, *Myth. Mon.*, 188.)

LINTON WORM

A **Dragon** of Scottish folklore. It coiled itself around Wormeston Hill near the village of Linton in the Scottish Borders, its poisonous breath destroying all life nearby, but was slain by a bold knight, the Laird of Lariston, who thrust a peat of burning pitch down its throat. The contractions of the dying monster are said to have left the indentations that can still be seen spiralling round the hill today. A much eroded medieval carving set above the porch door of the church of Linton shows the combat between knight and worm. The local Somerville family, who claim this knight as an ancestor, bear a dragon as their crest. (Hardwick, *Traditions*, 45; Henderson, *Notes*, 295–6; Scot, *Minstrelsy*, III, 295–6.)

LIZARD-HEADED FISH

The lizard-headed fish, also known as the Mississippi Pike or Armoured Snout, came to wider public notice when the curiosity cabinet of the Comte de la Tour d'Auvergne came up for sale in Paris in 1784. The catalogue described it as eel-shaped, with thick scales and a long head and jaw set with teeth, overall about 1.3 m (4¼ ft) in length. From the accompanying illustration, Dance conjectured that it was a sturgeon with the head of baby alligator. A certain Monsieur Gaillard snapped it up for six francs. (Dance, *Animal Fakes*, 116.)

LLAMHIGYN Y DWR

Welsh, 'the water leaper', a type of water spirit. It was described as being like a toad, but with wings and a tail instead of legs. In the nineteenth century, the father of a certain Ifan Owen claimed to have seen it many times in the vicinity of Llyn Gwynant, a lake in Snowdonia. (Rhys, *Celtic Folklore*, 79.)

LOCH NESS MONSTER

A creature supposed to inhabit the waters of Loch Ness, Scotland; since the 1930s known as the Loch Ness Monster, it's also affectionately called Nessie (Gaelic *Niseag*). The origins of the story are commonly traced back to a legend of St Columba recorded in the seventh century CE: the saint supposedly overcomes a water beast, *aquatilis bestia*, in the river Ness with the usual waving about of the cross and empty words. Local **Kelpie** legends were certainly known: 'It is reported that a horse [water-horse, or kelpie] used to frequent the road near Loch Ness, till a stout, brave Highlander, meeting the monster one night, drew his sword in the name of the Trinity, and finished the supposed kelpie forever' (Henderson, *Survivals*, 162; cf., Mackinlay, *Folklore*, 173–4); and an earlier story was reported in the *Aberdeen Journal* for 11 June 1879. That 'forever' lasted until 1933 when Hugh Gray's blurry photograph of a dark serpentine shape was published in the world's newspapers. Since then there have been various other sightings, photographs, films and sonar contacts, none of which bear any resemblance to a **Water-Horse**. Other sources have said that the loch harbours several specimen of water-bull, the **Tarbh-**

Uisge: 'Loch Ness is full of them' (Campbell, *Pop. Tales*, IV, 300). Over the years many theories have been proposed to explain the monster, including seismotectonics (Piccardi, 'Seismotectonic Origins'); survivals of species considered to be extinct, such as the plesiosaur (Binns, *Loch Ness*) or Tullimonstrum (Holiday, *Great Orm*); the simple misidentification of natural phenomena, including animals and optical effects; and of course outright hoaxes. Discussion on the topic is already vast and continues (see Hansen, 'Loch Ness'). Many other Scottish lochs have their reputed monsters, including Loch Awe, Loch Hourn (the **Wild Beast of Barrisdale**), Loch Lochy ('Lizzie'), Loch Morar ('Morag'), and Loch Oich ('Wee Oichy'), among others. (MacGregor, *Peat-Fire Flame*, 82.)

LOD-SILUNGUR

The Icelandic 'shaggy trout', a fish said to have reddish hair on its lower jaw and around the neck with additional hairy patches here and there along its body. Apparently it is poisonous and no dog nor bird of prey will eat of it. Davidson reported that one was washed up on shore in 1854 and was reported in the *Nordri* newspaper in 1855. ('Folk-Lore', 331.)

LÖWENMENSCH

The representation of a Stone Age *Löwenmensch*, 'lion-man', was discovered in Germany in the 1930s. It is a piece of worked mammoth ivory about 28 cm (11 in) in height of a human figure with a leonine head and may be as many as 40,000 years old, according to radiocarbon (C-14) dating. It was found by Gustav Riek during excavations in the Vogelherd cave in the Swabian Jura region in southern Germany in 1931. Due to the onset of World War II the object was not inventoried and it was not until 1969 that it was rediscovered by the archaeologist Joachim Hahn. Together with similar figurines discovered in the same area, it is one of the oldest examples of man-made representative art. (Curry, 'Dawn of Art', 28–33.)

LUCTIFER

Latin, 'grief-bringing' or 'ill-boding', a name given by the Romans to the owl (see **Strix**) because of its reputation as a bird of evil omen. (Seneca, *Herc. Fur.*, 687.)

LUMMEKOIRA

A creature of Finnish legend connected with the **Nixie** or **Nicker**. In this old Finnish spell 'To Discover the Cause', we read: 'I do not know at all just now, the reason I cannot surmise, why, Hiisi, thou hast entrance made, hast, devil (*Perkele*), made, thyself at home in a guiltless heart, in a belly free of blame. From waters of witches hast thou come, from the lilies on a landlocked lake, from Nixies' (*lummekoira*) haunts, from a water-Hiisi's hole, from the sea's black mud, a thousand fathoms deep, or from the heath of death (*kalma*), from the interior of the earth, from a dead man's belly, from the skin of one departed for eternity, from the armpit of a spectral form (*kalmalainen*), from beneath the liver of a shade (*manalainen*), hast thou been torn from

a cross's base, been conjured up from women's graves, beside a decorated church, from the edge of a holy field, or from great battle-fields, from the slaughter-fields of men?' (Abercromby, *Pre- Proto-Hist.*, 74.)

LYCAON

Lycaon, from the Greek *lycos*, 'wolf', can refer to two usages, one from Greek mythology, the other from early natural history: 1. In Greek mythology, Lycaon was turned into a wolf by the god Zeus after he poured the blood of a child over the altar as a sacrifice; ever after a man would be transformed into a wolf at the annual sacrifice to Lycaean Zeus, but may resume human form after nine years if he can abstain from human flesh (Pausanius, *Desc. Gr.*, 8.2). 2. According to Pliny (*Nat. Hist.* 8.52), an animal called *lycaon* is found in India; little is known of it, except that it can change its colour like a chameleon, including hair colour, and has a mane. Pliny grouped it with **Tarandus** and the wolf-like **Thos**. Previous translators have thought that he may have meant the Indian tiger, although it is hardly chameleon-like. The modern scientific genus *Lycaon* includes one extant species, the African hunting dog, *Lycaon pictus*.

LYNX

Also *once*, a precious-stone-urinating big cat. Pliny described the animal as being like a wolf in shape but with the leopard's spots: Pompey the Great first exhibited it at his games in 55 BCE (*Nat. Hist.*, 8.28). The product of this creature is first described in the fifth century BCE by Theophrastus (*On Stones*, 50) as *Lapis Lyncurius*: 'it is cold and very transparent'. Ovid mentioned it in his *Metamorphoses* as coming from India (15.391–417). Pliny (*Nat. Hist.*, 8.57), of course, gave the fuller account: 'In those countries where the Onces breed, their urine (after it is made) congealeth into a certain ycie substance, and waxeth dry, & so it comes to be a certain precious stone like a carbuncle, glittering and shining as red as fire, and called it is Lyncurium. And upon this occasion many have written, that Amber is engendred after the same manner. The Onces knowing thus much, for verie spight and envie, cover their urine with mould or earth, and this maketh it so much the sooner to harden and congeale.' *Once* is used by Philemon Holland in his seventeenth centuy translation of Pliny and, although more modern translators, e.g., John Bostock, prefer 'lynx', the name *once* is given by the French to the leopard and in Heraldry the leopard is sometimes called an 'ounce'. The leopard seems more probable as the lynx was once more widely distributed in Europe than it is now, whereas the leopard has always been a foreign species.

M

MACHLIS, SEE ACHLIS

MAIGHDEANN MHARA

The Scottish **Mermaid**, from the Gaelic meaning 'maid of the sea'; also *maighdean na tuinne, muirghin na tuinne*, 'maid of the wave'. The folk-lorist Alexander Carmichael collected a number of mermaid stories from apparently reliable and intelligent witnesses, first published in 1900 (*Carmina Gadelica*, II, 324–6):

(1) A crofter called Colin Campbell saw what he thought was an otter eating a fish on a reef in Coalas Cumhan, Barra. He raised his gun to fire, but now looking down the barrel he thought he could see a woman holding a child. Having a telescope with him, he was able to get a better view: 'he saw that the object before him had the head, the hair, the neck, the shoulders, and the breast of a woman, and was holding a child'. A noise startled her and, baby and all, she dived back into the waves. For the rest of his days, he remained sure that he had seen a mermaid.

(2) Another crofter, Neill MacEachain of Hough-beag, South Uist, was on his way home, sailing back from the Clyde. The wind dropped as he and his companions came out of the Sound of Mull and they drifted, becalmed, on the sea, as still and as smooth as a sheet of glass. Suddenly, 'all were astonished to see a creature about two yards from the side of the motionless skiff. Its head, neck, breast, and shoulders resembled those of a woman, though its hair was more coarse, and its eyes more glassy. All below the breast was in the water. The creature gazed at them for a minute or more with its large wondering eyes, and then disappeared into the sea as silently as it had come.'

(3) At Sgeir na duchadh, Grimnis, Benbecula, perhaps around 1830, a group of people were engaged in cutting seaweed. Before putting her stockings back on when she had finished, one of the women went out to a further end of the reef to wash her feet. She heard a splash and looking up 'she saw a creature in the form of a woman in miniature, some few feet away'. The woman cried out in alarm and her companions came up to see what was going on. The creature meanwhile amused herself by turning somersaults in the water. Some men tried to wade out and grab her, but she

easily evaded them. Boys started throwing stones and one struck her on the back. A few days later she was found dead on the beach at Cuile, Nunton, almost two miles away. It was now possible to examine her more thoroughly: 'The upper portion of the creature was about the size of a well-fed child of three or four years of age, with an abnormally developed breast. The hair was long, dark, and glossy, while the skin was white, soft, and tender. The lower part of the body was like a salmon, but without scales.' People came from all around to see her. Eventually a little coffin and shroud were made and she was buried not far from where she was found. Carmichael reported that 'There are persons still living who saw and touched this curious creature, and who give graphic descriptions of its appearance'.

MANTICORE

From the Greek μαρτιχώρα (μαρτιχώρας), *martikhora* ('*martikhoras*'); probably derived from the Old Iranian *Martijaqâra*, meaning 'man-eater': a monster of India with three rows of teeth set in a human head on a lion's body with a scorpion's tail. It was first described by the Greek writer Ctesias in the late fifth century BCE (*Anc. Ind.*, 11–12): 'Its face is like a man's – it is about as big as a lion, and in colour red like cinnabar. It has three rows of teeth – ears like the human – eyes of a pale-blue like the human and a tail like that of the land scorpion, armed with a sting and more than a cubit long. It has besides stings on each side of its tail, and, like the scorpion is armed with an

Manticore (1678)

additional sting on the crown of its head, wherewith it stings any one who goes near it, the wound in all cases proving mortal. If attacked from a distance it defends itself both in front and in rear – in front with its tail, by uplifting it and darting out the stings, like shafts shot from a bow, and in rear by straightening it out. It can strike to the distance of a hundred feet, and no creature can survive the wound it inflicts save only the elephant. The stings are about a foot in length, and not thicker than the finest thread. The name *martikhora* means in Greek ἀνθρωποφάγος ['man-eater'], and it is so called because it carries off men and devours them, though it no doubt preys on other animals as well. In fighting it uses not only its stings but also its claws. Fresh stings grow up to replace those shot away in fighting. These animals are numerous in India, and are killed by the natives who hunt them with elephants, from the backs of which they attack them with darts.' In the fourth century BCE, Aristotle included the creature in his *Historia Animalium* (2.3.10), adding 'if we are to believe Ctesias'. Pliny had read Ctesias, but not assiduously: 'Ctesias writeth, that in Æthiopia likewise there is a beast which he calleth Mantichora, having three rankes of teeth, which when they meet togither are let in one within another like the teeth of combes: with the face and eares of a man, with red eyes; of colour sanguine, bodied like a lyon, and having a taile armed with a sting like a scorpion: his voice resembleth the noise of a flute and trumpet sounded together: very swift he is, and mans flesh of all others hee most desireth' (*Nat. Hist.*, 8.30). Pausanius (*Desc. Gr.*, 9.21) identified this beast as the tiger, but the fantastical manticore continued to be described as such into the eighteenth century. Carolus Linnaeus included it as one of the **Animalia Paradoxa** in the 1740 edition of his *Systema Naturae*, describing it as having 'the face of a decrepit old man, the body of a lion, a tail ending with stinging stars' (66).

MARATHONIAN BULL,

SEE CRETAN BULL

MARES OF DIOMEDES

Four man-eating horses in Greek mythology, they feature in the Eighth Labour of Hercules: 'the horses of Diomedes, that greedily champed their bloody food at gory mangers with unbridled jaws, devouring with hideous joy the flesh of men' (Euripides, *Her.* 380). Diomedes was the son of the god Ares and Cyrene, and King of the war-like Bistones in Thrace. Hercules was sent by Eurystheus to bring Diomedes' fearsome horses to him in Mycemae. Hercules succeeded in capturing the horses, but the Bistones were alerted and gave pursuit. Hercules turned to battle the pursuers, leaving the horses

Hercules and the Mares of Diomedes (1608)

in the care of a boy called Abderus. Hercules slew them all, including Diomedes, but in the meantime the horses had turned on Abderus and dragged him to his death, although in art he is popularly depicted as being eaten by the horses. Hercules there founded the city of Abdera in his honour. He returned to Mycenae and presented them to Eurystheus; they were turned loose and devoured by wild beasts on the slopes of Mount Olympus (Apollodorus, *Library*, 2.5.8). Diomedes' manner of feeding the horses suggests the custom of human sacrifice and an earlier Thracian king, Lycurgus, was said to have been killed by horses as a means to restore fertility to the land (Apollodorus, *Library*, 3.5.1).

MARGYA

The **Mermaid** of Greenland, described by the Danish missionary Egede in the eighteenth century: 'the Middle upwards the Shape and Countenance or a Woman: A terrible broad Face a pointed Forehead, wrinkled Cheeks, a wide Mouth, large Eyes, black untrimmed Hair, two great Breasts, which shewed her Sex: She had two long Arms, with Hands and Fingers join'd together with a Skin, like the Feet of a Goose. Below the Middle she is like a Fish, with a Tail and Fins' (*Nat. Descr. Green.*, 86). For the male, see **Havestramb**.

MARI LLWYD

Also *Fari Lwyd*, Welsh, usually translated as 'Holy Mary', but older etymology derives it from *Marw*

Llwyd, meaning 'Grey Death'. It was a horse spirit represented at Yuletide by a horse skull born aloft on a pole by a man covered with a white sheet. The skull would be decorated with ribbons and streamers, and the jaws rigged so that the man could open and shut them, and so snap at bystanders during the procession – those it catches in its teeth have to a pay a fine to be released. The Mari Llwyd would lead a procession of youths with torches and boys dressed as rabbits, squirrels, foxes and bears round the village, knocking on every door and singing a song of woe. A contest of wit would ensue between the procession and the householders, with the procession demanding entrance; if the householders lost, then they would have to admit the whole party and supply them with beer and

Mari Llwyd (*c.*1910–1914)

cakes; riot ensued if the Mari Llwyd was not treated with due respect. It is equivalent to 'Old Hob' of Cheshire folk custom and the **Hooden Horse** of Kent, and further afield to the *Schimmel* (or *Schimmelreiter*) in various part of Germany. All are vestiges of ancient European horse worship. (Miles, *Christmas*, 200–1; Trevlyan, *Folk-Lore*, 31–3.)

MELEAGRIDES

The 'birds of Meleager', according to Pliny (*Nat. Hist.*, 10.26): 'Semblably, the birds named Meleagrides, doe fight a field in Bœotia. Now are these Meleagrides a kind of Turkey-cockes, and hens of Affricke, having a bunch on their backe, and bespotted with feathers of sundrie colours. Of all strange birds, comming out of forraine parts, these are last received and admitted to serve the table, by reason of a certaine harsh and unpleasant strong tast that they have. But it is the monument and tombe of Meleager which have given them that name and credite which they have.' The Meleagrides were the sisters of Meleager who mourned his death with such strength of feeling that they were transformed into black-plumed birds, their tears causing white spots to speckle the plumage: guinea hens. The myth is given by Apollodorus and here by Ovid (*Met.*, bk 8): 'The weeping sisters; but With Wings endu'd, | And horny beaks, and sent to flit in air; | Who yearly round the tomb in feather'd flocks | repair'. The tears of these birds were once thought to become amber: the Greek philosopher

Sophocles thought so, but Pliny rejected it. It is said that on the Greek island of Leros, linked to the myth of Meleager, that the meleagrides live around the temple of Artemis: birds of prey will not eat such birds; nor those who revere the gods. In 1850 Charles Lucien Boneparte gave the scientific name *Agelastes meleagrides* to the white-breasted guineafowl of West Africa. See also **Memnonides**. (Jackson, 'Callimachean', 236–40.)

MEMNONIDES

The 'birds of Memnon', from the Greek, Μεμνονίδες; Latin *Memnoniae aves*. 'Writers there be who affirme,' wrote Pliny (*Nat. Hist.*, 10.21), 'that every yeare certaine birds come flying out of Æthyopia to Ilium, and there, about the tombe or sepulchre of Memnon, skirmish and fight a battell. For which cause men call them Memnonides. And Cremutius avoucheth upon his owne knowledge, That every fift yeare the same birds do the like in Æthyopia, even before the roiall palace sometime of the said king Memnon.' Memnon was an Ethiopian king killed by the Greek hero Achilles during the siege of Troy. When his body was burnt on a funeral pyre it is said that the smoke and embers rose up and took on the form of birds; they divided into two flocks and fought each other before falling back down upon the ashes, and repeat the ritual every year. According to another story, it is Memnon's mourners who are turned into birds. Isidore of Seville (*Etym.*, 12.7.30) repeated the tale in the seventh century CE, having the

A 'Mermaid' on Show (1923)

birds more graphically 'tearing each other to pieces with their talons and beaks'. Similar to **Meleagrides**. (Graves, 'Greek Myths', 212–30.)

MERMAID

In 1868, the zoologist Francis (Frank) Buckland wrote that 'mermaids seem to have gone out of fashion about the same time as the dried heads of New Zealanders'. Despite that he was able to examine three specimens then being or having been exhibited in, or brought to, Britain: 1) the mermaid exhibited at the Egyptian Hall, London, before being bought by two Italian brothers who then sued the seller; 2) the 'Regent Street Mermaid' then on show at the Oriental Warehouse of Farmer and Rogers, 179 Regent Street, London; and 3) Captain Cuming's Yokohama mermaid. After examining the Regent Street Mermaid he concluded that 'the lower half of her body is made of the skin and scales of a fish of the carp family, neatly fastened on to a wooden body', the fingernails were made of ivory or bone, the teeth probably those of a young catfish set in double rows, and her ears pig-like. He noted that her hairstyle was 'submarine, and undoubtedly not Parisian'. Captain Cuming's mermaid, brought back from his recent travels, was made from half a monkey and 'a species of chub'. All three were, of course, of the **Jenny Haniver** species devised to dupe the paying public. Buckland forwarded the argument that stories of the mermaid originated with sailors' observations of the dugong and manatee, although this does not account for sightings and stories originating in areas where these species are unknown, as in the waters around Scotland, for example (see **Maighdeann Mhara**). For the Ancient Greek mermaid, see **Nereid** (female) and **Triton** (male); for the Greenland variety see **Havestramb** (male) and **Margya** (female). (Buckland, *Cur. Nat. Hist.*, 134–7, 144.)

FEEJEE MERMAID

A supposed mermaid from Fiji, which was once exhibited by the indubitable P.T. Barnum, as he tells the story: 'In the summer of 1843, Mr. Moses Kimball, of the Boston Museum, came to New York and showed me what purported to be a mermaid. He had bought it from a sailor, whose father, a sea captain, had purchased it in Calcutta, in 1822, from some Japanese sailors. I may mention here that this identical preserved specimen was exhibited in London in 1822, as I fully verified in my visit to that city' (*Am.*

Feejee Mermaid (1880)

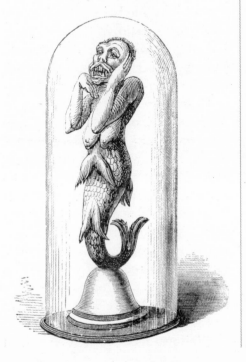

Mus., 60). Barnum used the mermaid to advertise his 'American Museum' and reported its success: 'The effect was immediately felt; money flowed in rapidly [...]' (ibid.).

MICE OF THE NILE

In the first century CE it was believed that the river Nile could engender living creatures – the so-called 'mice of the Nile' or 'water-mice' – by force of its own fertility. According to Pliny (*Nat. Hist.*, 9.58): 'the inundation of Nilus cleareth all these matters: the over-flowing whereof is so admirable, and so farre passeth all other wonders, that we may well beleeve these things. For when as this river falleth and returneth againe into his channell, a man may find upon the mud yong Mice halfe made, proceeding from the generative vertue of water and earth together: having one part of their bodie living alreadie, but the rest as yet mishapen, and no better than the verie earth.'

MINDI

The Mindi or 'Mallee Serpent' was a monster believed by the Australian Aborigines to haunt the Mallee scrub in Northern Australia. At 9 to 12 m (30 to 40 ft) long it was a somewhat smaller variety of **Bunyip** (or alternative name for the same). No one had ever seen one for the simple fact that to see it was to die. (Gould, *Myth. Mon.*, 180.)

MINOTAUR

In Greek mythology, the minotaur was born of the unnatural coupling of Pasiphaë and the **Cretan Bull**. To

The Minotaur in Dante's *Inferno* (1890)

cement his claim to the Cretan throne, Minos, the son of Zeus and Europa, said that he had received the kingdom from the gods and to prove it said that they would send him anything he prayed for. He prayed to Poseidon to send a bull out of the ocean with the promise that he would sacrifice it to him. A bull appeared, the famous Cretan Bull, but Minos found it such a fine specimen that he decided to keep it and sacrificed another bull in its place. Poseidon saw through the subterfuge and as a punishment he made the bull mad and Minos' wife Pasiphaë fall in love with it. To satisfy her desires, Pasiphaë enlisted the help of Daedalus, who built a wooden cow on wheels, covered with cow hide. Pasiphaë hid inside and the Cretan Bull mistaking it for a real cow mounted it. Nine months later, Pasiphaë gave birth to Asterius, named the Minotaur ('bull of Minos'). He had the face of a bull, but was otherwise human. Following the advice of the oracles, Minos hid the Minotaur within the Labyrinth 'that with its tangled windings perplexed the outward way', also made by Daedalus. Every year the Athenians sent seven youths and seven maidens into the Labyrinth as food for the monster. He was slain by Theseus, who had earlier also slain his father the Cretan Bull in its guise as the Marathonian Bull. (Apollodorus, *Library*, 3.1.4, 3.15; *Epit*. E.1.)

MISSOURIUM

In the first half of the nineteenth century, an enormous skeleton was exhibited in the Egyptian Hall in London's Piccadilly by Albert C. Koch. It was presented as the fossilised remains of some wondrous four-footed titan, but closer inspection revealed that it was a **Jenny Haniver** made up of the fossilised bones of elephants and mastodons. The British Museum purchased the assemblage and from it reconstructed the correct skeleton of a mastodon. Koch made a chequered career for himself with his fake fossils and after the Missourium imposture decamped for the USA where he 'discovered' another extinct species previously unknown to science, the **Hydrarchos Sillimannii**. (Mantell, *Illus. Lon.*)

MOLDWARPE

Pliny the Elder (*Nat. Hist.*, 8.29) tells us that there was a town in Thessally, Greece, 'undermined' by the fearsome Moldwarpes, at least according to his English translator Philemon Holland. This word comes from the German *Maulwurf* via Early Modern English variants such as *mouldywarp*, and is, of course, the city-destroying mole, a mighty subspecies of the humble gentleman in velvet, that is, thankfully, rarely met with. Moles were much used in magic, as a remedy for toothache and animal bites, for example (*Nat. Hist.*, 30.7).

MONGOLIAN DEATH WORM

Mongolian, *alter gorhai-horhai*, popularly known as the 'Mongolian Death Worm', a legendary monster of the Gobi Desert. Leading the Central Asiatic Expedition of the American Museum of Natural History in the

1920s, Roy Chapman Andrews was asked by the Mongolian Premier, the living Buddha Jalkhanz Khutagt Sodnomyn Damdinbazar, if he could catch this mysterious animal for him: 'None of those present ever had seen the creature, but they all firmly believed in its existence and described it minutely. It is shaped like a sausage about two feet long, has no head nor legs and is so poisonous that merely to touch it means instant death. It lives in the most desolate parts of the Gobi Desert, whither we were going. To the Mongols it seems to be what the dragon is to the Chinese.' (Andrews, *Trial*, 103.)

Mongolian Death Worm (*c*.2007)

MONOCEROS

Also *monocerote*, derived from the Greek *monoceros*, meaning 'single horn'; in Latin **Unicorn**. Conrad Gessner in his *Historia Animalium*, published in Zurich, 1551–87, used the spelling *Monocerote*. Into the seventeenth century, Edward Topsell discussed the monoceros in connection with other single-horned animals, the rhinoceros and the **Oryx**, leaning towards considering the ellusive monoceros an instance of the estab-

lished rhinoceros (*History*, 1658, 25, 462). In the first edition of his *Systema Naturae* published in 1735, Carolus Linnaeus listed it as an **Animalia Paradoxa**: 'body of a horse; feet of a wild animal; horn on forehead, long, spirally twisted. It is a fiction of painters: the Monodon [narwhal] of Artedi has the same manner of horn, but the other parts of its body are very different' (65).

MOONCALF

A thing without life or form, believed by the ancients – Pliny among them – to be created by the female only; a foetus made imperfect by the power of the moon; a phantom pregnancy; applied metaphorically to fools and deformed persons. Surprisingly, someone once wrote a poem on the subject (Drayton, *Miscellaneous Pieces*, 1627). (Dyer, *Folk-Lore*, 74; Farmer and Henley, *Slang*, IV, 348; Brand, *Pop. Antiq.*, 421.)

MORE

The horse-man of Irish legend: 'the More was an **Each-Uisge** or an each-coilleadh or a combination of both [...] More appears as (a) having horse's ears, (b) a king, (c) captain of a great fleet: he is horse-man, a monster sharing the qualities of both' (Henderson, *Survivals*, 119). See also **Centaur**.

MYRMEX INDIKOS

Myrmex Indikos, or Indian Ant: the ancient writers spoke of ants (Gr. Μύρμηξ, *myrmex*) that were not only of huge size but wondrously mined for gold and brought it to the surface. Writing in the fifth century BCE, Herodotus gave the first surviving account of them: 'in this desert and sandy tract are produced ants, which are in size smaller than dogs but larger than foxes, for there are some of them kept at the residence of the king of Persia, which are caught here. These ants then make their dwelling under ground and carry up the sand just in the same manner as the ants found in the land of the Hellenes, which they themselves also very much resemble in form; and the sand which is brought up contains gold. To obtain this sand the Indians make expeditions into the desert, each one having yoked together three camels [...] making calculations so that they may be engaged in carrying it off at the time when the greatest heat prevails; for the heat causes the ants to disappear under-ground. [...] When the Indians have come to the place with bags, they fill them with the sand and ride away back as quickly as they can, for forthwith the ants, perceiving, as the Persians allege, by the smell, begin to pursue them: and this animal, they say, is superior to every other creature in swiftness, so that unless the Indians got a start in their course, while the ants were gathering together, not one of them would escape' (*Hist.*, 3.102).

It sounded like a tall-tale, but was later apparently confirmed, at least in parts, by two travellers to the region: Nearchus (*c.*360–300 BCE), one of Alexander the Great's military commanders, a *navarch* (admiral); and Megasthenes (*c.*350–90 BCE), a Greek writer. After Alexander's Indian campaign of 326 to 324 BCE, Nearchus undertook a voyage from the Indus river to the Persian Gulf and made a detailed account of his travels. Possibly around 298 BCE, Megasthenes was sent as ambassador to the ancient city of Pataliputra in India by one of Alexander's generals, Seleucus, who by then had established himself as ruler over the territory in the Near East that Alexander had conquered before his death in 323 BCE. Nearchus' account is known through mention by other writers, especially Arrian; Megasthenes text survives in fragments, but it, too, was extensively referred to by later writers.

Luckily, amongst these fragments we still have Megasthenes' description of the giant gold-digging ants. It differs from that of Herodotus and may thus represent a different source: 'Among the Derdai, a great tribe of Indians, who inhabit the mountains on the eastern borders, there is an elevated plateau of about 3,000 stadia in circuit. Beneath the surface there are mines of gold, and here accordingly are found the ants which dig for that metal. They are not inferior in size to wild foxes. They run with amazing speed, and live by the produce of the chase. The time when they dig is winter. They throw up heaps of earth, as moles do at the mouth of the mines. The gold-dust has to be subjected to a little boiling. The people of the neighbourhood, coming secretly with beasts of burden, carry this off. If they came openly the ants would attack them, end pursue them if they fled, and would destroy both them and their cattle. So, to effect the robbery without being observed, they lay down in several different places pieces of the flesh of wild beasts, and when the ants are by this device dispersed they carry off the gold-dust' (McCrindle, *Anc. Ind.*, 94–5). In another fragment he says that they throw up so many heaps of shining gold that it is impossible to look towards the sun without destroying one's eyesight.

In his famous *Geography*, Strabo (*c.*63 BCE–24 CE) referred to both Nearchus' and Megasthenes' accounts of these ants. Arrian, the principal historian of the campaigns of Alexander the Great writing in the second century CE, based his book *Indica* largely on the travels of Nearchus and Megasthenes. Both relate that Nearchus had only seen the reputed skins of these ants; Strabo (XV.I.44) adds that he decribed them as being 'as large as the skins of leopards'. Their report of Megasthenes conforms to that given in the surviving fragments, but Arrian adds that it is only hearsay (Arrian Bk VIII (*Indica*), XV).

When Pliny came to write of them in the first century CE, the ants had moved up a step in size, closer to Nearchus' leopard skins than Herodotus' small dogs: 'In the countrey of the Northerne Indians named Dardæ, the Ants doe cast up gold above ground from out of the holes and mines within the earth: these are in colour like to cats, and as big as the wolves of Ægypt. This gold beforesaid which thy worke up in the winter time, the Indians do steale from them in the extreame heat of Summer,

waiting their opportunitie, when the Pismires lie close within their caves under the ground, from the parching Sun: yet not without great daunger. For if they happen to wind them and catch their sent, out they goe, and follow after them in great hast: and with such furie they flie upon them, that oftentimes they teare them in peeces; let them make way as fast as they can upon their most swift Camels, yet they are not able to save them. So fleet of pace, so fierce of courage are they, to recover gold that they love so well' (*Nat. Hist.*, 11.36). Pliny also recorded that some relics of another giant ant were on display in the Ionian city of Erythrae in Asia Minor (nowadays Turkey): 'In the temple of Hercules at Erythræ, there were to bee seene the hornes of a certain Indian Ant, which were there set up for a wonder to posteritie.'

In the seventh century CE, Isidore of Seville (*Etym.*, 11.36) relocated the ants, inexplicably, to Ethiopia, but retained their giant form and gold-digging proclivities. With so many writers of authority propounding on the subject, the idea of giant ants became firmly fixed in the Medieval mind. In the manuscript known as Marvels of the East, dating from the tenth to twelfth centuries, they are described as being as big as dogs, red and black in colour, with the feet of locusts and 'they are so swift that you might think they were flying' (Druce, 'An Account', 347–64). In Guillaume le Clerc's *Bestiaire* of the thirteenth century we find the influence of Isidore in placing the giant ants in

Ethiopia, but he added a new and ingenious method of stealing their gold: 'There is another kind of ant up in Ethiopia, which is of the shape and size of dogs. They have strange habits, for they scratch into the ground and extract therefrom great quantities of fine gold. If any one wishes to take this gold from them, he soon repents of his undertaking; for the ants run upon him, and if they catch him they devour him instantly. The people who live near them know that they are fierce and savage, and that they possess a great quantity of gold, and so they have invented a cunning trick. They take mares which have unweaned foals, and give them no food for three days. On the fourth the mares are saddled, and to the saddles are fastened boxes that shine like gold. Between these people and the ants flows a very swift river. The famished mares are driven across this river, while the foals are kept on the hither side. On the other side of the river the grass is rich and thick.

Here the mares graze, and the ants seeing the shining boxes think they have found a good place to hide their gold, and so all day long they fill and load the boxes with their precious gold, till night comes on and the mares have eaten their fill. When they hear the neighing of their foals they hasten to return to the other side of the river. There their masters take the gold from the boxes and become rich and powerful, but the ants grieve over their loss' (Kuhns, 'Bestiaries'). In the fourteenth century, Sir John Mandeville relocated the ants once again, this time to a place he called Taprobane (Sri Lanka), but kept Guillaume's innovation. When McCrindle published his translations of Megasthenes and Arrian in 1877, he added a footnote to the story of the ants, explaining that they were Tibetan miners.

MYRMECOLEON,

SEE FORMICOLEON

N

NĀGA

Sanskrit meaning 'cobra'; in Indian mythology a race of demi-gods who lived in the depths of the waters, or an underworld called Patala Land, and had the power to raise storms and guarded hidden treasure. They were believed to be able to take human shape and are often represented as having the upper parts of a person and the lower part of a snake. A form of worship grew up around them. (Ingersoll, *Dragons*, 42ff.)

NÄKKI

The Finnish form of the Germanic water spirit **Nicker**; also used in Estonia and among the Livonians of Lithuania. He is a man with the legs of a horse; a dog with a long beard; or a huge billy-goat with netting strung between his horns; or a tree trunk or log with a single eye as big as a plate and a mane growing down its back. It might be a tree floating in the water that carries anyone climbing on to it under the surface; his teeth have also been described as being made of iron.

For the Estonians he is a white or grey foal that tries to lure children to ride on its back and so takes them into the sea. Entering the water in Finland, one says, 'The Näkki is as heavy as iron; I am as light as a leaf', and on leaving it the charm is reversed: 'The Näkki is as light as a leaf; I am as heavy as iron'. Swimmers put a knife in their mouths or leave it on the shore with the edge turned to the water. When horses are taken to the water, metal is thrown in, or a fire-steel is tied to the tail, or a bell is hung about the neck. Crosses were also scratched on the hooves of horses and cattle. Calling the name of those who had been drowned or of the Näkki itself were also said to be efficacious. Holmberg believes that the Näkki is a borrowing from Germanic folklore and not indigenous, so to speak; nonetheless, it has found a ready home here. (Eiichirô, 'Kappa', 29; Holmberg, *Wassergottheiten*, 161, 191, 194, 197–8.)

NAUTILOS

A sort of fish with sails, from the Greek meaning 'sailor' (Latin, *Nautilus*). Pliny (*Nat. Hist.*, 9.29): 'But among the greatest wonders of Nature, is that fish, which of some is called Nautilos, of others Pompilos. This fish, for to come aloft above the water, turneth upon his backe, and raiseth or heaveth

Nautilos (1868)

himselfe up by little and little: and to the end he might swim with more ease, as disburdened of a sinke, he dischargeth all the water within him at a pipe. After this, turning up his two foremost clawes or armes, hee displaieth and stretcheth out betweene them, a membrane or skin of a wonderfull thinnesse: this serveth him in stead of a saile in the aire above water: with the rest of his armes or clawes, he roweth and laboureth under water; and with his taile in the mids, hee directeth his course, and steereth as it were with an helme. Thus holdeth he on and maketh way in the sea, with a faire shew of a foist or galley under saile. Now if he be afraid of any thing in the way, hee makes no more adoe but draweth in water to ballaise his bodie, and so plungeth himselfe downe and sinketh to the bottome.' Such a fish does not exist but was a mistaken interpretation of the behaviour of the genus *Argonauta*, a group of several species of pelagic octopuses, the female of which produces a distinctive eggcase from tentacle secretions.

NDZOODZOO

The **Unicorn** of sub-Saharan Africa. Joseph John Freeman (1794–1851), a missionary noted for his researches on Madagascar in the early nineteenth century, received information from a native somewhere north of Mozambique (the reason for this vagueness is not made clear): 'The *Ndzoo-dzoo* is by no means rare in Makooa. It is about the size of a horse, extremely fleet and strong. It has one single horn projecting from its forehead, from twenty-four to thirty inches in length. This is flexible when the animal is asleep; it can be curled like the trunk of the Elephant, but becomes perfectly firm and hard when the animal is excited, and especially when pursuing an enemy. Its disposition is extremely fierce, and it universally attacks man if it sees him. The usual method of escape adopted by the natives is, to climb up a dense and high tree, so as to avoid, if possible, being seen. If the animal misses his sight of the fugitive, he immediately gallops off to his haunt; from whence it may be inferred that he is not endowed with the power of a keen scent. Should he, however, espy his object in the tree, woe to the unfortunate native, – he begins to butt with his horns, – strikes and penetrates the tree, and continues piercing it till it falls, when his victim seldom escapes being gored to death. Unless the tree is of a large girth, he never fails in breaking it down. Having killed his victim, he leaves him without devouring the carcase. The male only is provided with the horn. The female has not anything of the kind' (Freeman, *Sth. Afr. Ch. Rec.*, 33). The Scottish zoologist, Sir Andrew Smith, KCB (1797–1872), who quoted this account, saw in it a fanciful description of the rhinoceros (*Illus. Zoo.*, 20).

NECK, SEE NICKER

NEMEAN LION

A monstrous lion of Ancient Greek mythology with a skin that was invulnerable to weapons. It was the offspring of **Echidna** by her own son, the double-headed dog **Orthus**. Hesiod was the first to describe the beast: 'the Nemean lion, which Hera, the good wife of Zeus, brought up and made to haunt the hills of Nemea, a plague to men. There he preyed upon the tribes of her own people and had power over Tretus of Nemea and Apesas: yet the strength of stout Heracles overcame him' (Hesiod, *Hes., Hom. Hym.*, 103). Hercules' combat with the beast was the first of his celebrated Twelve Labours: he overcame it by choking it death. In his *Geography* (8.6) first published in 7 BCE, Strabo described the Nemean Games still being held in Nemea in honour of this legendary event. (Apollodorus, *Library*, 2.5.)

NEREID

The Greek and Roman **Mermaid**, usually used in the plural to refer to the fifty (or later, one hundred) daughters of the sea-god Nereus and Doris, the daughter of Oceanus. Some were known by name, especially Amphitrité, wife of Poseidon, 'silver-footed' Thetis, Galatea, and Doto. First mentioned in Homer's *Iliad* (18.141) and *Odyssey* (24.58). In the first century CE, Pliny took the nereids seriously enough to include them in his *Natural History* (9.4): 'And for the Meremaids called Nereides, it is no fabulous tale that goeth of them: for looke how painters draw them, so they are indeed: only their bodie is rough and skaled all over, even in those parts wherin they resemble a woman. For such a Meremaid was seene, and beheld plainely upon the same coast neere to the shore: and the inhabitants dwelling neer, heard it a farre off, when it was a dying, to make piteous mone, crying and chattering very heavily. Moreover, a lieutenant or governour under Augustus Cæsar in Gaule, advertised him by his letters, That many of these Nereides or Meremaids were seene cast upon the sands, and lying dead.'

NESSIE, SEE LOCH NESS MONSTER

NICKER

'The nickers lie there on the sloping rocks of the ness, monsters that at mid-day go out into the open sea' (Brooke). A malevolent water spirit of Northern Europe, source of the term 'Old Nick' for the Devil. Believed to descend from the hypothetical Old Teutonic word *nikwiz* or *nikuz*, possibly from the root word *nig* 'to wash', it is found in all the Germanic languages: Old Norse *Nikr*, Old English *Nicor*, Old High German *Nichus*, Middle Low German *Nicker*, *Necker*, Norwegian *Nök*, also *Nykk*, Icelandic *Nykur* (or **Hnikur**), Swedish *Neck*, Danish *Nök* or *Nökke*, Dutch *Nikker*, modern German *Nixe*, also *Nix*, *Nixie* (but not *Nixi*). Odin was sometimes called *Nikarr* or *Hnikarr* and *Nikuz*. Odin was also on occasion identified with the Roman god Neptune (Greek Poseidon); a thirteenth-century Low German glossary translates Neptune as Necker. The earliest written reference is in the Old English epic poem *Beowulf*, composed between the eighth and eleventh centuries. The hero fights a gang of nicors, usually translated as 'sea-beasts', off the coast of Finland: 'they set upon me all together, near the bottom of the sea [...] Yet I had the fortune to slay with my sword nine nicors: never have I heard of a harder battle by night under concave of heaven, nor of a man more wretched on the ocean streams.' However, the form these nicors took is not described. Later, setting out after the monster Grendel, Beowulf leads his men 'over the steep stone-cliffs, the narrow road, the confined solitary paths, the unknown road, the precipitous promontories, a multitude of Nicor-houses'. They find the armour of one of the men taken by Grendel lying on a cliff above the sea, below 'the flood boiled with blood, with hot poison, the people looked on: from time to time the horn sang a dirge, a terrible song; all the troop sat down; they saw there amid the water many a kind of snake, strange sea dragons swim, and also on the promontories nicors lie'. From here Beowulf launches into his battle with Grendel's Mother. The nicors play a minor role, but the marsh-dwelling Grendel and especially Grendel's Mother (*brimwylf*, 'she-wolf of the breakers', she is called) should also be seen as evil water spirits; it is on 'the track of Grendel's kinsman', i.e., his mother, that Beowulf sees nicors. Of the Norwegian Nök it is said that it frequently took the form of half a horse lying on the bank, although it might also appear as half a boat in the water or as gold and other precious things. As *nennir* or *nikr* in Old Norse, it is a dapple-grey horse with hooves pointing the wrong way. He can, however, be caught and put to work: 'A clever man at Morland in Bahus

fastened an artfully contrived bridle on him, so that he could not get away, and ploughed all his land with him; but the bridle somehow coming loose, the "neck" darted like fire into the lake, and drew the harrow in after him' (Grimm).

Although most often portrayed as a horse, the Nicker has also been described as an old man with a long beard, green hat and green teeth (Denmark), or as a wild boy with shaggy hair or yellow curls under a red cap, sometimes with fish's teeth; the Finnish **Näkki** has iron teeth. According to Kemble: 'The beautiful Nix or Nixie who allures the young fisher or hunter to seek her embrace in the wave which brings his death; the Neck who seizes upon and drowns the maidens who sport upon his banks; the river-spirit who still yearly, in some part of Germany, demands tribute of human life, are all forms of the ancient Nicor.' A Norwegian charm against the Nyk shows the power of metal over the spirits: 'Nyk, Nyk, needle in water! The Virgin Mary casts steel in water! You sink and I flee'. The Nicker is always connected with death by drowning: it was a superstition that the redness of face of the drowned was a sign of their blood having been sucked by the Nicker, usually through the victim's nostrils (Hazlitt). Possibly connected with some form of washing ritual (lustration-rite), particularly involving water as a means of purifying children; or ancient rites of human sacrifice intended to appease the spirits of the waters. The Roman Neptunalia was celebrated on 5 December; even into the Christian period, German millers were said to throw offerings into the water on 6 December, St Nicholas' Day; and Anichkof connects St Nicholas with Nicor and Neck, recording also the German usage of the name Nickel and Nickelmann for the same; and as Nick is short for Nicholas we are back with the Devil again. Other authors connect the spirit with the Cornish Nickynan-Night (also Nickanan Night) celebrated on the Monday before Lent, a local mischief night like Hallowe'en (Hazlitt). The poisonous water-hemlock is known in Sweden as the neck-wort. The creature gives its name to the river Neckar in Germany, a 367-km (228-mile) long tributary of the Rhine that flows through Stuttgart and Heidelberg. Brooke argued that the nickers in *Beowulf* were 'the great seals and walruses', but also a metaphor for 'the monstrous fury of the waves, of the lower powers of the wintry sea'; in other contexts, whales and hippopotamuses have also been inferred. In connection with the horse-form of this monster we should mention the onomatopoeic 'nicker' for that sound made by horses. See also **Kelpie**. (Antichkof, 'St. Nic.', 108–20; Anon., *Beowulf*, xvii, 24, 58; Brooke, *History*, 42–3, 62,76; Grimm, *Teut. Myth.*, II, 488–9; Hazlitt, *Brand's Pop. Antiq.*, II, 459; Kemble quoted in Mackinlay, *Folklore*, 163; M 'Kenzie, 'Child. Wells', 253–82; Thorpe, *North. Myth.*, II, 20ff, 81–2.)

NÍDHÖGGR

Also *Nidhogg, Nidhogger, Nithhogger*, etc., in Norse mythology a **Serpent** or **Dragon** that lives within a well called Hvergelmir in Niflheim ('Home of Mists'), the underworld. Here it gnaws the roots of the World Tree, Yggdrasil, and tears apart the bodies of the dead. See also **Jörmungandr** ('Gylfaginning', §16, §52, in Sturrleson, *Prose Edda*, 30–1, 82.)

NIGHT-HAWK

Hewbrew, *tahmas*, meaning 'to scratch or tear the face'; one of the unclean birds listed in the Bible (Lev. 11:16; Deut. 14:15). Interpreted either as the night-jar (**Caprimulgus**) or owl (**Strix**). (Easton, *Ill. Bib. Dict.*)

NIGHT-LIZARD

The zoologist Dr John F. Gray, FRS and President of the Entomological Society, brought an unusual example of the 'night lizard', or *Geeko Reevesii*, to notice when he reported on the activities of certain Chinese collectors in fabricating specimens of **Jenny Haniver**: 'there was a stuffed specimen of a Night Lizard (*Geeko Reevesii*) which had a square tuft of hair from some mammal stuck on the back of its neck'. It was part of a consignment that also included an unusual snake 'which had the claw of a mammal surrounded with fur inserted on each side of its neck just behind the head, so as to make it appear as if it had rudimentary feet armed with large claws'; and 'several of the Coleopterous insects, especially the larger Cerambyces, were painted, so as to give them quite a different appearance from the usual and natural colour of the species'. Gray considered the forgeries to be so badly executed as to be immediately obvious to anyone but the most naïve collector. There is a real zoological family of night lizards (family *Xantusiidae*) and a gecko called *Geeko Reevesii* (named by Gray, incidentally), all of which are, of course, entirely unrelated. (Gray, 'On a New Genus', 90–2.)

NIGHT-RAVEN

In a seventeenth-century work of ornithology we read: 'In the night time it cries with an uncouth voice, like one that were straining to vomit [...] that bird our common people call the Nightraven, and have such dread of, imagining its cry portends no less than their death, or the death of some of their near relations.' (Willughby, *Ornith.*, 279, 283). Old English, *nihthræfn*, *næhthræfn*; German *Nachtrab*, *Nacht Rabe*; Norwegian *Nattskärran*. The Greeks called this bird *Nycticorax* ('night-raven') for its nocturnal habits and harsh crow-like call; properly, it is the black-crowned night heron (*Nycticorax nycticorax*, also called *Nycticorax griseus*), the only species of night heron to be found in Europe. However, the night-raven (or night-crow) seems to have become a supernatual class of bird quite distinct from its zoological counterparts. According to Danish tradition, every exorcised spirit becomes a night-raven. Thorpe describes the process: 'At the spot where a spirit has been exorcised, a sharp stake is driven in to the earth, which passes through the left wing of the raven, causing a hole in it. It is only through the most frightful swamps and morasses that the night-raven ascends. It first begins under the earth with the cry of "Rok! Rok!" Then "Rok op! Rok op!" And when it has thus come forth, it flies away screaming "Hei! Hei! He—i!" When it has flown up it resembles a cross, and at first hops on the ground like a magpie, and cries "Bav! Bav! Bav!" It afterwards flies towards the east, to approach the holy sepulchre, because if it can come hither, it will get rest. When it flies over head, care must be taken not to look up; for if any one sees through the hole in its left wing, he himself becomes a night-raven and the night-raven is released. In general the night-raven is harmless, and strives only to go farther towards the east' (Thorpe, *North. Myth.*, II, 210–11). In Danish legend the first *nat-ravn* was a maiden who betrayed the lovers Hagbard and Signe to Signe's father, King Sigar, which leads to their deaths. In punishment the maiden was buried alive and her soul continues to fly above the grave in the form of a *nat-ravn*; her grave is called the *nat-ravn* hole or 'night-jar hole' (Schütte, 'Dan. Pag.', 364). The great poets of the English language – Shakespeare, Milton, Spenser – all speak of the night-raven (Harrison, 'Two of Spenser's', 232–5). In *Much Ado about Nothing* (II, 3), Shakespeare reveals his knowledge of the bird's reputation: '[...] and I pray God his bad voice bode no mischief. I had as lief have heard the night-raven, come what plague could have come after it.' In the sixteenth century, William Turner associated it with Aristotle's **Caprimulgus** ('goat-sucker'). Willughby identified the bittern as the 'night-raven'. Other writers have suggested the owl, nightjar and cormorant. Goldsmith (*Hist.*, II, 368) also thought that it was the bittern, but recorded some interesting folklore: 'I remember, in the place where I was a boy, with what terror this bird's note affected the whole village [...] if any person in the neighbourhood died, they supposed it could not be otherwise, for the night-raven had foretold it.' In Norse mythology the raven was sacred to Odin. In Greek mythology it was sacred to Apollo. For other birds portending death or misfortune, see **Lich-Fowl**, **Whistler**.

NINTU

Also *Nintud*, Summerian, 'Lady of Birth' or 'Queen Who Gives Birth'; she is also Ninmah, 'great queen', and Ninhursag, 'queen of the mountain', and is probably identical with the earlier earth goddess Ki. An important Mesopotamian goddess, half woman from her head to her loins, half **Serpent**, or scaled like a serpent, from her loins to her feet, with a horn projecting from her head, she is usually depicted with a baby suckling at her breast. She is described as the 'mother of the land', that is, the goddess of the earth, who plays a key role in the Mesopotamian agricultural myth of creation. She copulated with the god Enki to produce freshwater streams and waterways that fertilise the fields; their union is also said to have produced the other gods. Her son Ninurta defeats the primordial **Dragon** of chaos, **Kur**. (Jastrow, *Sum. Myth.*, 112, 120; Kramer, *Sum. Myth.*, 41, 56, 82; Mackenzie, *Myth. Bab.*, 76.)

NIXIE

Also *Nix*, *Nixy*, but not *Nixi*; modern German *Nixe*; see **Nicker**. Usually female, this water spirit was said to sit on the rocks in the sun, combing her hair, or was seen bobbing in the water showing a beautiful figure above the waves whilst hiding her fishtail below it. Male nixes are also known; like the female they might bob in the water, human above and horse below, or display some other unusual characteristic. Under the heading *nixe*, Grimm recorded the following tale: 'On the grass by the shore a girl is seized by a pretty boy wearing a handsome peasant's belt, and is forced to scratch his head for him. While she is doing so, he slips a girdle round her unperceived, and chains her to himself; the continued friction, however, sends him to sleep. In the meantime a woman comes up, and asks the girl what she is about. She tells her, and, while talking, releases herself from the girdle. The boy was more sound asleep than ever, and his lips stood pretty wide apart; then the woman coming up closer, cried out: "why, that's a neck, look at his fish's teeth!" In a moment the neck was gone' (*Teut. Myth.*, II, 491, 497). The German nixe is also found in wells; children who fall in are given tangled flax to spin. In Northern Germany, Bavaria and Brandenburg (where they are small grey men) they are said to kidnap healthy babies and replace them with changelings, just like the *Wassermann* or *Wasserwieb* of Hungary; in Oldenburg, the *Schinonte* in the German Black Forest is one reputed haunt. (Blind, 'Scottish', 189;

M'Kenzie, 'Child. and Wells', 274–5.)

Njogel

The Shetland **Water-Horse**, also *njuggel, njogli, neugle, nigle, nygel,* or *water-njogel,* all local variations on **Nicker**. 'This being is described as similar in size and shape to a horse or pony of the Shetland type, well proportioned, and of great strength and fleetness. Generally he was fat and sleek, and of handsome appearance; but occasionally he appeared as a very thin, worn-out, old horse. His color was gray, usually rather dark gray, but sometimes lighter or darker, and approximating to white or black. He differed from ordinary horses in that his hair grew and lay in the opposite direction to the hair of other horses; his fetlocks grew upwards instead of downwards; his mane was stiff and erect; his hoofs were also reversed and pointed backwards; and his tail was shaped like the rim of a wheel. Why the tail was so peculiar in form seems to be unknown; but the people say that it must have been of special utility to him in some way, perhaps used for propulsion in the water or to accelerate his speed on land, or perhaps to stop water-mills in some way. Some claim that his naturally very long tail was dragged behind, and occasionally rolled up like a hoop or the rim of a wheel, between his legs, or on his back. He could roll it up at will', and generally did so to hide his true nature (Teit, 'Water-Beings', 183). For these reasons, the Njogel preferred to come out at night to loiter about the river banks and loch sides, and lonely byways, waiting for his victim. The Njogel would disappear into the water in a blue light. As well as tricking passers-by into riding him, the Njogel would also annoy millers. His noted trick was to stop the water-mill even as the water continued to run over the wheel in full flow. The remedy was to throw a lighted torch down what was called the 'lighting-hole' in something called the 'looder': the Njogel would let go of the wheel and the machinery would turn as before. It was not unknown for him to combine the two: when the wheel stopped the miller would come to investigate and finding a beautiful pony, all saddled and bridled, would jump up and so be carried off to a watery grave. He was afraid of iron. Teit said that he knew three or four people who claimed to have seen the Njogel, one of them had even ridden upon it and lived to tell the tale. Sometimes differentiated as a fresh-water variant of the sea-dwelling **Tangie**, or the other way round: the distinction does not always hold true. It is notable that Tangie is black, like an **Each-Uisge**, whilst the Njogel is generally grey. (Black, *Country*, III, 189–1903; Teit, ibid., 183–6.)

Noctifer

From the Latin, meaing 'night bringer'; the Spirit of the Dark Ages, according to Charles Waterton (1782–1865), the man who invented it. It was a taxidermical concoction 'made of the gorget and legs of a bittern, and the head and wings of an eagle owl, so skilfully blended that no one but an ornithologist could have detected the playful imposition'. It is now in the Wakefield Museum. See also **Waterton's Nondescript**. (Waterton, *Nat. Hist. Ess.*, 126.)

NÖK, SEE NICKER

NUCKELAVEE

The 'Devil of the Sea' of the Orkneys: half man, half horse, all monster. Although the word is derived from **Nicker**, this **Water-Horse** has a unique description. It had the head of a man, although ten times larger than normal, and one huge red eye; its mouth projected like a pig's snout and opened as wide as a whale's, the lower part was like that of a horse, often described as having fins, and it entirely lacked skin: 'The whole surface of the monster appeared like raw and living flesh, from which the skin had been stripped. You could see the black blood flowing through his veins, and every movement of his muscles, when the horrid creature moved, showed white sinews in motion' (Dennison, 'Nuckelavee', 132). As befits such a fearsome form, the Nuckelavee had an evil reputation. (Douglas, *Scot. Fairy*, 19, 197–201.)

O

OANNES

A **Sea Monster** of ancient Babylon described as having the body and head of a fish with a human head underneath the fish head and human feet underneath the tail, and with the power of human speech. According to Berosos, a priest in the Temple of Bel in Babylon during the reign of Alexander the Great, this monster instructed the people in writing, science and art, teaching them how to build cities and temples, how to make laws and how to gather (or produce) their food (Barton, 'Tiamat', 16). For a destructive Babylonian sea monster, see **Tiamat**.

OCTOPUS, GIANT

In the first English translation of Pliny's *Natural History* (9.30) we read of 'Many-feet fishes called Polypi', otherwise known as octopuses, and of one in particular, a beast – the Polype of Carteiath – that troubled the fishermen and merchants of Carteia, a Roman town at the head of the Bay of Gibraltar, by stealing their salted fish.

As well as being a crafty and determined thief, 'this Polype fish was of an unmeasurable and incredible bignesse: and besides, hee was besmeared and beraied all over with the brine and pickle of the foresaid salt-fish, which made him both hideous to see to, and also to stinke withall most strongly. Who would ever have looked for a Polype there, or taken knowledge of him by such markes as these? Surely they thought no other, but that they had to deale and encounter with some monster: for with his terrible blowing and breathing that he kept, he drave away the dogges, and otherwhiles with the ends of his long stringed winding feet, he would lash and whip them; somtimes with his stronger clawes like arms he rapped and knocked them well and surely, as it were with clubs. In summe, he made such good shift for himselfe, that hardly and with much adoe they could kill him, albeit he received many a wound by trout-speares which they launced at him. Well, in the end his head was brought and shewed to Lucullus for a wonder, and as bigge it was a good round hogshead or barrell that would take and containe 15 Amphores: and his beards (for so Trebius tearmed his clawes and long-stringed feet) carried such a thicknes and bulke with them, that hardly a man could fathom one of them about with both his armes, such knockers they were, knobbed and knotted like clubs, and withall 30 foot long. The concavities within them, and hollow vessels like great basons, would hold four or five gallons apeece; and his teeth were answerable in proportion to the bignes of his bodie. The rest was saved for a wonder to be seen, and waighed 700 pound weight.' Lucullus was Lucius Licinius Lucullus, a former Roman consul and governor of Hispania: he was noted for his extravagant feasts. Pliny also reported more brief accounts from the second-century BCE writer Trebius Niger 'that Cuttels also and Calamaries have been cast upon that shore, full as bigge. Indeed, in our sea there be Calamaries taken of five cubits long, and Cutrels of twaine, in length'.

ODONTOTYRRANOS

Meaning something like 'tooth-tyrant': a monster named by Palladius of Galatia (*de vita Bragmanorum*) in the fifth century CE (Derrett, 'History of Palladiaus', 100–35), but corresponding to the earlier description given by Ctesias in the fifth century BCE (*Anc, Ind.*, 27–8): 'there is bred in the Indian river [the Ganges] a worm like in appearance to that which is found in the fig, but seven cubits more or less in length, while its thickness is such that a boy ten years old could hardly clasp it within the circuit of his arms. These worms have two teeth – an upper and a lower, with which they seize and devour their prey. In the daytime they remain in the mud at the bottom of the river, but at night they come ashore, and should they fall in with any prey as a cow or a camel, they seize it with their teeth, and having dragged it to the river, there devour it. For catching this worm a large hook is employed, to which a kid or a lamb is fastened by chains of iron. The worm being landed, the captors hang up its carcase, and placing vessels underneath it leave it thus for thirty days. All this time oil drops from it, as much being got as would fill ten Attic *kofylai*. At the end of tho thirty days they throw away the worm, and preserving the oil they take it to the king of the Indians, and to him alone, for no subject is allowed to get a drop of it. This oil [like fire] sets everything ablaze over which it is poured and it consumes not alone wood but even animals. The flames can be quenched only by throwing over them a great quantity of clay, and that of a thick consistency.'

ONCE, SEE LYNX

ONCHÚ

Irish, believed to derive from *on-*, 'water', and *cú*, 'dog', hence a water-dog. The Irish call the otter, *dobharchú*, 'water dog', but the onchú finds itself listed among venomous creatures such as toads, scorpions, dragons and serpents in the twelfth-century *Cogadh Gaedhel re Gallaibh* ('War of the Irish with the Foreigners'), for example. In other medieval manuscripts it is noted for its 'wildness' and 'fearsomeness'. In Irish legend an onchú terrorised the pasturage between Loch Con and Loch Cuilinn. It was said to have killed nine people before Muiredach, pursuing it into one of the lakes, slew it. Near Glendalough in County Wicklow, there is a Loch na nOnchon, 'Lake of the Water Monster' (in English, Lough Nahanagan). It was used as a device on the battle flag of the Irish, noted in 1595 after the English recapture of Enniskillen, and can be traced back as a seal of the O'Kennedys in 1337. O'Flaherty (Hardiman, *Chor. Descr.*, 19–20) recorded the form *anchu* in use in County Mayo in the seventeenth century. There is also an unconnected St Onchu, who nonetheless has a sacred well at Killonaghan. (Curtis, 'Some Med. Seals', 6; Williams, 'Of Beasts', 62–78.) See also **Dobhar-Chú**.

OPINICUS

Heraldry, a rare beast like a winged **Griffin** with lion's legs and a short tail. (Woodward, *Treatise*, II, 696.)

ORTHUS

Also Orthrus in later sources: a double or many-headed dog of Ancient Greek mythology first referred to by Hesiod in his *Theogony* of c.700 BCE (*Hes. Hom. Hym.*, 103). The earliest depictions date from the seventh century BCE; a red-figure kylix (drinking bowl) dated to 550–500 BCE (now in the Staatliche Antikensammlungen, Munich) shows a two-headed Orthus with a snake for a tail (revealing his parentage). He was the offspring of **Typhon** and **Echidna** and later with Echidna fathered the leonine **Sphinx** and **Nemean Lion**. He became the hound of the three-headed (sometimes three-bodied) giant **Geryon** and was slain by Hercules (Apollodorus, *Library*, 2.5.10). For a similar creature, see also his brother **Cerberus**.

ORYX

The oryx is a genus of large antelope found in Africa and the Arabian Peninsula, and formerly believed to be possessed of only one horn; rest assured it has two. To Ctesias' description of the single-horned wild ass of India (**Unicorn**) from the late fifth century BCE, Aristotle (384–322 BCE) added the single horned oryx in his influential *Historia Animalium*. Pliny the Elder probably had the oryx in mind when he described the *oryges*, a type of goat, 'said to be the only animals that have the hair the contrary way, the points being turned towards the head' (*Nat Hist.*, 8.79), although he did not mention the reputed number of horns.

OSCHAERT

The name of a particular *something* that once troubled the town of Hamme, near Dendermonde in Flanders. It could be a huge horse, a **Black Dog**, a rabbit or an ass with blazing eyes, and would leap onto the backs of travellers and so burden them until they came to a crossroads or statue of the Virgin. Those with a guilty conscience felt most its weight, the sharpness of its claws and the fiery breath that scorched their necks. It was exorcised by a priest and banished to the coast for ninety-nine years – a term which has surely now expired. (Henderson, *Notes*, 273.)

OTTER, GIANT

Also the 'master otter', a creature well-known in Irish folklore. Glenade Lough was said to harbour two such beasts up until the early eighteenth century. According to the story, one of them killed Grace Connolly as she washed clothes in the lake. Her husband killed it, but he and a companion were driven off by the otter's mate, although they later killed that, too. Supposedly, a representation of the battle can be found on the tomb of Grace Connolly in Conwall cemetery, Drummans. A species of giant otter (*Pteronura brasiliensis*) is found in South America that can grow up to 1.6 m (5.6 ft) long. Among the native Achuar and Shuar people of the Amazon region it is believed to be a form taken by *Tsunki*, the first shaman who gives shamans their power. In Scotland it is believed that the **Maighdeann Mhara** can take the form of an otter. (Williams, 'Of Beasts', 62–78.)

MASTER OTTER

The skin of the master otter is said to protect a house from fire, a ship from drifting, and a body from blade and bullet. He sometimes appears with a host of other animals about him, like a king with his court. It is said that one was seen at Dhu-Hill and another on an island in Clew Bay. Similar beliefs were once found in Scotland: 'there is a king or leader among the otters, spotted with white and larger. They believe that it is never killed without the sudden death of a man or some animal at the same instant; that its skin is endowed with great virtue, as an antidote against infection, a preservative of the warrior from wounds, and insures the mariner from all disasters upon the sea'. (Daniel, *Rur. Sp.*; Wood-Martin, *Traces*, 122.)

P

PADFOOT

A **Black Dog** the size of a donkey with long shaggy hair and eyes as big as saucers, it could walk on two legs, or run on three; sometimes it was a sheep or a woolpack rolling along of its own volition, occasionally invisible, sometimes dragging chains, sometimes roaring like no earthly animal, but always with the soft pad, pad, pad of its feet following behind the one destined to die, or simply fated to be frightened. Its territory was the area around Leeds in Yorkshire. Henderson reported that 'Old Sally Dransfield' was a 'firm believer': she claimed to have seen it several times on the road from Leeds to Swillington. A man in Hornby once saw a white padfoot: 'He was going home by Jenkin, and he saw a white dog in the hedge. He struck at it, and the stick passed through it. Then the white dog looked at him, and it had "great saucer e'en"; and he was so "flayed" that he ran home trembling and went to bed, when he fell ill and died' (Henderson, *Notes*, 273–4). (Wright, *Rust.* Sp., 194).

PAN

Ancient Greek, Πάν, an archaic pastoral god, also associated with forests and the wilderness, ultimately and speculatively related to 'the all', τὸ πᾶν, the universe. Herodotus (*Hist.*, 2.145) said that he lived 800 years before him, i.e., around 1200 BCE. There are various accounts of his parentage: Herodotus (ibid.) says of Hermes and Penelope, Apollodorus (*Library*, 14.1) says of Zeus and Hybris; they say that his mother fled when she saw his horns, bear, snub nose, tail and goat's hooves. He was worshiped first in Arcadia, but his cult spread throughout Greece. The invention of the syrinx, or shephard's flute, was attributed to him. The Romans identified him with their god Faunus. Connected to the Egyptian god Mendes, depicted with the head and legs of a goat (Herodotus, *Hist.* 2.46), and in later times the so-called 'Goat of Mendes' in Satanic worship. He was later multiplied into Pans, plural, and largely unidentifiable from the tribes of **Satyr**s and Fauns. (Homer, *Hom. Hym.*; Smith, *Dict.*, III, 107.)

PAPILIO ECCLIPSIS

When, in 1763, the celebrated zoologist Carolus Linnaeus published *Centuria Insectorum* ('One Hundred Insects'; this was actually the thesis of his student Boas Johansson, although

Linnaeus has appropriated its authorship), he included a new species of butterfly he called *Papilio ecclipsis*. It has bright yellow wings with black spots and blue crescent markings, and appears to be a type of Brimstone butterfly. Linnaeus had a specimen in his cabinet and also included it in the twelfth edition of his *Systema Naturae* in 1767. It was only after Linnaeus' death that one of his former students, the entomologist Johan Christian Fabricius, expressed some doubt as to its authenticity. The unusual markings had been painted on. For another of Linnaeus's embarrassments see the **Legless Bird of Paradise**. (Dance, *Animal Fakes*, 104.)

PARDALOCAMPUS

The rare sea-panther of Ancient Greek and Roman mythology: from the Greek, *pardalo-*, 'panther', and *kampos*, 'crooked', usually Latinised as pardalocampus. Two Roman mosiacs from the first or second century CE (Gaziantep Arch. Mus.) show a female lying on the back of a sea-panther. A name above one identifies her as the **Nereid** Galatia; the other may also be a Nereid or possibly a figure being carried off on the back of a sea-bull. She may be a Nereid, or Astypalaia being abducted by Poseidon in the form of a fish-tailed leopard, notably also having a pair of bird's wings.

PEGASUS

Ancient Greek winged horse. The story of Pegasus is first told by Hesiod (*Theog.* 270) in the fourth century BCE. When Perseus suceeds in cutting off

Medusa's head, 'there sprang forth great Chrysaor and the horse Pegasus who is so called because he was born near the springs of Ocean'. Pegasus immediately flies off and came to the deathless gods: 'and he dwells in the house of Zeus and brings to wise Zeus the thunder and lightning'. Pegasus returned to earth to carry Bellerophon in his fight against the **Chimæra** (Hesiod, *Theog.*, 304). In the first century CE, the Roman writer Pliny the Elder reported that 'horses with wings, and armed with hornes, which they call Pegasi' were to be found in Africa ('Æthiopia breedeth them'); although he later called them fowls 'headed like horses' and put them in Scythia, and discounted them altogether as mere fables (*Nat. Hist.*, 8.21, 10.49).

PHOENIX

Ancient Greek fabulous bird, probably derived from the Ancient Egyptian **Bennu** mentioned in *The Book of the Dead*, dating from 1600 to 1200 BCE. It symbolises rebirth and was later taken up by Christian writers to represent the resurrection. However, where the Bennu was more like a heron, the phoenix appears quite different. The earliest surviving mention of the 'phoenix' as such is in Herodotus' *The Histories* of 440 BCE, but he drew on an older work, the *Periegesis* by Hecataeus of Miletus written in the late sixth or early fifth century BCE. According to Herodotus, the phoenix 'is a great rarity, even in Egypt, only coming there (according to the accounts of the people of

Heliopolis) once in five hundred years, when the old phoenix dies.' He goes on to describe it: 'The plumage is partly red, partly golden, while the general make and size are almost exactly that of an eagle'. Herodotus relates a further story of the bird, 'which does not seem to me to be credible', concerning how 'he comes all the way from Arabia, and brings the parent bird, all plastered over with myrrh, to the temple of the Sun, and there buries the body. In order to bring him, they say, he hollows out the ball, and puts his parent inside, after which he covers over the opening with fresh myrrh, and the ball is then of exactly the same weight as at first; so he brings it to Egypt, plastered over as I have said, and deposits it in the temple of the Sun'.

Pliny the Elder, writing in the first century CE (*Nat. Hist.*, 10.2), gives a more embellished and somewhat divergent description, but like Herodotus he expresses reservations: 'The birds of Æthyopia and India, are for the most part of diverse colours, and such as a man is hardly able to decipher and describe. But the Phœnix of Arabia passes all others. Howbeit, I cannot tell what to make of him: and first of all, whether it be a tale or no, that there is never but one of them in the whole world, and the same not commonly seen. By report he is as big as an Ægle: for colour, as yellow & bright as gold; (namely, all about the necke;) the rest of the bodie a deep red purple: the taile azure blew, inter-mingled with feathers among, of rose cornation colour: and the head bravely adorned with a crest and pennache finely wrought; having a tuft and plume thereupon, right faire and goodly to be seene. Manilius, the noble Romane Senatour, right excellently well seene in the best kind of learning and litterature, and yet never taught by any, was the first man of the long Robe, who wrote of this bird at large, & most exquisitely. Hee reporteth, that never man was knowne to see him feeding: that in Arabia hee is held a sacred bird, dedicated unto the Sunne: that hee liveth 660 yeares: and when hee groweth old, and begins to decay, he builds himselfe a nest with the twigs and branches of the Canell or Cinamon, and Frankincense trees: and when he hath filled it with all sort of sweet Aromaticall spices, yeeldeth up his life thereupon. He saith moreover, that of his bones & marrow there breedeth at first as it were a little worme: which afterwards prooveth to bee a pretie bird. And the first thing that this yong new Phœnix doth, is to performe the obsequies of the former Phœnix late deceased: to translate and carie away his whole nest into the citie of the Sunne neere Panchæa, and to bestow it full devoutly there upon the altar. The same Manilius affirmeth, that the revolution of the great yeare so much spoken of, agreeth just with the life of this bird: in which yeare the starres returne againe to their first points, and give signification of times and seasons, as at the beginning: and withall, that this yeare should begin at high noone, that very day when the Sunne entreth the signe Aries. And by his saying, the yeare of that revolution was by him shewed, when P. Licinius and M. Cornelius were Consuls. Cornelius Valerianus writeth, That whiles Q. Plautius and Sex. Papinius were Consuls, the Phœnix flew into Ægypt. Brought he was hither also to Rome in the time that Claudius Cæsar was Censor, to wit, in the eight hundred yeare from the foundation of Rome: and shewed openly to bee seene in a full hall and generall assembly of the people, as appeareth upon the publicke records: howbeit, no man ever made any doubt, but he was a counterfeit Phoenix, and no better.'

When Tacitus (*Annals*, 6.28) came to write of the phoenix he said 'All this is full of doubt and legendary exaggeration. Still, there is no question that the bird is occasionally seen in Egypt'. Carolus Linnaeus included it as one of the **Animalia Paradoxa** in the 1740 edition of his *Systema Naturae* (66): but he saw through the story and described it as being in actuality the date palm. The Musæum Tradescantianum, the first museum open to the public to be established in England, in Vauxhall, south London, once boasted two phoenix feathers in its collection. For the bird known as the Chinese Phoenix, see **Fenghuang**.

PHORCYS

Greek, primordial sea-god, father of monsters; mentioned in Homer's *Odyssey* as the god 'who rules over the unresting sea' (1.44) and 'the old man of the sea' (13.93, 329). In a mosaic from the Trajan Baths of Acholla now in the Bardo Museum, Tunis, he is shown as having a human head, albeit

with two horns, and torso, and a long fish body from which, in place of legs, two crab-like arms with pincers emerge. According to Hesiod (*Theog.*, 304), 'Ceto was joined in love to Phorcys and bore her youngest, the awful snake who guards the apples all of gold in the secret places of the dark earth at its great bounds' (see **Ladon**); their other offspring were the Graiae and the Gorgons (*Theog.*, 270).

PHYSETER

A **Sea Monster** of the Atlantic described by Pliny (*Nat. Hist.*, 9.4): 'In the French Ocean there is discovered a mightie fish called Physeter, (i.e., a Whirlepoole) rising up aloft out of the sea in manner of a columne or pillar; higher than the very sailes of the ships: and then he spouteth, and casteth forth a mightie deale of water as it were out of a conduit, ynough to drowne and sinke a ship.' What Pliny was describing was the sperm whale, known to be able to grow over 20 m (over 65 ft) in length, and the largest toothed predator. In the eighteenth century, Linnaeus gave it the scientific name of *Physeter macrocephalus*. Icelandic fishermen also sometimes counted it among the **Illhvel**, or 'wicked whales'.

PIAST (PÉIST)

An Irish **Worm** (**Dragon**) or **Serpent**; in Irish *Péist*, known in English as Piast. It is said that such a creature still lives in the waters of Lough Nahanagan (from the Irish *Loch na hOnchon*, meaning 'Lake of the Water Monster') in County Wicklow, Ireland

(Williams, 'Of Beasts', 62–78). In 1963, a certain 'L.R.' told the press that he and a friend had seen 'a creature which could only be described as a monster' in Lower Lough Bray. It had 'a large hump like the back of a rhinoceros [...] a head something like a tortoise only many times bigger' with a circular body some 3 to 3.6 m (10 to 12 ft) in circumference and a 'dark greyish colour'; the friend thought its head was more like that of a swan (quoted in Costello, *In Search*). See also **Wurrum**.

PICKTREE BRAG

A most bizarre animal found in and around the village of Picktree, Washington, County Durham. It is said that 'Sometimes it was like a calf, with a white handkerchief round its neck, and a bushy tail; sometimes, in form of a coach-horse, it trotted "along the lonin afore folk, settin' up a great nicker and a whinny now and then". Again it appeared as a "dick-ass", as four men holding up a white sheet, or as a naked man without a head. Sir Cuthbert's informant, an ancient dame, told him how her uncle had a white suit of clothes, and the first time he ever put them on he met the Brag, and never did he put them on again but some misfortune befell him. Once, in that very suit, returning from a christening, he encountered the Brag, and being a bold man, he leapt upon its back; "but, when he came to the four lonin ends, the Brag joggled him so sore, that he could hardly keep his seat; and at last it threw him into the middle o' the pond, and ran away,

setting up a great nicker and laugh, just for all the world like a Christian"' (Henderson, *Notes*, 270). It is an animal to rival the **Hedley Kow**.

PICTISH BEAST

A mythological creature found on Pictish carved stones, possibly intended to be a **Dragon** or **Water-Horse**; sometimes described in archaeological writing as an 'elephant'. No one knows for sure what it is or was intended to mean, but its frequent appearance on the carved stones points to high significance. Animals depicted on Pictish stones are generally drawn from nature – wolves, horses, serpents, stags – and so it is likely that the Beast is also meant to be a real animal. It has four legs ending in curling, flipper-like

Pictish Beast on the Maiden Stone (1890)

and a long nose like a dolphin. northern waters, it is more plausible that the seal is intended, or that it is perhaps a memory of the walrus of more northerly waters. Most of the Pictish Beast stones are found furthest from the sea and are concentrated in the districts of Aberdeen, Banff and Buchan, Gordon, and Kincardine and Deeside in north-eastern Scotland. Important examples include: the Maiden Stone outside Pitcalpe, Aberdeenshire; the Meigle 4 and Meigle 5 Pictish Stones, now in the Meigle Sculptures Stone Museum, Perth and Kinross; the Dyce 1 Symbol Stone at Dyce in Aberdeenshire; the Eassie Stone in Eassie churchyard, Angus; Rodney's Stone, Moray; and the Strathmartine Castle Stone from Angus, now in the McManus Galleries in Dundee. The Picts were known as the *Pechs*, *Pechts* or *Peghts* in Scotland, and believed by some to be fairies due to their similarly diminutive size and mysterious habits. (Alcock, 'Pictish Stones', 1–21; MacRitchie, 'Memories', 123.)

PIG-FACED LADY

In 1829, a certain J.R. wrote to the *Magazine of Natural History* about 'a monstrosity of the human species from the deserts of Arabia' being exhibited in a caravan in London: the so-called Pig-Faced Lady. The author of the piece had correctly deduced that it was, despite being called Madame Stevens, neither a pig nor a lady, but a 'female bear, shaven and dressed as a woman'. (J.R., 'Zoo. Imp.', 189.)

PISMIRE

An old word for the ant, from Middle English *pisse*, 'urine', and *mire*, 'ant' (compare Old Norse, *maurr*, 'ant'); a term derived from the smell of the ants' formic acid. It was used from the fourteenth century up until the seventeenth century, at least. It was also another term for the heraldic ant, the **Emmet**. The ancients described particularly impossible species; see **Formicoleon**, **Myrmex Indikos**.

PONGO

A Mediterranean **Sea Monster**. It was described as being half tiger, half shark – although evidently not a tiger shark – that preyed on the inhabitants of a certain part of Sicily, devouring everyone within a twenty-mile radius. (Bassett, *Legends*, 206–7.)

PRISTES

A fish of great size once believed to swim the Indian Ocean. Another of Pliny's animals, he says little about it except its location and size: 'Pristes are two hundred cubites long.' The name comes from the Ancient Greek for 'saw' or 'one who saws' (*Nat. Hist.*, 9.3). Pliny's specimen is likely the sawfish. In Ancient Rome a cubit was equal to about 44 cm, so 200 cubits would equal some 88 m. In 1758 Linnaeus categorised the now critically endangered common sawfish as *Pristis pristis*. It has been known to grow over 7 m (23 ft) in length, but is more usually under three.

PRESTER

A type of fantastic **Serpent** first described by Lucan (*Phars.* 9.722), then notably by Isidore of Seville (*Etym.*, 12.4.16): 'The prester is an asp who goes with its mouth always open and steamy, as the poet mentions [Lucan]: *Oraque distendens avidus fumantia preseter* (The greedy prester stretching forth foaming jaws). Stricken by this snake, a person becomes distended, and dies from his enormous corpulence; decay follows the swollen condition.'

PYGMY BISON

The Pygmy Bison or American Ox first came to notice in Britain in 1829. It was supposed to be like a normal male bison in every regard, except its size: it was only some 18 to 20 cm (7 or 8 in) high. A stuffed specimen was in the possession of Mr Murray, dealer in curiosities, who valued it at forty guineas. Someone known only as 'V' examined it and found it to be a wooden model covered with the skin of a pug-dog, long hairs plucked from a young bear, and horns and hooves made from buffalo horn (V., 'Notice', 218–19).

PYRALIS

The 'fire fly', *pyralis* or *pyrausta*, was thought, literally, to live in fire. Pliny (*Nat. Hist.*, 11.36): 'The fire also, a contrarie element to generation, is not without some living creatures engendred therein. For in Cypres, among the forges and furnaces of copper, there is to be seen a certaine foure-footed creature, and yet winged, (as big as the greater kind of flies) to flie out of the very middest of the fire: and called it is of some Pyralis, of others Pyrausta. The nature of it is this: So long as it remaineth in the fire, it liveth: but if it chaunce to leape foorth of the furnace, and to flie any thing far into the aire, it dieth.'

PYTHON

A she-**Dragon** of Ancient Greek mythology defeated by the god Apollo. The earliest surviving reference to Python is in the 'Hymn to Apollo', a poem in the epic meter dating from about the sixth century BCE and part of the so-called Homeric Hymns. She is described, rather unflatteringly, as 'the bloated, great she-dragon, a fierce monster wont to do great mischief to men upon earth, to men themselves and to their thin-shanked sheep; for she was a very bloody plague' (Hesiod, *Hes. Hom. Hym*, xxx). She guarded a spring on the slopes of Mount Parnassus in Greece near the site chosen by Apollo to site a temple to himself. He kills her with an arrow; special attention is paid in the poem to her rotting away. In the second century CE, the Greek writer Pausanius (*Desc. Gr.*, 10.6.5) derived the name Python from the verb 'to rot'. The site is thereafter called Pytho and Apollo is given the name of Pythian. According to Apollodorus (*Library*, 1.4), Python was the guardian of an earlier oracle at Delphi and tried to prevent Apollo from approaching; again he killed the dragon and took over the oracle. The historical and archaeological record confirms that there was an older sacred site at this location, dating from the

Late Bronze Age, dedicated to Athena/Gaia. Python was also known as Delphine or Delphyne: Delphinia was a surname of Artemis at Athens; Delphinius was later adopted by Apollo after his defeat of the dragon; it is probably derived from the site name Delphi. Evidence for the cult of Pythian Apollo dates from the eighth century BCE. The oracles of Apollo were delivered via a priestess termed Pythia. The dragon-slayer motif echoes both the earlier Babylonian conflict between **Tiamat** and Marduk and the later combat between St George and the Dragon. (Smith, *Dict.*, II, 627-8.)

Apollo and Python (1589)

Immensum certis strauit Pythona sagittis
Nec meruit minimum Cynthius arte decus,

Latonae matri monstrum Iunonis ob iram
Et terra infestum dum necat atq mari

Q

QUETZALCOATL

Mesoamerican, 'feathered **Serpent**' or 'plumed serpent'; the feathers come from the resplendently coloured *quetzal* bird (genus *Pharomachrus*). The name dates from the pre-Aztec, Toltec culture, although depictions of a feathered serpent can be found in the first Mesoamerican civilisation, that of the Olmecs, which lasted from about 1400 to 400 BCE. To the Aztecs, he was the bringer of knowledge – particularly of how to work jadeite and, in later myths, of the cultivation of maize – and the inventor of the *Tonalamatl*, or 'Book of Fate'. In several myths he is credited as the creator of the cosmos and all living things; he seeks bones in the underworld with which to make humankind. There are a large number of stories concerning Quetzalcoatl, not all of them in agreement. Seen as a more civilised god, who required blood purification rather than human sacrifice and cannibalism, Quetzalcoatl was forced to abandon his country due to the intrigues of sorcerers, sailing away on a raft of snakes, which would seem to represent the usurpation of his cult by rivals. Before leaving, he told his disciples that, one day, he would return. When the Conquistador Hernán Cortés landed on the shores of the New World (Yucatán Peninsula) in 1519, the Aztec Emperor, Moctezuma II, believed that he was the god Quetzalcoatl returned and so sent him the ceremonial dress of Quetzalcoatl; the turquoise snake mask can today be seen in the British Museum. Quetzalcoatl corresponds to the Mayan Kukulkan and Gucumatz of the Guatamalan Kiché. (Spence, *Gods Mexico, passim.*)

The Mask of Quetzalcoatl (1400–1521 CE)

R

RAM-FISH

Also translated as 'sea-ram', another of Pliny's mysterious creatures: 'This fish is a very strong theefe at sea, and makes foule worke where he commeth: for one while he squatteth close under the shade of bigge ships that ride at anker in the bay, where he lieth in ambush to wait when any man for his pleasure would swim and bath himselfe, that so he might surprise them: otherwhiles he putteth out his nose above the water, to spie any small fisher boats comming, & then he swimmeth close to them, overturneth and sinketh them' (*Nat. Hist.*, 9.44). One translator thought that Pliny might have been referring to the dolphin, but this sort of behaviour does not sound typical of the dolphin, a species that Pliny was otherwise quite familiar with.

RANA-PISCIS

Also *Ranae in Piscem Metamorphosis*: one of Carolus Linnaeus's 'contrary animals' (**Animalia Paradoxa**) listed in the first edition of his *Systema Naturae* published in 1735. This creature is a real South American animal: a green and rather ordinary looking frog, however, unlike normal frogs it was believed to metamorphose from a frog into a fish, hence the names *Rana-Piscis*, 'frog-fish', or *Ranae in Piscem Metamorphosis*, 'frog changing into fish'. Linnaeus was sceptical, arguing that nature does not allow changing from one class of animal to another. He was right to be so: the origin of this story comes from the fact that the frog in its tadpole state is considerably larger than in its adult frog state; and because the adult animal is normally always larger than the immature, so the idea arose that the frog went from being a frog to being a fish (tadpole). Linnaeus changed its name to *Rana paradoxa* and it is now classified as *Pseudis paradoxa*, still a paradoxical frog.

RAT KING

From the German, *Rattenkönig*. The reputed phenomenon of several rats becoming entangled to form one large mass of rats, usually black rats (*Rattus rattus*); although Conrad Gessner was more literal: 'Some would have it that the rat waxes mighty in its old age and is fed by its young: this is called the rat king' (*Hist. Anim.*). In 1682 Drugulin (*Hist. Bild.*, 270) published a depiction of a rat king of six rats found in a cellar in Strassburg. In 1883 another was

The Strasburg Rat King (*c.*1683)

found in Lüneburg, Germany, and apparently kept in the Natural History Collection there (Verein, *Führer Lüneburg*, 68). The Zoological Museum of Göttingen University, Germany, has its rat king: the *Rattenkönig* of Rüdershausen/ Eichsfeld. The scientific museum Mauritianum in Altenburg, Germany, has a particularly gruesome specimen on display, showing a group of mummified rats knotted together at the tails. It was supposedly found in a miller's fireplace in Buchheim in 1828. A smaller rat king of nine interwoven rats is held by the museum of Nantes in France, and the Museum of Fine Arts and Natural History, Chateaudun, has a knot of six rats preserved in alcohol. The Natural History Museum of Maastricht owns a rat king of seven rats found in Limburg in 1955. Despite the existence of such specimens, the rat king is more probably a species of **Jenny Haniver**, although Miljutin documents a find in Estonia in 2005: the Rat King of Saru. This was originally a group of sixteen rats, thirteen of which have been preserved in the original knot, and is now on display in the Natural History Museum at the University of Tartu, Estonia. From examination of this specimen, Miljutin concluded that it was genuine and had probably been caused by an initial freezing together of the tails and subsequent knotting

together as the rats tried to free themselves ('Rat Kings', 77–81). Examples
of cats knotted at the tails have also
been published; see **Katzenknäuel**.

RAVEN

The raven appears throughout the old
European myths and legends. He is the
sacred bird of the Greek Apollo; as
Huginn and Muninn, 'Thought' and
Memory', they perch on the shoulders
of Norse Odin and each morning fly
out to bring him news of the world;
the bird is associated with the Celtic
war-goddess Morrigan and the Welsh
(British) god Bran (meaning 'raven').
Bran's head was buried under the
Tower of London as a magical charm
against invasion and the ravens gather
there to this day in his honour;
according to tradition, if they should
ever leave, or be removed, then the
Kingdom of Great Britain will fall.
Among the old Finnish legends there
are accounts of 'The Origin of the
Raven' (Abercromby, *Pre- Proto-Hist.*,
314–15), that put a new and zoologically impossible complexion on this
bird: the raven is born on a pile of
charcoal, bred from the charcoal itself;
its head is made from potsherds, its
belly from a beggar's sack, its legs from
crooked sticks. Lempo, an erotic
demon figure, provides his spinning
wheel for the raven's breastbone, his
sail for the bird's tail, his needle-case
for the guts, whilst Hiisi, the Finnish
Devil, gives his weaving stool for the
bird's neck and in one version his old
glove for the bird's body; its crop is a
worn-out kettle, a sorcerer's arrow-
head forms the beak; it has mussel

pearls for eyes, and its tongue is the axe
of Kirki. Pliny (*Nat. Hist.*, 8, 10.21),
of course, had some odd things to say
about the raven: that the bird could
treat itself for poisoning by adminis-
tering laurel; that 'they conceive and
engender at the bill'; that a pregnant
woman eating a raven's egg will
likewise give birth through her mouth;
that they can foretell disaster. Finally,
Pliny also had a story about a talking
raven that lived in a cobbler's shop in
Rome during the reign of Tiberius and
would visit the Forum every morning
to salute the Emperor and greet
passers-by. Pliny himself had witnessed
a crow express itself in words and
sentences. There was also a hunter
called Craterus Monoceros of Erizena
who went hunting with ravens
perching on his shoulders; these birds
would fly off and round up all the wild
ravens, and bring them to him. See
also **Night-Raven**.

RAVENS OF OWAIN

In the medieval Welsh Mabinogion,
the ravens are an army three hundred
strong who fight for the legendary
Owain (Sir Ywain), the son of Urien
and Morgan le Fay; in one tale they
attack King Arthur's squires in retal-
iation against their assaults. (Guest,
Mabinogion, 311.)

RAVEN, WHITE

'In the year 1548, in the month of
August,' wrote William Turner, 'I saw
two white Ravens from the same nest,
and handled them at the very place in
Cumberland of our Britain, bred on
the property of a lord of that county,

and trained for bird-catching just like hawks. For they had been taught both to sit quietly on the arm of the falconer, and when loosed to fly as quickly as possible to his call and sign even from a distance. Nothing unlucky followed them […]' (*Turner Birds*, 49–50). There are several myths that posit that the raven was originally white, but turned black due to some crime. In Ovid we read: 'The raven once in snowy plumes was drest, | White as the whitest dove's unsully'd breast, | Fair as the guardian of the Capitol, | Soft as the swan; a large and lovely fowl; | His tongue, his prating tongue had chang'd him quite | To sooty blackness, from the purest white.' Apollo had fallen in love with the nymph Coronis, 'fairest of the fairer kind', but Coronis was unfaithful and Apollo's white raven had seen it all. The raven tells Apollo and in his rage he shoots Coronis with an arrow. As she lies dying she tells him of the child she is carrying. Repenting of his rashness, he saves the child, but 'in his fury black'd the raven o'er, | And bid him prate in his white plumes no more'. In Chaucer's retelling in the *Canterbury Tales*, Phoebus (Apollo), plucks the white feathers and throws the bird to the Devil – 'And for this cause be all crowes black' – with the moral 'Keep well thy tongue, and think upon the crow'. In the Welsh myth cycle, the Mabinogion, the name of Bran the Blessed's sister, Branwen, means 'white raven'. In the Bible (Genesis 8:6–12), Noah sends out a raven from the ark to find land; according to an Arabic commentary on the text (sixteenth century), the raven

sees dead bodies floating in the water and stops to feed on them. Three months later he returns, having forgotten to look for land, and Noah curses him so that he becomes black. In other legends, for example, those of the Timagami Ojibwa of north-eastern Ontario, Canada, and the North Mansi in West Siberia, the raven (or crow) turns black because he eats carrion. In Jewish tradition the ravens' 'young are born with white feathers, wherefore the old birds desert them, not recognising them as their offspring. They take them for serpents. God feeds them until their plumage turns black, and the parents return to them. As an additional reward, God grants their petition when the ravens pray for rain' (Ginzberg, *Legends Jews*, I:113, V:142–3). (Korotayev et al., 'Return', 203–35.)

RAWUZEL

A shaggy black-haired bear-like monster with devilish face and horns comparable to the **Krampus**. The Metropolitan Museum of Art in New York has a small colour lithograph by the Hungarian artist Josef Diveky dated 1911 called 'Der Rawuzel'. Rawuzel or Rawuzeln (Raunigel) is also the name given to a type of coconut-flake covered confectionary in Austria. (Schröer, 'Myth. Gest.', 426.)

RE'EM

A giant horned animal of Jewish folklore. Only one breeding pair exists at a time because the world could not feed more of them. They copulate once every seventy years, an act that finishes off the male; and twelve years later the female gives birth to twins, an act that finishes off the female. As soon as they are born, the offspring travel in different directions, east and west, and after seventy years find each other again to begin the cycle anew. Translated as **Unicorn** in English versions of the Bible. (Ginzberg, *Legends Jews*, I, 30–1.)

RHINOCEROS BIRD,

SEE TRAGOPANADES

RIVER-DRAGON

'Thus with ten wounds | The river-dragon tam'd at length submits | To let his sojounrers depart [...]': in John Milton's *Paradise Lost* (bk 2), the river-**Dragon** is an allusion to the crocodile and a passage in the Book of Ezekiel concerning 'the great dragon that lyeth in the midst of his rivers'.

RIVER-WHALE

When translating Pliny's *Natural History* (9.15), Philemon Holland created a genus of monstrous fish called 'the "river-whale" with three species: the river-whale called Silurus, in Nilus; the Lax, in the Rhene; the Attilus, in the Po'. By Silurus, he meant what we call the catfish: Linnaeus gave the name *Silurus* to the genus of eighteen catish species native to Europe and Asia. Found from Khazakstan to the United Kingdon, the wels catfish (*Silurus glanis*) can grow to 4 m (13 ft) in length and has been known to attack people (usually with provocation). Pliny went on: 'As for the Silurus, a cut-throat hee is

The River-Whale of the Ossiacher See, Austria (1666)

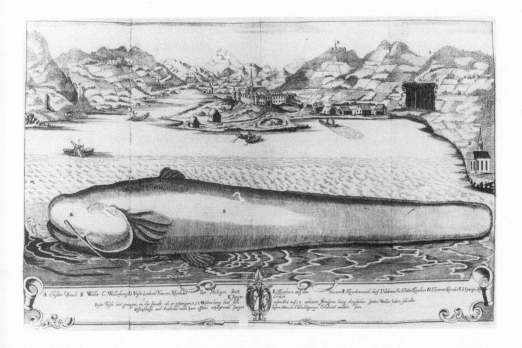

wheresoever hee goeth, a great devourer, and maketh foule worke: for no living creatures come amisse unto him, he setteth upon all indifferently. The very horses oftentimes as they swim, he devoureth.' Some have argued that the **Loch Ness Monster** is a wels catfish. Lax is probably the German *Lachs*, the salmon, and Rhene, the river Rhein, although another translator gave pike for Pliny's original *isox*. Linnaeus gave the name *Esox* to the genus of fish we call pikes. Both types of fish can grow over a metre in length, with some species pushing two. Over the years there have been accounts of pike attacking people, dogs and calves (Daniel, *Rur. Sp.*, 266). According to Pliny, the Attila 'groweth so fat with ease and lying still, that otherwiles it weigheth a thousand pounds: and being taken with a great hooke fastened and linked to a chaine, cannot be drawne forth of the river but with certaine yokes of oxen.' This has been translated as the sturgeon: the Beluga sturgeon (*Huso huso*) can grow over 7 m (23 ft) in length.

ROC

Also *rokh*, *rukh*; a gigantic bird of Persian folklore made famous in 'The Seven Voyages of Sinbad the Sailor' (Lang, *Arabian Nights'*, 131ff). It was reputed to be so large that it could carry off elephants. Coming to Madagascar during his voyages, Marco Polo heard tell of the creature: 'The people of the island report that at a certain season of the year, an extraordinary kind of bird, which they call a *rukh*, makes its appearance from the southern region. In form it is said to resemble the eagle, but it is incomparably greater in size; being so large and strong as to seize an elephant with its talons, and to lift it into the air, from whence it lets it fall to the ground, in order that when dead it may prey upon the carcase. Persons who have seen this bird assert that when the wings are spread they measure sixteen paces in extent, from point to point; and that the feathers are eight paces in length, and thick in proportion'. Marco Polo thought it might be the fabled **Griffin**, but the people he questioned were adamant that it was some form of giant eagle. The Grand Khan of Malabar at this time apparently acquired several 'feathers' (*Travels*, ed. Masefield, 393). The roc was duly illustrated in Ulisse Aldrovandi's *Ornithologia* of 1599. The 'claw of the roc bird' was listed in the collection of John Tradescant (*c.*1570–1636), the man who opened the first public museum in Britain (Hagen, 'History', 88). It has been suggested that the legend originated with the aepyornis, an extinct flightless Madagascan bird, an egg of which was discovered by d'Abbadie in 1850 (Hazlitt, *Faiths*, 1); such an egg can be seen in the British Museum today. More recently, it has been proposed that the legend is based on the Malagasy crowned eagle (*Stephanoaetus mahery*), a large bird of prey formerly inhabiting Madagascar until becoming extinct around 1500 CE (Goodman, 'Description', 421–8). The largest African eagle, the martial eagle (*Polemaetus bellicosus*), can have a

Roc (1900)

wingspan of almost 260 cm (8 ft 6 in). The giant bird is a frequent motif in mythology, from the **Garuda** of India to the **Zu Bird** of Mesopotamia.

RORE-TROLD

A shape-shifting spirit of the north: 'In the Rorevand in Nedenaes, a lake enclosed within steep mountains, and much exposed to squalls of wind, a Troll, called the Rore-trold, has his abode. He appears under various forms, sometimes as a horse, sometimes as a load of hay, sometimes as a huge **Serpent**, and sometimes as a number of persons. In the winter, and when the ice is thickest, there may be seen, on one night, a long, broad chasm, with fragments of ice lying in it, all of which is the work of the Rore-trold'. (Thorpe, *North. Myth.*, II, 23.)

S

SALAMANDER

Aristotle, writing in the fourth century BCE, seems to be the source of the impossible salamander: 'The fact that certain animal structures exist which really cannot be burnt is evident from the salamander, which, so they say, puts the fire out by crawling through it' (*Hist. Anim.*). Pliny (*Nat. Hist.*, 10.86) expanded on the theme: 'He is of so cold a complexion, that if hee do but touch the fire, hee wil quench it as presently, as if yce were put into it. The Salamander casteth up at the mouth a certaine venomous matter like unto milke, let it but once touch any bare part of a man or womans bodie, all the haire will fall off: and the part so touched will change the colour of the skin to the white morphew'; and 'some engender not at all, as the Salamanders: for there is no distinction of sex in them no more than in Yeeles, and in all those which neither lay egs, ne yet bring forth any living creatures.' The translator, Philemon Holland, added his remark that this latter was 'found untrue by experience'.

SALPUGA

Pliny (*Nat. Hist.*, 29.29): 'There is a kind of venomous ant, by no means common in Italy; Cicero calls it "solipuga", and in Bætica it is known as "salpuga". The proper remedy for its venom and that of all kinds of ants is a bat's heart.' They re-appear in Lucan's *Pharsalia* (9.734) when he says 'And who would fear thy haunts, *Salpuga*? Yet the Stygian Maids have given thee power to snap the fatal threads'. In 1815 the naturalist William Leach classified a family of *Solpugidae*, or sun spiders, of the order *Solifugae*, 'those that flee from the sun', a type of insect between scorpion and spider.

SAPAKSHA-SIMHAH

Indian winged lion. A variation is the rarer winged and horned lion seen on the Sanchi reliefs. (Murthy, *Myth. An. Ind.*, 8.)

SASSU-WUNNU

A Babylonian **Sea Monster**, one of the forms taken by the god Ea. He had the head of a **Serpent**, the ears of a **Basilisk**, twisted horns, the body of a fish that was 'full of stars', and clawed feet. (Mackenzie, *Myth. Bab.*, 62.)

SATYR

First mentioned by Hesiod (*Fragments*, 277), 'the tribe of worthless, helpless

Satyrs', with pointed ears, horns and a tail. They were followers of Dionysus (Bacchus) and fond of wine. Older ones, bald and heavily bearded, were called Silens; the younger, Satyrisci. In later ages they became confounded with Pans and Fauns, and took on a more goatlike aspect (Smith, *Dict.*, III, 727). The ancient writers Pausanias (*Desc. Gr.*, 1.23.5–6) and Aelian (*Nat. An.*, 16.21) both mentioned the satyr as an actual creature in their scholarly works. For Pausanias, satyrs were a kind of wild man, having red hair and horsetails, inhabiting the islands named Satyrides after them: they had a reputation for lasciviousness. On the authority of Pausanias, Conrad Gessner even included an illustration of a satyr, looking like a hare with a man's face and bird's feet (*Hist.*, I, 978). From these sources, Carolus Linnaeus included the *satyrus* as one of the **Animalia Paradoxa** in the second edition of his *Systema Naturae* in 1740, with the description: 'tailed, hairy, bearded, human-like body, gesticulating much, very fallacious, is a species of monkey, if ever one has been seen' (65); he later used the binomial classification *Simia satyrus* for the orangutan (now classifed as genus *Pongo*).

SCITALIS, SEE SCYTALE

SCOPES

In the *Odyssey*, Homer made mention of birds called 'scopes' (σκῶπές). Pliny (*Nat. Hist.*, 10.70) was wont to dismiss the idea: 'Homer maketh mention of certaine birds called Scopes: but I cannot conceive those Satyricall gestic-ulations of theirs like Antikes when they are perched, which so many men talke of: neither doe I thinke otherwise, but that these birds are out of knowledge now adaies.' Describing the island of the nymph Calypso, Homer (*Odyssey*, 5(E), 1.66) wrote about a wood 'wherein birds long of wing were wont to nest, owls and falcons and sea-crows with chattering tongues, who ply their business on the sea'. Homer's original is translated with 'owls' and there is indeed a scops owl (e.g., *Otus scops*); the screech-owl (**Strix**) was once included in this category. It was said that it could be captured by its tendency to mimic the movements of someone dancing in front of it, 'those Satyricall gesticu-lations'; and hence was also the name of a dance in which the movements of an owl were mimicked.

SCORPION

The entirely possible scorpion was the source of some impossible ideas in antiquity. In the first century CE, Ovid thought that: 'If you remove the hollow claws of land-crabs, and put the rest under the soil, a scorpion, with its curved and threatening tail, will emerge from the parts interred' (*Met.*, 15, 369–71). Also writing in the first century CE, Pliny the Elder said of them that 'Scorpions are a plague and a curse from Africa. Their tails have a sting that is always in motion, ready to strike. Their sting is always fatal to girls and usually fatal to women, but only fatal to men if they are stung in the morning when the poison is strongest. Victims take three days to die. A drink made of the ashes of the scorpion mixed with wine is said to be a cure for their sting. The south wind gives scorpions the power of flight; it supports them when they stretch out their arms like oars' (*Nat. Hist.*, 11.30). In the seventh century CE, Isidore of Seville added some new features: 'Scorpions do not strike at the palm of the hand' (*Etym.*, 12.4:3); and 'If ten crabs are tied with basil, all of the scorpions in that area will gather together' (12.6:17). For the Babylonian scorpion-man, see **Girtablilu**; for the Ancient Egyptian scorpion-goddess, see **Serqet**.

SCYLLA

A six-headed **Sea Monster** of Ancient Greek mythology, Scylla is first mentioned in Homer's *Odyssey* (12.142–259; in Palmer, 189–92), dating from the eighth century BCE, but undoubtedly based on an older oral tradition. The story relates Odysseus' adventures on his voyage home after the siege of Troy (recounted in the *Iliad*). With the aid of the god Hermes, he subdues the sorceress Circe, who then tells him how to evade Scylla, amongst other things. Scylla forms a pair with another moster, **Charybdis**, and the two are never encountered separately. Odysseus' passage between the two equal dangers gave rise to the expression 'between Scylla and Charybdis', meaning a choice between two equally unpleasant alternatives. Circe tells Odysseus that Scylla was once a beautiful nymph, but after she roused the anger of the gods, Circe herself transformed her into a monster. She describes her to Odysseus as having twelve feet and six necks ending in heads with three rows of teeth. According to another legend, Hercules had already killed her for eating one of **Geryon**'s cattle, but **Phorcys**, her father, had returned her to life; and so she lay in Odysseus' path. After escaping the **Sirens**, Odysseus and his crew sailed on: 'Soon after we left the island [of the sirens], I observed a smoke, I saw high waves and heard a plunging sound. From the hands of my frightened men down fell the oars, and splashed against the current. There the ship stayed, for they worked the tapering oars no more. Along the ship I passed, inspiriting my men with cheering words, standing by each in turn [...] But Scylla I did not name – that hopeless horror – for fear through fright my men might cease to row, and huddle all together in the hold. I disregarded, too, the hard behest of Circe, when she had said I must by no means arm. Putting on my glittering armour and taking in my hands my two long spears, I went upon the ship's fore-deck, for thence I looked for the first sight of Scylla of the rock, who brought my men disaster. Nowhere could I descry her; I tired my eyes with searching up and down the dusky cliff. [...] And now it was that Scylla snatched from the hollow ship six of my comrades who were best in skill and strength. Turning my eyes toward my swift ship to seek my men, I saw their feet and hands already in the air as they were carried up. They screamed aloud and called my name for the last time, in agony of heart. As when a fisher, on a jutting rock, with long rod throws a bait to lure the little fishes, casting into the deep the horn of stall-fed ox; then, catching a fish, flings it ashore writhing, even so were these drawn writhing upon the rocks. There at her door she ate them, loudly shrieking and stretching forth their hands in mortal pangs towards me. That was the saddest sight my eyes have ever seen, in all my toils, searching the ocean pathways.' Modern attempts to identify Scylla suggest that she was some sort of giant squid infesting the Straits of Messina.

SCYTALE

A type of fantastic **Serpent** first mentioned by Lucan (*Phars.*, ix.1.717), then by Pliny (*Nat. Hist.*, 32.19) in passing and expanded upon by Isidore of Seville (*Etym.*, 12.4.19): 'The snake named scytale shines conspicuously in the great variety of colour of its back. Thanks to those markings, it slows down those who look at it. Because it is slower in creping, and unable to chase prey, it captures those stupified by amazement. It has such great heat that even in winter it sheds the skin from its burning body'.

SEA BISHOP

De pisce Episcopi habitu, a 'fish in the clothing of a bishop', a fish resembling a Catholic bishop described in the mid-sixteenth century. Guillaume Rondelet, regius professor of medicine at the university of Montpellier, is credited with its identification in his 1554 book *Libri de Piscibus Marini*: 'I set forth another monster much more marvellous, which I received from Gisbertus Germanus.

This he had received from Amsterdam along with letters which affirmed that in 1531 a sea monster clothed like a bishop had been brought before the King of Poland'. Rondelet reserved his judgement, although he chose not to publish further information he had received about the creature on the grounds that it seemed simply fabulous. (Gudger, 'Jenny Hanivers', 511–23.)

SEA CALF

Pliny (*Nat. Hist.*, 8.49): 'The Sea-calfe likewise liveth both in the sea, and upon the land: and hath the same nature and qualitie that the beiver is, for hee casteth up his gall, which is good for many medicines: and so he doth his runnet in the maw, which is a singular remedie for the falling sicknesse: for well is he ware, that men seeke after him for these two things.' A sea-calf like a beaver? Later Pliny tells us exactly what he is talking about: 'the Sea-calves or Seales, which the Latines call *Phocæ*'. Pliny also reports that 'their right finnes or legs are thought to have a power and vertue to provoke sleepe, if they be laid under ones beds head'. The souls of the drowned are said to be embodied in a monster in the form of a calf that appears in a lake in Poland (Bassett, *Legends*, 215).

SEA COW, SEE CRO SITH

SEA DOG

Also called *hound-fish* or *sea-hound*, described by Pliny (*Nat. Hist.*, 9.46): 'these fishes have a certain dim cloud or thin web, growing and hanging over their heads, resembling broad, flat, and gristly fishes, which clingeth them hard, and hindreth them from retiring backe and giving way [...] these fell, unhappie, and shrewd monsters'. Pliny described an aggressive animal that was capable of killing swimmers, especially sponge divers. To avoid such a fate a diver would tie a rope about his middle and tug on it when in danger as a signal to his comrades to be pulled up, but 'unlesse they give him a sodaine jerke and snatch him up quickly, they may be sure to see him worried and devoured before their face'. Sea lions are often called sea dogs because of their canine appearance, but it is unlikely that Pliny was referring to this animal. He may have meant a) the family of sharks called dogfish, although one would have expected him to also mention their venom-coated dorsal spines; or b) either of two species of catshark known as the lesser and greater-spotted dogfish, both of which are found in the Mediterranean. Pliny also mentioned animals the translator called 'sea-foxes', but gave very little detail as to what these are; they are probably also dogfish. Dogs are associated with water deities in mythology: with the Irish Nuada, and the British equivalent Nodons (or Nodens), venerated at Lydney Park in Gloucestershire on the River Severn; and with the goddess Coventina at her sacred well at Carrawbrough, Northumberland, and elsewhere. Williams ('Of Beasts', 73) argues that these water-hounds are in fact otters; in Irish the otter is called *madra uisce*, 'water dog'. Other names include the

Irish *eascú, eascann*, 'waterfall hound' and **Dobhar-Chú**. In 1635, a monster was seen in the river Don, or so it was said, having 'the head of a dog, arms, body and hands of a man, and tail of a fish' (Bassett, *Legends*, 212). In heraldry, the sea-dog 'is depicted like a talbot in shape, but with the tail like that of a beaver, the feet webbed and the whole body scaled like a fish, a scalloped fin continued along the hack from the head to the tail' (Vinycomb, 275). The noted expert on Heraldry, Fox-Davies, thought that the animal was an early attempt to depict the beaver. The Irish surname MacNamara is an anglicised form of *Mac con mara*, itself a contraction of *Mac Con na Mara*, meaning 'Son of the Sea Hound'.

SEA EAGLE

Aqulia Marina, described and depicted in Pierre Belon's *De Aquatilibus* published in 1553 and in Ulyssi Aldrovandi's *De Piscibus* of 1613, among others. This was the European or common eagle ray (*Myliobatis aquila*), but in both cases had been manipulated to present a more exaggerated appearance. The eagle ray is distributed across the Eastern Atlantic, including the waters of the North Sea and Mediterranean, and can reach almost 2 m (6 ft 6 in) in length, including the long, whip-like tail. Belon's specimen is considered to be one of the earliest published examples of a **Jenny Haniver**.

SEA ELEPHANT

Almost every sort of land animal seemed to be able to take the prefix 'sea'; and so Pliny added some more: 'sea-Elephants and Rams, with teeth standing out; and hornes also, like to those of the land, but that they were white like as the foresaid teeth' (*Nat. Hist.*, 9.4).

SEA HARE

The *lepus marinus* (Latin), a poisonous fish found in the waters off India; according to Pliny (*Nat. Hist.*, 9.48): 'the Sea-hare, which keepeth in the Indian sea, is so venimous, that the very touching of him is pestiferous; and presently causeth vomiting and over-turning of the stomacke, not without great daunger. They which be found in our sea, seeme to be a peece or lumpe of flesh without all forme and fashion, in colour onely resembling the land Hare. But with the Indians they be full as big, and resemble their Hare, onely it is more stiffe and hard. And verily they cannot possibly be taken there alive.' The Sea-hare is a type of large sea slug (marine gastropod), the largest species of which (*Aplysia vaccaria*) can grow to a length of 75 cm (30 in) and weigh 14 kg (31 lb).

SEA MONK

In his account of the fairies written in 1692, Robert Kirk said, somewhat in passing, 'There be fishes sometimes at sea resembling monks of late order in all their hoods and dresses' (Kirk, *Sec. Com.*, 49). The creature had been earlier described and illustrated by Guillaume Rondelet in 1554: 'In our time there has been caught in Norway, after a great tempest, an ocean monster, to which all who saw it incontinently affixed the name of monk: for it had a man's face, rude and ungraceful, with a bald, shining head; on the shoulders, something like a monk's hood; long winglets, instead of arms; the extremity of the body terminated in a tail' (quoted in Bassett, *Legends*, 206–7). See the similar, **Sea Bishop**.

SEA MONSTER

In the churning seas and crashing waves, sailors saw such sights as they could hardly describe: huge fins cutting through the brine, spouting jets of water reaching to the skies, bodies as big as islands, gaping maws of gigantic creatures. They found names for some – **Balaena**, **Physeter**, **Whirlepoole** and the rest – but for others no words seemed fitting, except 'sea monster'. In the *Enumu Elish*, the Babylonian Creation Myth dating from 2000 BCE, the universe is created out of the body of a sea monster called **Tiamat**. She would be the basis for the great sea monster of the Old Testament, **Leviathan**. To the ancients, the sea thus represented primordial chaos and evil. In the second half of the first century CE, Pliny the Elder (*Nat. Hist.*, 9.5) wrote that during the reign of the Emperor Tiberius (14 CE – 37 CE) 'in a certain Island upon the coast of the province of Lions, the sea after an eb, left upon the bare sands three hundred sea monsters and above, at one flote together, of a wonderfull varietie and bignesse, differing asunder. And there were no fewer found upon the coast of the Santones.' From a report Pliny ascribes to Turanius he

Iconismus II. Ponatur è regione pag. 401.

Fig. I. Triton.

Fig II.
Monstrum Marinum effigie Monachi.

Fig. III.
Vir Marinus
Episcopi habitu

Fig. IV
Satyrus Marinus

Sea Monsters (1662): I. Triton; II. Sea Monk; III. Sea Bishop; IV. Sea Satyr

also writes, 'That a monster was driven and cast upon the coast of Gades, betweene the two hindmost finnes whereof in the taile, were sixteene cubites: it had 122 teeth, whereof the biggest were a span or nine inches in measure, and the least halfe a foot.' Pliny also claimed that 'M. Scaurus among other strange and wonderfull sights that he exhibited to the people of Rome, to doe them pleasure in his Ædileship, shewed openly the bones of that sea monster, before which ladie Andromeda (by report) was cast to be devoured: which were brought to Rome from Ioppe, a town in Iudæa: and they caried in length fortie foot: deeper were the ribs than any Indian Elephant is high, and the tidge-bone a foot and halfe thicke.' Piny also described monstrous fish-like trees and wheels: 'In the Ocean of Gades, betweene Portugall and Andalusia, there is a monstrous fish to be seene like a mightie great tree, spreading abroad with so mightie armes, that in regard thereof onely, it is thought verily it never entred into the streights or narrow sea there by of Gibraltar. There shew themselves otherwhiles fishes made like two great wheeles, and therupon so they be called: framed distinctly with foure armes, repre-senting as many spokes: and with their eies they seeme to cover close the naves from one side to the other, wherein the

Sea Monsters (*c.*1544)

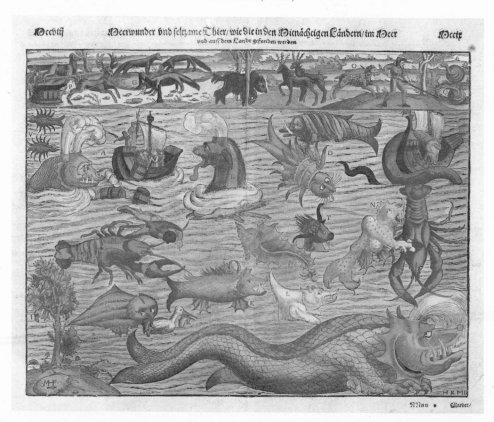

said spokes are fastened.' Not many years after Pliny, John of Patmos wrote the Book of Revelation featuring a **Beast of the Apocalypse** that rises out of the waves. In Ancient Greek and Roman mythology, a number of different monsters dwell in the sea. There were otherwise ordinary land animals who had extraordinarily developed fish-tails, such as the Aigikampos (sea-goat), **Hippocampus** (sea-horse), **Leocampus** (sea-lion), **Pardalocampus** (sea-leopard), and **Taurocampus** (sea-bull). Their names are based on *kampos*, meaning 'crooked'; see **Campe**.

SEA MOUSE

According to Icelandic folklore the *Chimæra monstrosa*, otherwise known as the 'sea mouse' or 'rabbit fish', is a sea monster to be reckoned with. They say it can swallow a boat whole, so large is its mouth; luckily it can most often be seen aproaching because so fast is its movement that it causes the sea to foam before it. It will chase a boat right up onto the shore and take any number of bullets before swimming off, unhurt, with the next tide. (Davidson, 'Folk-Lore', 328–9.)

SEA SERPENT

Also sea **Dragon**, the first and greatest sea dragon is the Babylonian **Tiamat**, dating from Sumerian myths of the third millennium BCE. There have, of course, been many more besides. In the first century CE, Pliny the Elder described a species that he also called the *Cornuta* on account of its horns: 'There is another Fish that putteth

forth hornes above the water in the sea, almost a foot and a halfe long, which thereupon tooke the name Cornuta. Againe, the sea Dragon if he be caught and let goe upon the sand, worketh himselfe an hollow trough with his snout incontinently, with wonderfull celeritie' (*Nat. Hist.*, 9.27). It is not entirely clear what sort of fish he was describing. Pliny (9.48) also talked about another marine creature that he called 'the dragon or spider of the sea' that was covered in poisoned spines; this was also Isidore of Seville's *draco marinus* with 'stingers on its arms, facing its tail' (*Etymologies*, XII.6.42). This has also been tranlsated as the weaver or weever fish, several species of the family *Trachinidae* known for their poisonous spines. The greater weever is known scientifically as *Trachinus draco*. Coming into the modern era, the evidence for sea dragons was apparently more plentiful than even in Babylonian times. In 1749 the *Gentleman's Magazine* carried news of a two-legged, hoofed and winged variety complete with illustration. It was apparently being toured round the counties by a fisherman who claimed to have lost the use of his arm due to a hideous bite wound when he captured it off the coast of Suffolk. A more astute observer, Edward Donovan, recognised it as a **Jenny Haniver** made out of the distorted skin of the angel shark (*Squalus squatina*). A similar monster appeared under the name of the **Extraordinary Fish** in 1861. A certain Albert C. Koch exhibited his considerably larger 'extinct marine serpent', the **Hydrarchos Sillimannii**, in New York in 1845, and afterwards in Dresden, Germany. But they were not all hoaxes; see **Halsydrus Pontoppidani**. (Dance, *Animal Fakes*, 59–63.)

SELEUCIDES

A locust-eating bird that appears out of nowhere at a time of need (which would be during a plague of locusts). According to Pliny (*Nat. Hist.*, 10.26): 'The birds called Seleucides, come to succour the inhabitants of the mountaine Casius, against the Locusts. For when they make great wast in their corne and other fruits, Iupiter at the instant praiers and supplications of the people, sendeth these foules among them to destroy the said Locusts. But from whence they come, or whether they goe againe, no man knoweth: for never are they seene but upon this occasion, namely, when there is such need of their helpe.' In 1800, Francois Marie Daudin gave the scientific name *Seleucidis melanoleucus* to the twelve-wired bird-of-paradise, the sole species of the Genus *Seleucidis*.

SELKIE

A seal that can assume human form, particularly found among the Orkneys. Seals were of two sorts: the common seal, or 'tang fish', that had no power of shape-shifting, and larger seals – great seal, rough seal, Greenland seal, crested seal and grey seal – that comprised the 'Selkie Folk'. Various accounts of them are given: that they are fallen angels whose crimes were too trivial to warrant hell; that they were once humans, punished for some offence and condemned to assume seal-form; or that they were seals, first, who could take human shape. (Dennison, 'Selkie', 171–7.)

SENMURV, SEE SIMURGH

SEPS

A fabulous snake with flesh-dissolving venom. This monster was first described by Lucan in the first century CE: 'Seps whose poisonous juice | Makes putrid flesh and frame'. He describes the effect on a certain Sabellus, a soldier in Cato's army, bitten in the Libyan desert: 'Clinging to his skin | A Seps with curving tooth, of little size, | He seized and tore away, and to the sands | Pierced with his javelin. Small the serpent's bulk; | None deals a death more horrible in form. | For swift the flesh dissolving round the wound | Bared the pale bone; swam all his limbs in blood; | Wasted the tissue of his calves and knees: | And all the muscles of his thighs were thawed | In black distilment, and file membrane sheath | Parted, that bound his vitals, which abroad | Flowed upon earth: yet seemed it not that all | His frame was loosed, for by the venomous drop | Were all the bands that held his muscles drawn | Down to a juice; the framework of his chest | Was bare, its cavity, and all the parts | Hid by the organs of life, that make the man [...]' (*Phars.*, 9, ll 848–9, 896–913). Isidore of Seville perpetuated the fearsome seps in the seventh century CE, writing: 'The deadly seps devours a man quickly so that he liquifies in its mouth' (*Etym.*, 12.4:17).

SERAPIS

Also *Sarapis*, a **Serpent** with a human head. Serapis was a multifunctional, composite god made up of the Egyptian Osorapis (Osiris plus **Apis**) and a host of Greek gods, including Zeus, Hades, Helios, Dionysos and Asklepios. Evidence of his worship dates from the time of Ptolemy I (305–285 BCE). (Shaw and Nicholson, *Dict. Anc. Eg.*, 261.)

SERPENT

It was the belief among the ancients that snakes were born of the marrow of a dead man's spine. This is attributed to Pythagoras in the sixth century BCE and Ovid mentions it in his *Metamorphoses* (15.389–90): 'There are those who believe that when the spine has putrified in the closed sepulchre, human marrow is changed into a snake'. Pliny the Elder had heard the story as well and gave an account of it in his *Natural History*, adding 'and well it may be so'. In the seventh century CE, Isidore of Seville repeated it, adding incongruously, 'It is said that a serpent does not dare to touch a nude person' (*Etym.*, 12.4.48). The Roman poet and political intriguer Lucan explained the poisonous nature of the snakes known in North Africa: 'Malevolent nature from [Medusa's] body first / Drew forth these noisome pests; first from her jaws | Issued the sibilant rattle of serpent tongues; | Clustered around her head the poisonous brood' (*Phars.*, 9, 739–41). A number of unusual, if not to say impossible, species have been described: the two-headed **Amphisbaena**; the

Aspis that can cover its ears; the horned **Cerastes**; the smoking **Chelydros**; the **Haemorrhois**; the flying **Jaculus**; the steamy-mouthed **Prester**; the flesh-dissolving **Seps**; the parthenogenic **Tirynthian Serpent**. The Greek historian Herodotus also described a flying variety (see below). The 'king of serpents' was the **Basilisk**. Various gods and goddesses were depicted with snake attributes, such as **Apep**, **Glycon**, **Heptet**, **Quetzalcoatl**, **Serapis** and **Uatchet**; see also **Uraeus**. In general there was a confusion with the **Dragon**.

SERPENT, WINGED

Writing in the fifth century BCE, Herodotus (*Hist.*) described certain 'winged serpents of Arabia' that he himself had seen: 'I went once to a certain place in Arabia, almost exactly opposite the city of Buto, to make inquiries concerning the winged serpents. On my arrival I saw the backbones and ribs of serpents in such numbers as it is impossible to describe: of the ribs there were a multitude of heaps, some great, some small, some middle-sized. The place where the bones lie is at the entrance of a narrow gorge between steep mountains, which there open upon a spacious plain communicating with the great plain of Egypt. The story goes, that with the spring the winged snakes come flying from Arabia towards Egypt, but are met in this gorge by the birds called ibises, who forbid their entrance and destroy them all. The Arabians assert, and the Egyptians also admit, that it is on account of this service thus rendered that the Egyptians hold the

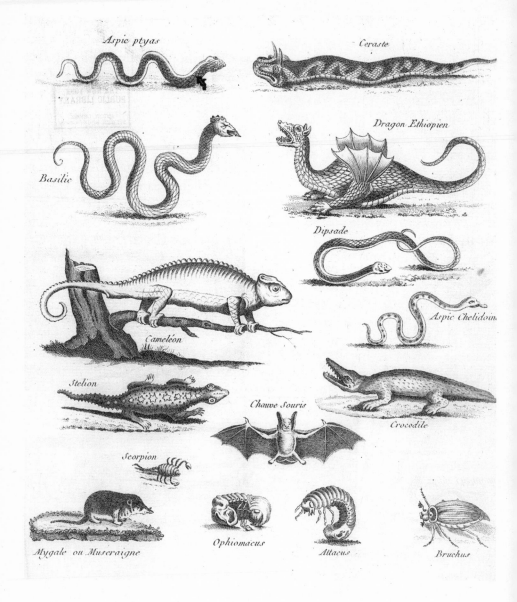

Serpents (1784): 'Aspic Ptyas'; 'Ceraste' (Cerastes); 'Basilic' (Basilisk); 'Dragon Ethiopien';
'Dipsade'; 'Aspic Chelidoine' (Chelydros); note also the 'Stelion' (Stellio)

ibis in so much reverence'. Buto was an ancient city in Egypt, now ruined, some 95 km (59 miles) to the east of Alexandria. Its patron deity was the snake-headed goddess **Uatchet** whose hieroglyph was the cobra. In the seventh century CE, Isidore of Seville (*Etym.*, 12.4.12) picked up the story in distorted form: 'In Arabia there are snakes with wings, which are called sirens. They are said not only to run from horses, but also to fly. Their virulence is such that death follows a bite as quickly as its pain.' The translator of Herodotus, George Rawlinson, suggests that these winged serpents were locusts.

SERQET

Also *Serket*, *Selqet*, the Ancient Egyptian scorpion-goddess. She stood with the forces of evil, but also assisted the dead in the afterlife and was connected with Isis. Isis in turn was connected with the scorpion, for it was said that the scorpion never stung the women who worshipped Isis at her temples. (Budge, *Gods*, 377–8.)

SET

An animal-headed god of Ancient Egypt. He was the son of Seb and Nut, brother of Osiris, Isis and Nephthys, as well as the latter's husband, and father of **Anubis**, according to some accounts. Associated or contrasted with Horus as the powers of light and darkness; later identified with **Typhon**. The etymology of the name is unclear, but the parallel with Horus, 'he who is above', would suggest 'he who is below'. Further, the animal head he bears is likewise mysterious: it is camel-like, but with long pointed ears, sometimes squared at the end; when depicted in full animal shape he has a four-legged, dog- or jackal-like body with a straight or erect tail divided in two at the end. No one knows what it is; it is simply called the 'set-animal', or *sha*. Certain other animals were also associated with Set: the fabulous **Akhekh**, the serpent **Apep** (Apophis), the ass, the crocodile, the hippopotamus, the pig and the turtle, among others. (Budge, *Gods*, 241ff.)

SEVEN WHISTLERS,

SEE WHISTLER

SHAMIR

According to Jewish legend, the Shamir was created by Yahweh at twilight on the sixth day. It is the size of a barley corn, but can cut even diamond. It was used to inscribe the names of the twelve tribes onto the stones set in the breastplate of the high priest. Because the law prohibited the use of iron tools, the Shamir was used to hew the stones of the Temple of Solomon. It was kept wrapped in wool inside a lead container filled with barley, and guarded in paradise until Solomon should need it. When the Temple was destroyed, the Shamir was found no more. See also **Tahash**. (Ginzberg, *Legends Jews*, I, 34.)

SHEDU

Akkadian, *šēdu*: a Babylonian demon in the form of a bull with a human head. Originally destructive, the shedu was later harnessed to protect buildings against other demons and human adversaries. The name is also found in magic texts. Its counterpart is the **Lamassu**. (Jastrow, *Rel. Bab.*, 263–4, 257, 290; Mackenzie, *Myth. Bab.*, 65.)

SHELLYCOAT

A Scottish water spirit, so named from its being covered in shells – Grimm connects it with the German *Schellenrock* ('skirt of bells') – apparently of humanoid shape and gigantic size, the clacking of his coat would put fear in the stoutest hearts. Widespread throughout Scotland, although two places are to be noted: the old house of Gorinberry on the river Hermitage in Liddesdale; and the old docks at Leith in Edinburgh had a Shellycoat Stane until it was removed at the building of the new docks. (Douglas, *Scot. Fairy*, 181–2; Campbell, *Hist. Leith*, 223; Grimm, *Teut. Myth.*, 479.)

SHOOPILTEE

The **Water-Horse** of the Shetlands, from *shelty* meaning a small horse. Like all of his kind, the Shoopiltee would try and lure people to mount him and then dash off into nearby waters and drown the rider. A glass of beer is given as an offering to this spirit. (Kohl, *Travels*, 200; Thorpe, *North. Myth.*, II, 22, 209.)

SIGGAHFOOPS

A bird resembling the corncrake seen by moonlight or in the wee small hours. It may be coaxed from cover 'by the recitation, in a firm voice, of verse'.

The bird was, of course, a spoof: someone called 'R.L.' sent it to *Scottish Field* and, strangely, they printed it.

SIMURGH

Also *Senmurv*, from Middle Persian (Pahlavi), *Sênô-mûrûv*; Avestan, *Saênô Mereghô*: a mythical bird, often translated as **Griffin** and described as 'dog-bird' or 'peacock-dragon'. It was believed to suckle its young and 'to be of three natures like the bat'. (West, *Pahlavi*, 112.) In the eleventh-century Iranian *Shahnameh* ('Epic of Kings') we read: 'Now there standeth far from the haunts of men the Mount Alberz, whose head toucheth the stars, and never had mortal foot been planted upon its crest. And upon it had the Simurgh, the bird of marvel, builded her nest. Of ebony and of sandal-wood did she build it, and twined it with aloes, so that it was like unto a king's house, and the evil sway of Saturn could not reach thereto' (Zimmern, *Epic*, 34–5).

SIREN

Usually referred to in the plural, the Sirens are first mentioned in Homer's *Odyssey*, dating from the eighth century BCE, but undoubtedly based on an older oral tradition. The story relates Odysseus' adventures as he attempts to return home after the siege of Troy (the subject of the *Iliad*). With the help of the god Hermes, he overcomes the sorceress Circe, who then tells him how to evade the sirens, amongst other things: '[...] our staunch ship swiftly neared the Sirens' island; a fair wind swept her on. On a sudden

Siren (Thirteenth Century)

the wind ceased; there came a breathless calm; Heaven hushed the waves. My comrades, rising, furled the sail, stowed it on board the hollow ship, then sitting at their oars whitened the water with polished blades. But I with my sharp sword cut a great cake of wax into small bits, which I then kneaded in my sturdy hands. Soon the wax warmed, forced by the powerful pressure and by the rays of the exalted Sun, the lord of all. Then one by one I stopped up the ears of my crew; and on the deck they bound me hand and foot, upright upon the mast-block, round which they wound the rope; and sitting down they smote the foaming water with their oars. But when we were as far away as one may call and driving swiftly onward, our speeding ship, as it drew near, did not escape the Sirens, and thus they lifted up their penetrating voice: "Come hither, come, Odysseus, whom all praise, great glory of the Achaeans! Bring in yor ship, and listen to our song. For none has ever passed us in a black-hulled ship till from our lips he heard the ecstatic song, then went by his way rejoicing and with larger knowledge. For we know all that on the plain of Troy Argives and Trojans suffered at the gods' behest; we know whatever happens on the bounteous earth." So spoke they, sending forth their glorious song, and my heart longed to listen. Knitting my brows, I signed [to] my men to set me free; but bending forward, on they rowed. And straightway Perimedes and Eurylochus arose and laid upon me still more cords and drew them tighter. Then, after

passing by, when we could hear no more the Sirens' voice nor any singing, quickly my trusty crew removed the wax with which I stopped their ears, and set me free from bondage.' Homer did not describe the sirens, but in later Greek art they are shown as birds with the heads of women, as on an Attic vase from Starnos dated around 490 BCE, now kept in the Biritsh Museum, where two sirens perch on overhanging rocks whilst a third swoops over Odysseus' ship.

In the first century CE, the Roman writer Pliny the Elder was more doubtful: 'As touching the birds Syrenes, I will never beleeve there be any such, let Dino the father of Clitarchus that renowned writer, say what he will: who avoucheth for a truth, that they be in India: and that with their singing they will bring folke asleepe, and then flie upon them and teare them in peeces' (*Nat. Hist.*, 10.49). For Isidore of Seville (*Etym.*, 12.4.12) the siren was a type of fantastic snake: 'In Arabia there are snakes with wings, which are called sirens. They are said not only to run from horses, but also to fly. Their virulence is such that death follows a bite as quickly as its pain.' This is undoubtedly derived from the winged serpent (see **Serpent, Winged**) described by Herodotus. Citings of the creature in works of natural history continued into the seventeenth and eighteenth centuries, but the avian characteristics disappeared to be replaced by aquatic ones. The Danish physician Thomas Bartholin, famed for his discovery of the human lymphatic system, classified a species of sea-animal, *homo marinus* or 'marine human', he called *Sirene*, with a lengthy discussion of cases and even an illustration of a bald-headed, human female-breasted, fish-like creature (*Hist. Anatom.*, 169ff). The Swedish naturalist Peter Artedi, considered the 'father of ichthyology', took this into his *Philosophia Ichthyologica* (1738): 'Two fins only on all the body, those on the chest. No finned tail. Head and neck and chest to the umbilicus have the human appearance' (81). His friend Carolus Linnaeus included it as one of the **Animalia Paradoxa** in the second edition of his *Systema Naturae* in 1740. Citing the earlier classifications, he was nonetheless sceptical:

'So long as it is not seen living, nor seen dead, nor faithfully and perfectly described, it is called into doubt' (66). See also **Mermaid**.

SIRRUSH, SEE MUSHUSSU

SJÖHÄSTEN, SEE BÄCKAHÄST

SKRIKER, SEE TRASH

SLEIPNIR

'Sleipnir is best, which Odin has; he has eight feet': from the Old Norse meaning 'the slipper', as in 'one who slips', suggesting speed rather than accident, Sleipnir is the grey eight-

Sleipnir (700–900 CE)

legged horse ridden by Odin, chief among the Norse gods. It is said that he had runes carved on his teeth (Grimm). Images of Sleipnir have been identified dating back to the eighth century CE – two carved stones on Gotland, Sweden – with written sources appearing in the twelfth and thirteenth century – e.g., Saxo Grammaticus's *Gesta Danorum* (twelfth century), the *Saga of Hervör and Heidrek* (thirteenth century) and particularly Snorri Sturluson's *Prose Edda* (c.1200). Sleipnir is the offspring of the god Loki (in the form of a mare) and the magical stallion **Svaðilfari**. In Iceland, the horseshoe-shaped depression of Asbyrgi is also known as 'Sleipnir's Hoofprint', the folk explanantion being that it was formed by one of Sleipnir's hooves touching the ground. Swedish farmers once left a sheaf of grain in their fields as fodder for Sleipnir (Grimm; Thorpe), although others cast doubt on this (Davidson). Symbolically, Sleipnir's eight legs convey the ability to gallop at great speed. He is frequently referred to as a superior animal in Norse writings. In the *Prose Edda* we read that 'Odin is the best of the Æsir, Sleipnir of horses' and 'this horse is the best among gods and men'. However, the duplication of the legs also suggests the ability to move between the two worlds of the living and the dead. When the god Baldr dreams of his own death, Sleipnir is the horse that carries Odin to Hel to look for answers. When Baldr is killed, Sleipnir is the horse that carries Odin's son Hermódr to Hel to look for his spirit. H.R. Ellis Davidson suggested that the number of Sleipnir's legs was a *kenning* (metaphor) for the funeral bier carried by four men (eight legs). And we should add that speed again is implied, for nothing is as fast as death: 'the dead ride fast' (Grimm). Odin himself is a god of the dead and led the spirits of the dead through the sky in the Wild Hunt. Sleipnir's grey coat also connects him with death: Kirsten Wolf notes that in two Norse sagas figures appearing in dreams portending death are mounted on greys; and grey can more generally mean supernatural power. Helmut Nickel makes the connection between Odin riding Sleipnir and the fourth horseman of the Apocalypse: Death riding a pale horse. The gallows were once called *horva Sleipnir*, 'Sleipnir of flax-ropes', because they would carry their rider to the land of the dead (see Hagen, 'Origin and Meaning', 61).

If we look at the beliefs of shamanic religion we find the **Abaasy** ('evil spirits') of the Yakut also having only one eye and riding on eight-legged horses, just like one-eyed Odin on Sleipnir. The Russian anthropologist L.P. Potapov argued that the *bura* ('ghost horses') painted on the drums of Siberian shamans of the Sajan-Altai region were intended to carry the shamans on their spiritual journeys; they were regularly red, white, black and grey (like Sleipnir), these being the colours of the four cardinal directions. Otto Höfler, as early as 1934, had already made the connection between Sleipnir and the shaman's spirit horse. An eight-legged elk is known among the Tungus shamans. (Davidson, *Pag.*

Scan., 125; Grimm, *Teut. Myth.*, II, 656, 844; Höfler, *Kult.*, 234ff; Nickel, 'And Behold', 179–83; Potapov, 'Pferdekult', 473–88; Sturluson, 'Gylfaginning', §15, 41, 42, 49, *Prose Edda*, 28, 53, 55, 72; Thorpe, North. Myth., 50; Wolf, 'Color Grey', 235.)

SNAKE, SEE SERPENT

SNAKESTONE

Neither snakes, nor always stones, snakestones are a curious blend of imaginative misidentification and magic. There are two sorts of such stones: a) the fossils of ammonites having a spiral form suggestive of a snake; and b) a stone said to come from the heads of snakes. Ammonites are particularly plentiful around Whitby in Yorkshire and local legends have grown up to explain them. In the seventh century CE, St Hilda turned all the snakes into stones to clear a building plot for her convent, thus accounting for the absence of snakes and the abundance of snakestones. The fact that the stones have no head is attributed to the curse of St Cuthbert. Local collectors and dealers, however, frequently 'restored' the stones by carving heads on them; the British Museum has a fine example. Of the second sort, the seventeenth-century traveller Jean-Baptiste Tavernier described seeing the snakestone whilst in India: 'which is nearly of the size of a double doubloon [a Spanish gold coin], some of them tending to an oval shape, being thick in the middle and becoming thin toward the edges. The Indians say that it grows on the heads of certain snakes' (*Travels*, II). He rather thought that they were of human manufacture. From other sources it appears that their composition was of the ashes of the roots of a type of plant mixed with clay, of charred bone, or, according to Kunz ('Madstones'), of tabasheer (a white substance found in the nodal joints of some bamboo species). The stones were supposed to be a remedy for snake bite and all kinds of venomous wounds, including those of poisoned arrows. (Bassett, 'Formed Stones', 2–17.)

SPHINX

A monster of Ancient Egyptian and Ancient Greek mythology: the word itself is Greek and thought to derive from σφίγγω, 'the throttler'. The Egyptian and Greek versions are distinguished by being usually male and wingless, and female and winged, respectively. The difference between the Egyptian and Greek forms led Herodotus (*Hist.*, 2.175) to call the Egyptian version ἀνδρόσφιγξ, 'anthrosphinx', or 'man-sphinx'; other forms were called criosphinx (ram-headed) and hierarcosphinx (falcon-headed). The Great Sphinx of Giza in Egypt is the oldest representation of the monster, as well as being the oldest monumental sculpture, dating from the Old Kingdom probably in the reign of the Pharaoh Chephren around 2558 to 2531 BCE. However, the original name by which it was known has not been preserved. In the New Kingdom (c.1550 BCE to c.1077 BCE) it was called *Hor-em-akhet*, 'Horus of the Horizon', Hellenised as Harmachis.

The Great Sphinx of Giza (1878)

Between the paws of the Great Sphinx there is a temple and in the temple there is a stela of red granite, and on the stela is inscribed the dream attributed to Thothmes IV that tells the tale of the sphinx. Purported to date from about 1400 BCE, it is undoubtedly later, but still wonderfully ancient. Part of the stela reads: 'Of stone was this mighty figure, hewn out of the living rock, his face the face of a man, stern and majestic, turned to the rising sun, his body the body of a lion; upon his brow is the death-dealing snake with head erect, ready to strike. Men call this figure Harmachis, and the Sphinx, and the Father of Terrors. Great and exalted is this figure of the God, resting in his chosen place; mighty is his power, for the Shadow of the Sun is upon him. The temples of Memphis and the temples of every town on both sides adore him, they stretch out their hands to him in adoration, sacrifices and libations are made before him' (Murray, *Anc. Egyp. Leg.*, 21). The 'deadly Sphinx' of the Ancient Greeks is first referred to in literature in Hesiod's *Theogony* of *c.*700 BCE as the offspring of **Typhon** and **Echidna**. Pseudo-Apollodorus says 'she had the face of a woman, the breast and feet and tail of a lion, and the wings of a bird.' This sphinx was supposed to have plagued the city of Thebes and could only be defeated by the answering of her riddle: 'what is that which has one voice and yet becomes four-footed and two-footed and three-footed?' All those who got it wrong were devoured by her, and Thebes lost many men this way until Oedipus correctly guessed the answer, thereby winning the kingdom and unknowingly marrying his mother. Pliny included the sphinx in his *Natural History* (8.30), describing it as having 'brown hair and two mammae on the breast'; it has been supposed that he was referring to some species of monkey, such as *Simia troglodytes* (the common chimpanzee). This was the interpretation of Isidore of Seville (*Etym.*, 12.2.31), writing in the seventh century CE: he gave the name sphinx to a species of ape. For other combinations of human and lion forms see the Stone Age **Löwenmensch**, lion-headed **Ugallu**, and **Urmahlilu**.

STELLIO

Also *stelliones*, from the Latin *stella*, 'star', the so-called 'star-lizard' named for its spotted skin. Pliny said of them that they 'cast their old coat, like as snakes doe, but when they have so done, they eat it up againe, and so prevent men of the helpe thereby for the said falling evill. He reporteth besides, that their stings and bitings in Greece be venomous and deadly: but in Sicilie harmelesse.' It supposedly lived on a diet of dew and spiders (11.31). Pliny added that 'stellio' was also used for a cheat or rogue: 'there being no creature, it is said, that resorts in its spite to more cunning devices for the deception of man; a circumstance owing to which, the name of "stellio" his been borrowed as a name of reproach' (30.27). This creature was known to the Greeks as *ascalabos* or *ascalabotes* from the myth of the transformation of Ascalabus, the boy turned into a lizard by Demeter

because of his rudeness (Ovid, *Met.* v.1.450). With such a poor reputation, it is surprising that the stellio also appears as an heraldic beast. John Bossewell in his *Works of Armorie* of 1572 says that the 'Stellio is a beaste like a lysard, having on his back spotts like starres' (Vinycomb, *Fict. Sym.*, n.p.). The supporters of the Ironmongers' Company of London are Stelliones. Known as the stellion or star lizard is a real lizard called *Stellagama stellio* by Linnaeus in 1758. A wondrous variation is also recorded: the 'stellione-serpent', which is a **Serpent** with a weasel's head. Such a creature appears on the coat of arms of the family Baume. This possibly comes from the strange recipe given by Pliny: the gall of a star-lizard beaten in water attracts weasels (29.22).

STOORWORM

A huge **Sea Serpent** of Scottish folklore, said to be so huge that it reached halfway round the world with a tongue hundreds of miles long and glowing red eyes. When it snapped its jaws, earth and sea shook. Its breath was lethal to all life. It could swallow islands and could certainly make a meal of Scotland; and one day that is what it intended to do. He was defeated by a young boy called Pattle, who sailed down its throat and poured hot coals onto its liver. The monster's death throes created various features of the northern landscape; it coiled itself up and finally died, becoming Iceland, and the coals still burn deep within its belly. Compare **Jörmungandr**, said to encompass the whole world. (Williams, *Fairy Tales*, 49–76.)

STRIX

Greek, στρίξ, 'screech-owl', plural *striges*; in antiquity, a creature believed to suck the blood of infants. The oldest account of the strix is traced back to the fourth century BCE, when the Greek writer Boio told the story of Polyphonte – she mates with a bear and produces cannibal sons – who is punished by the gods and turned into 'a strix that cries by night, without food or drink, with head below and tops of feet above, a harbinger of war and civil strife to men' (in Oliphant, 'Story Strix', 133–4). Ovid (*Fasti*, vi.131–42) gives the classic account: 'Large are their heads, fixed is their gaze, for plunder are their beaks adapted; on their wings a greyish colour, crooked talons are on their claws. By night they fly, and they seek the children unprotected by the nurse, and pollute their bodies, dragged from their cradles. With their beaks they are said to tear the entrails of the sucklings; and they have their maws distended with the blood which they have swallowed. "Striges," are they called; and the origin of this name is, the fact, that they are wont to screech in the dismal night.' He left open the question as to whether they were creatures of nature or enchantment; despite this, folk belief answered that the striges were witches in the shape of birds. In Ovid's *Metamorphoses*, the wings and flesh of a strix, along with the entrails of a werewolf and other supernatural unsavouries, are used by Medea in concocting a magic potion to rejuvenate Aeson, the father of Jason. In the early years of the first century CE,

Seneca the Younger wrote that the striges dwelt on the fringes of Tartarus, giving them the title of **Luctifer**, 'grief-bringing'. When talking of the strix, Pliny mentioned a belief (that he dismisses) concerning its coming in through the open window and 'ejecting milk from its teats upon the lips of infants', which seems to be entirely contrary to the general folk belief of the time (*Nat. Hist.*, 11.95). When talking specifically of the owl Pliny uses the terms Noctua, Bubo and Ulula, generally supposed to be the *Strix otus*, *Strix bubo* and the *Strix aluca* of Linnaeus, respectively. The Bubo is a 'monster of the night', according to Pliny (*Nat. Hist.*, 10.16) and the subject of much superstition: 'The Scritch-owle betokeneth alwaies some heavie newes, and is most execrable and accursed, and namely, in the presages of publick affaires: he keepeth ever in deserts: and loveth not onely such unpeopled places, but also that are horrible and hard of accesse. In summe, he is the verie monster of the night, neither crying nor singing out cleere, but uttering a certaine heavie grone of dolefull mourning. And therefore if he be seene to flie either within cities, or otherwise abroad in any place, it is not for good, but prognosticateth some fearfull misfortune. Howbeit I my selfe know, that hee hath sitten upon many houses of privat men, and yet no deadly accident followed thereupon. He never flieth directly at ease, as hee would himselfe, but evermore sidelong and byas, as if he were carried away with the wind or somewhat else. There fortuned one of them to enter the very secret sanctuarie within the Capitoll at Rome, in that yeere when Sext. Papellio Ister and L. Pedanius were Consuls: whereupon at the Nones of March, the citie of Rome that yeere made generall processions to appease the wrath of the gods, and was solemnly purged by sacrifices.' Pliny did not give any physical description and there are more than twenty species of screech-owls (Family *Strigidae*, Genus *Megascops*); the name is also sometimes given to the barn owl (*Tyto alba*). In any event, Oliphant prefers identification with the bat: Boio well described its manner of hanging upside down, and Pliny's reference to its mammalian suckling habits, instead of a wild fancy about a bird, are a more or less accurate allusion to the bat; but by then it was too late; the image of the screech-owl and the strix had become inseparably one. (Oliphant, 'Story Strix', 133–49.)

STYMPHALIDES

Greek Στυμφαλιδες, man-eating birds found near the Stymphalian lake in Arcadia. The oldest account of them is by Apollonius Rhodius (Argonautica 2 1052ff) in the third century BCE, recounting the sixth of the mythical Labours of Hercules: 'Herakles when he came to Arkadia, was unable with bow and arrow to drive away the birds that swam on the Stymphalian Lake. [...] What he did was to take his stand on a height and make a din by shaking a bronze rattle; and the astounded birds flew off into the distance screeching for fear'. It was said that they had been reared by the war-god Ares (Serv. *ad Aen.* viii. 300) and that their wings were made of brass and could fire off feathers like arrows, and their beaks could pierce armour (Apollodorus, *Library*, ii. 5. § 2; Pausanius, *Desc. Gr.*, 8.22.4; Hyginus, *Hygini Fabulae 30; Schol. ad Apollon. Rhod.* ii. 1053). According to another version, they were not birds, but the women and daughters of Stymphalus and Ornis, who were murdered by Hercules because he thought they were rude to him (Mnaseas in *Schol. ad Apollon. Rhod.* ii. 1054).

SUHURMASU

Akkadian, also written *suhumāšu*, from the original Sumerian *suĝur-máš*, 'goat-fish', or literally 'carp-goat': a Mesopotamian monster spawned by the sea-dragon **Tiamat**. The creature was enlisted in her army of eleven evil monsters that she sent against the god Marduk, as told in the Babylonian Creation Myth, the *Enuma Elish*. Suhurmasu is also the name for the zodiacal constellation we know as Capricorn. (Green, 'Note Ass. "Goat-Fish"', 25–30.)

SVADILFARI

Meaning 'unlucky traveller' in Old Norse, Svaðilfari sired **Sleipnir** on Loki in the form of a mare. His story is told in the thirteenth-century *Prose Edda*. The Æsir, the high gods of the North, in the first days of their rule, shortly after having forged Midgard, were approached by a builder (a giant) who offered to construct a citadel for them in just three seasons that would protect them against the other giants. In return he wanted the goddess Freyja, the sun and moon. After much deliberation, the gods agreed, on Loki's advice and on condition that he build it in one winter without the aid of another man, although they consented to let him have the help of his stallion, Svaðilfari; and so he started work. However, the gods were astonished to see what the horse could achieve. By the time there were only three days of winter left, the citadel was almost complete and every indication was given that it would be finished within the allotted time. The gods had no intention of giving up Freyja, or the sun and the moon, so, laying the blame at Loki's feet they threatened him with violence unless he could find a way to break the contract. Loki turned himself into a mare on heat and led Svaðilfari away. Furious at being tricked, the builder turned to confront the gods, but Thor had returned from afar and now brought down his hammer, Mjollnir, on the giant's skull, sending him straight away down into Niflheim: 'But Loki had such dealings with Svadilfari, that somewhat later he gave birth to a foal, which was gray and had eight feet; and this horse is the best among gods and men'. (Sturluson, 'Gylfaginning', §42, *Prose Edda*, 53–5.)

T

TACHARAN

Also *Tachran*, *Tacharain*. Described as a diminutive form of **Kelpie**. There are several places named after it: 'Clachan an Tacharain', Islay; the Ford of the kelpie, Islay; and 'Poll an Tacharain', the Pool of the Kelpie, Perthshire. (Carmichael, *Carm. Gad.*, II, 367; Watson, 'High. Myth.', 68.)

TAHASH

According to Jewish legend, this creature was created by Yahweh with the sole purpose of using its skin for the Tabernacle. It is only briefly described: 'It had a horn on its forehead, was gaily coloured like the turkey-cock, and belonged to the class of clean animals'. (Ginzberg, *Legends Jews*, I, 34.)

TANGIE

Also *Tangi*, a **Water-Horse** of Shetland; the name comes from *tang*, 'seaweed', with which this creature is said to be covered. The Tangie is sometimes, and mostly unsuccessfully, differentiated as a fresh-water variant of the sea-dwelling **Njogel**, and the other way around. The notable fact is that Tangie is black, whilst the Njogel is generally grey. A black horse who would graze the clifftop paths by night and if anyone should unwisely mount him, he would charge off the nearest cliff, taking his rider with him in a mysterious flash of blue light. Another curious feature was that he was said to have cloven hooves. Teit conjectured that Tangi was actually a personal name or nickname as it was always referred to as just 'Tangi' and never 'the Tangi'. A certain infamous person called Black Eric was once said to be in league with the Devil and that Tangie was a demon at his command, carrying him from the top of Fitful Cliff to his cave: the sailors had seen the blue lights flashing up and down the rockface. See **Nicker**. (Eric, *Rur. Rhym.*, 62; Dyer, *Folk-Lore*, n.p.; Stewart, *Shet. Fire.*, 117–40; Teit, 'Water-Beings', 180–201.)

TANIWHA

Also *tanewa*, the Maori name for a **Sea Monster** or gigantic fish that was reputed to swallow the natives. It was also believed to live in rivers and pools. Its huge head was described as resembling that of a bird; it had a scaly neck, some 1.8 m (6 ft) in circumference; it had two short powerful legs; fins projected from its body, which ended in a tail like that of a grey duck. See also **Bunyip**. (Morris, *Austral English*, 457.)

TANYSIPTERA NYMPHA

The genus *Tanysiptera*, the paradise kingfishers of Australasia, acquired a new member in 1841 when the famous ornithologist George Robert Gray, FRS, described an odd **Jenny Haniver** bought in Paris. It was cunningly contrived from at least five different birds: 'on examining the specimen carefully, some doubt arose as to the fact, whether it had not been, in part, at least, artfully dressed in its present showy plumage [...] the wings were decidely those of an *Alcedo Senegalensis* [woodland kingfisher] [...] A further examination proved that the downy feathers (which are of a rich salmon colour) of the uropygium, and most of those beneath the body, had been taken from a specimen of *Trogon Duvaucelii* [scarlet-rumped trogon]; while on the sides these latter feathers are mixed with others from the neck of a young bird of *Alcedo leucocephala* [grey-headed kingfisher] [...] it may reasonably be concluded that the feet by which the specimen is attached to its perch, have also been added to complete it' ('Remarks', 237–8). However, amongst the assemblage, Gray spotted feathers that appeared to be genuinely unique. He named this *Tanysiptera nympha* and subsequent discoveries confirmed the existence of this new species. The original is kept in the British Museum.

TARANDUS

A large colour-changing ox-sized stag-headed herbivore of Central Eurasia, according to Pliny the Elder: 'In Scythia there is a beast called Tarandus, which chaungeth likewise colour as the Chamæleon. [...] The Tarandus is as bigge as an oxe, with an head not unlike to a stagges, but that it is greater, namely, carrying braunched hornes: cloven hoofed, and his haire as deepe as is the Beares. The hide of his backe is so tough and hard, that thereof they make brest-plates. He taketh the colour of all trees, shrubs, plants, flowers, and places wherein he lieth when he retireth for feare; and therefore seldome is he caught. But when he list to looke like himselfe and be in his owne colour, he resembleth an Asse. To conclude, straunge it is that the bare bodies of a beast should alter into so many colours: but much more straunge it is and wonderfull, that the haire also should chaunge' (*Nat. Hist.*, 8.52). Pliny related it to other supposedly hair-changing animals, the **Lycaon** and the **Thos**. The reindeer is known by the scientific name of *Rangifer tarandus*.

TARANTULA SEA SPIDER

In 1829, a certain M.C.G. of Margate wrote to the *Magazine of Natural History* with the news that 'one day last month, as a fisherman on this coast was dragging up his net, he found an intruder had entangled itself in the meshes of it; which said intruder has since been exhibited under the denomination of a "Tarantula Sea Spider".' It had eight, unjointed legs, two eyes, which, because it had no head, were on the back of the thorax; the mouth was beneath the abdomen and held a spiral tongue that was 'nearly half a yard long' ending 'with a pair of forceps'; it had a large spinner and weighed in all

5¼ pounds (2 kg). When alive it could supposedly 'run with the velocity of a race horse, and changed colour every instant'. The owner, a Mr Murray, intended to take the spider to London and exhibit it at the Bazaar in Portman Street North.

TARASQUE

A monster of Tarascon in Provence, France. It had the head of a lion and the tail of a **Dragon**. A mysterious Christian saint – St Martha – is said to have saved the people of Tarascon from the ravages of this fearsome monster. She reputedly subdued it with only a cross and a dash of holy water, and, leading it back into town, the people stoned it to death. Two annual processions – *La Fête de la Tarasque* on the last Sunday in June and St Martha's Day on 29 July – were instituted in 1469 to mark the occasion. (Spicer, *Festivals*, ch. 3.)

TARBH-UISGE

The Scottish 'water-bull', from the Gaelic; synonymous with *tarbh-baoidhre*. It was said to be a harmless creature, living in the remote tarns in the hills. It only appeared at night and might come down to graze with ordinary cattle. In the Highlands they say that calves born with short ears or ears that look as though they have been cut are the offspring of the *tarbh-uisge*: for the water-bull has no ears at all, and the calves are called 'knife-eared' or 'half-eared'. Should anyone be so minded, they can only be killed with silver: in the old days, a farmer might load his shotgun with sixpences to this purpose (MacGregor, *Peat-Fire Flame*,

79; Mackinlay, *Folklore*, 178). For the Ancient Greek version see **Taurocampus**.

TATZELWURM

German, from *Tatzen*, 'claws', and *Wurm*, 'worm': the clawed **Worm** or **Dragon** of the German-speaking alpine districts of southern Germany, Switzerland and Austria. Magical powers were said to reside in its claws, which were something like the wishing-hat of Fortunatus. It is said that large rewards have been offered for its capture, although, and perhaps of course, it has never been found. Notwithstanding that fact, legend has it that the skeleton of such a beast was once suspended from the ceiling in the castle of Marquartstein; and an ancient votive tablet was formerly preserved at Unken in Austria 'on which was represented the death of a peasant, the result of his horror at meeting two such creatures, which were depicted in the form attributed to them by the imagination of a village painter'. A staff made from the wood of the ash was said to ward off all serpents in these parts. Other terms for it include *Stollenwurm* and *Springwurm*. It is also equated with the Bergstutz, the 'Stag of the Mountain'. In 1915, Porsche built a super-tractor capable of pulling twenty trailers and called it the Tatzelwurm. (Doblhoff, 'Altes und Neues', 142–67; Schmid, *Bav. High.*, 178–9.)

TAUROCAMPUS

The sea-bull of Ancient Greek and Roman mythology: from the Greek, *tauro-*, 'bull', and *kampos*, 'crooked', usually Latinised as *taurocampus*. A Roman mosiac from the first or second century CE shows a female figure being carried off on the back of a sea-bull. She may be a **Nereid**, or Europa being abducted by Zeus in animal form. (Gaziantep Arch. Mus.)

THOS

The naked wolf, according to Pliny: 'As for the Thos (which are a kind of wolves somewhat longer than the other common-wolves, and shorter legged, quicke and swift in leaping, living altogether of the venison that they hunt and take, without doing any harme at all to men) they may be said, not so much to chaunge their hew, as their habite and apparell: for all winter time they be shag-haired, but in summer bare and naked' (*Nat. Hist.*, 8.52). Pliny grouped them with the **Lycaon** and **Tarandus**.

THOTH

The ibis-headed god of knowledge and writing in Ancient Egyptian mythology, sometimes, and especially earlier, also represented as a baboon. He was associated with the moon: his head-dress was crowned with a disc and crescent representing the phases of the moon; it is also conjectured that the long curving beak of the ibis was seen as a lunar symbol, as well as possibly representing the reed pen. He recorded the verdict at the weighing of the souls of the dead. (Shaw and Nicholson, *Dict. Anc. Eg.*, 268–9.)

THUNDER BIRD

A widespread avian deity of the Native Americans: called *Tootooch* in British Columbia, he stands upon the top of the totem pole of the Raven Clan; he is *Wuchowsen*, the Great Wind Bird of the Algonquin in New England; he is *Hurakan* among the people of the Gulf of Mexico. A creator god who offers protection, peace and plenty. The darting glance of his bright eye is the lightning. When he flaps his wings, the storm (hurricane) is unleashed, driving evil spirits to the far corners of the world. Compare the Norse **Hrae-Svelgr**. (Leland, *Algonquin*, 111–13; Stratton, *Storm God*, 1–7; Webster, *Thunder*, 20–1.)

TIAMAT

Babylonian primordial deity; chaos, mother of dragons and monsters; the personification of the sea. Although usually described as a **Dragon** herself, the earliest written account of her, the Babylonian creation story known as the *Enuma Elish*, does not specify her shape or form. Other Mesopotamian myths do, however, name Tiamat as a dragon or **Serpent**; and representations in sculpture and seals show a **Sea Monster** with the head of a lion or **Griffin**, wings, claws and a tail. A neo-Assyrian cylinder seal in the British Museum (BM 138129), dating from 800 to 600 BCE and showing an archer aiming an arrow at a crested serpent, is usually interpreted as Marduck fighting Tiamat. An older Neo-Assyrian cylinder seal (BM 89589) from 900 to 750 BCE shows a similar scene with a larger horned serpent, apparently with forelegs, and an archer armed with a thunderbolt, along with other figures; again the serpent is considered to be

Tiamat. According to the *Enuma Elish*, after her fellow chaos-god, Apsu, is killed by a rebellious new order of gods, she gives birth to an army to defeat them: 'she spawned huge serpents, | Sharp of tooth, pitiless in attack. | She filled their bodies with venom instead of blood. | Grim, monstrous serpents, arrayed in terror, | She decked them with brightness, she fashioned them in exalted forms, | So that fright and horror might overcome him that looked upon them, | So that their bodies might rear up, and no man resist their attack, | She set up the Viper, and the Snake, and the god Lakhamu, | The Whirlwind, the ravening Dog, the Scorpion-man, | The mighty Storm-wind, the Fish-man, the horned Beast [bull-man] | They carried the Weapon which spared not, nor flinched from the battle' (Budge, First tablet, lines 114–23). These nine plus the weapon (perhaps the thunderbolt) and the god Kingu (Tiamat's first-born son and husband), to whom Tiamat had given the Tablets of Destiny to wear as a breastplate, comprise the eleven allies of Tiamat. Despite this formidable force, Tiamat is defeated in battle by the winged hero-god Marduk and he creates the physical universe out of her body: 'He slit Tiâmat open like a flat (?) fish [cut into] two pieces, | The one half he raised up and shaded the heavens therewith, | He pulled the bolt, he posted a guard, | He ordered them not to let her water escape.' Fragments of the *Enuma Elish* were rediscovered by Austen Henry Layard during excavations in the ruins of the ancient city of Nineveh in the years 1848 to 1876.

It is written in cuneiform on seven clay tablets and consists of about a thousand lines. This version dates from about the seventh century BCE, although it is generally considered to be based on earlier Sumerian stories possibly going as far back as 2000 BCE. Tiamat and her eleven allies are interpreted as the signs of the Zodiac; indeed, one of the later acts of Marduk is to set the stars of the Zodiac in the heavens, but they are not specifically related to Tiamat and the eleven. It is more probable that Tiamat represented what we call the Milky Way, but she is also connected to the constellation of Hydra. The Babylonian Creation Myth is the prototype of the Old Testament version; in the Apocryphal Book of Enoch, the serpent is named as Tabaet (pronounced *tavaet*), seen as a corruption of Tiamat influenced by the story of the creature **Oannes**. She is also connected with the Old Testament **Leviathan** and the New Testament **Beast of the Apocalypse**. The names of the monsters created by Tiamat are Basmu ('venomous snake'), **Girtablilu** ('scorpion-man'), **Kulullu** ('fish-man'), **Kusarikku** ('bull-man'), Musmahha (the horned serpent), **Ugallu** (a lion-headed monster), **Uridimmu** ('rabid dog/lion'), Usumgallu ('great dragon') – all of Tiamat's demon brood became beneficent apotropaic demons used to ward off evil. (Barton, 'Tiamat', 1–27; Budge, *Bab. Leg. Cr.*, 114–23; King, *Sev. Tab. Cr.*, 116–17.)

TIRYNTHIAN SERPENT

A type of parthenogenic **Serpent** of Greece described by Pliny (*Nat. Hist.*,

8.84): 'certaine Serpents in Tirinthe, which are supposed to breed of themselves out of the very earth.' Pliny's translator meant Tiryns in Greece, called *Tirynthus* in Latin, or *Tirynthe* in French; no zoologist has ever found one of these snakes.

TRAGOPANADES

Also *tragopomones*, from *tragus*, 'goat' and the name of the Greek god Pan: an iron-coloured bird of great size – 'many men affirm to bee greater than the Ægle,' said Pliny – with ram's horns on either side of its red-plumed head. He was drawing on Pomponius Mela's earlier brief mention of 'wonderful birds, such as *tragopomones* which have horns'. Pliny (*Nat. Hist.*, 10.60) classed this one with the **Pegasus** and **Griffin**, as mere fable, but today it is seen as only an exaggerated description of the tropical hornbill (*Bucerotidae*), a family of birds characterised by their long downward curving bills, with some species having additional horny protuberances (called casques) on top. Aldrovandi (*Ornithologia*, 12.20.10.7) saw one of the beaks that had been brought to Europe and termed the bird *Rhinoceros Avis*. Their modern scientific name comes from *buceros*, Greek for 'cow's horn'. There is also a type of 'horned pheasant' of the genus *Tragopans*, so named because of the fleshy horns on either side of the head that become erect during courtship displays. Like Pliny's *tragopanades*, they generally have a reddish plumage. They are found along the Himalayas and in other parts of South Asia and the Far East.

TRASH

A death omen in the shape of a dog reported from Burnley in Lancashire, possibly derived from *thurse* (giant, demon), or onomatopoeic, like 'splash'; also known as *Skriker*. According to Hardwick (*Traditions*, 173–4): 'The appearance of this sprite is considered a certain death-sign, and has obtained the local names of "Trash" or "Skriker". He generally appears to one of the family from which death is about to select his victim, and is more or less visible according to the distance of the event. I have met with persons to whom the barghaist [**Barghest**]has assumed the form of a white cow or a horse; but on most occasions "Trash" is described as having the appearance of a large dog, with very broad feet, shaggy hair, drooping ears, and "eyes as large as saucers". When walking, his feet make a loud splashing noise, like old shoes in a miry road, and hence the name of "Trash". The appellation, "Skriker", has reference to the screams uttered by the sprite, which are frequently heard when the animal is invisible. When followed by any individual, he begins to walk backwards, with his eyes fixed full on his pursuer, and vanishes on the slightest momentary inattention. Occasionally he plunges into a pool of water, and at other times he sinks at the feet of the person to whom he appears with a loud splashing noise, as if a heavy stone was thrown into the miry road. Some are reported to have attempted to strike him with any weapon they had at hand, but there was no substance present to receive the blows, although the Skriker kept his ground. He is said to frequent the neighbourhood of Burnley at present, and is mostly seen in Godly Lane and about the Parochial Church; but he by no means confines his visits to the churchyard, as similar sprites are said to do in other parts of England and Wales.' Hardwick connects this with the legend of Odin's stray hound.

TRITON

Ancient Greek sea god, later reduced to the Roman merman. Hesiod (*Theog.* 901): 'And of Amphitrite and the loud-roaring Earth-Shaker was born great, wide-ruling Triton, and he owns the depths of the sea, living with his dear mother and the lord his father in their golden house, an awful god.' According to Pliny (*Nat. Hist.*, 9.5): 'In the time that Tiberius was Emperour, there came unto him an Embassador from Ulyssipon, sent of purpose to make relation, That upon their sea coast there was discovered within a certain hole, a certain sea goblin, called Triton, sounding a shell like a Trumpet or Cornet: & that he was in forme and shape like those that are commonly painted for Tritons.' He goes on: 'I am able to bring forth for mine authors divers knights of Rome, right worshipfull persons and of good credite, who testifie that in the coast of the Spanish Ocean neere unto Gades, they have seene a Mere-man, in every respect resembling a man as perfectly in all parts of the bodie as might bee. And they report moreover, that in the night season he would come out of the sea abourd their ships: but look upon what part soever he setled, he waied the same downe, and if he rested and continued there any long time, he would sinke it cleane.' In the second century CE, the geographer Pausanius (*Desc. Gr.*, 9.21.1) claimed to have seen one for himself: 'I saw another Triton among the curiosities at Rome, less in size than the one at Tanagra. The Tritons have the following appearance. On their heads they grow hair like that of marsh frogs not only in colour, but also in the impossibility of separating one hair from another. The rest of their body is rough with fine scales just as is the shark. Under their ears they have gills and a man's nose; but the mouth is broader and the teeth are those of a beast. Their eyes seem to me blue, and they have hands, fingers, and nails like the shells of the murex. Under the breast and belly is a tail like a dolphin's instead of feet.' A sub-species with horse's feet instead of arms was known as an **Ichthyocentaur**. See also **Mermaid**.

TURTLE, GIANT

According to Pliny (*Nat. Hist.*, 9.10): 'There be found Tortoises in the Indian sea so great, that one only shell of them is sufficient for the roufe of a dwelling house. And among the Islands principally in the red sea, they use Tortoise shells ordinarily for boats and wherries upon the water.' The translator used the word tortoise where we would ordinarily understand turtle nowadays. The largest species of such animals was the Late Cretaceous era *Archelon ischyros* from about 80 million years ago, which has been measured at almost 5 m (over 15 ft) long. The largest turtle today, the Arrau turtle of South America, can reach a length of one metre.

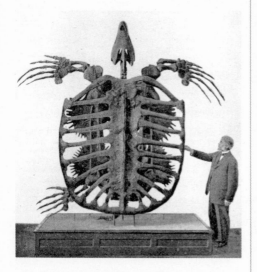

Giant Turtle (*Archelon ischyros*) (1901)

TYPHON

Ancient Greek Τυφῶν, Typhon, also *Typhaon*, *Typhoeus*: a monstrous being of Ancient Greek mythology first referred to in Homer's *Iliad* (2.782) in the eighth century BCE. Homer said little about what he called Typhoeus, locating him in an unknown country called Arimi. In his *Theogony* (ll. 306–32) of *c*.700 BCE, Hesiod differentiated between Typhoeus and Typhaon. Of Typhoeus he says: 'Strength was with his hands in all that he did and the feet of the strong god were untiring. From his shoulders grew an hundred heads of a snake, a fearful dragon, with dark, flickering tongues, and from under the brows of his eyes in his marvellous heads flashed fire, and fire burned

from his heads as he glared. And there were voices in all his dreadful heads which uttered every kind of sound unspeakable; for at one time they made sounds such that the gods understood, but at another, the noise of a bull bellowing aloud in proud ungovernable fury; and at another, the sound of a lion, relentless of heart; and at another, sounds like whelps, wonderful to hear; and again, at another, he would hiss, so that the high mountains re-echoed.' Born of Gaia and Tartarus, Typhoeus rises to challenge the supremacy of Zeus. After a terrible battle, Zeus casts Typhoeus into the lowest hell (also called Tartarus) under Mount Aetna. This is vividly depicted on a Greek vase from around 550 BCE (now in the Staatliche Antikensammlungen, Munich), showing Zeus hurling thunderbolts at a winged monster with human head and intertwined snake-tails for legs. Even after defeat, Typhoeus was the source of all the ill winds, giving him the epithet 'father of the Harpies' and a lingering currency in the word typhoon (etymologically derived from the Chinese *tai fung*). In Aristophanes' *Frogs* (845) written in 405 BCE, one of the characters calls for a black sheep to be sacrificed to avert a typhoon. By the first century CE, Pliny the Elder says that a certain type of storm like a hurricane (or typhoon) is called Typhon (*Nat. Hist.*, 2.49). Typhaon, called by Hesiod 'the terrible, outrageous and lawless', mated with the snake-woman **Echidna** to produce the two-headed dog **Orthus**, the fifty-headed **Cerberus**, the **Lernæan Hydra**,

Typhon with Harpies (Seventeenth Century)

and **Chimæra**. Smith argues that Hesiod depicted Typhaon as the son of Typhoeus, but this is not evident in the text and the differentiation between the two as separate beings is probably not correct. Herodotus, writing in the fifth century BCE, identified Typhon with the Egyptian god **Set** and said he was buried under Lake Serbonis (nowadays Lake Bardawil). Later writers introduced a number of different themes and locations. For example, Pseudo-Apollodorus writing in the first or second century CE described him thus: 'In size and strength he surpassed all the offspring of Earth. As far as the thighs he was of human shape and of such prodigious bulk that he out-topped all the mountains, and his head often brushed the stars. One of his hands reached out to the west and the

other to the east, and from them projected a hundred dragons' heads. From the thighs downward he had huge coils of vipers, which when drawn out, reached to his very head and emitted a loud hissing. His body was all winged: unkempt hair streamed on the wind from his head and cheeks; and fire flashed from his eyes. Such and so great was Typhon when, hurling kindled rocks, he made for the very heaven with hissings and shouts, spouting a great jet of fire from his mouth.' His account of the battle between Zeus and Typhon also mentions 'the she-dragon Delphyne, who was a half-bestial maiden'. For other dragon-like monsters defeated by hero-gods, see **Python** and the Babylonian **Tiamat**; and comparison can be made to the Christian **Beast of the Apocalypse**.

U

UATCHET

Alternatively, *Wadjet*: a **Serpent**-headed goddess of the Ancient Egyptians. She was a major deity associated with the **Uraeus** and had a cultic centre at Per-Uatchet (known as Buto by the Greeks). She was connected with other goddesses in the form Mut-Uatchet-Bast and later absorbed into Isis. See also **Heptet**. (Budge, *Gods*, 24, 92, 93, 440.)

UGALLU

Ugallu is Akkadian, meaning, 'big weather beast', but from its form is usually called the 'great lion' or 'lion demon': a Babylonian lion-headed, eagle-clawed monster spawned by **Tiamat** to serve in her army of evil creatures. In earlier depictions, Ugallu is sometimes also shown with human feet, but from the Old Babylonian period the avian talons become dominant; there is some evidence that he may also have been depicted with donkey's ears. The earliest literary reference is in the Babylonian Creation Myth, the *Enuma Elish*, believed to

date back to Sumerian stories as old as 2000 BCE. Ugallu appears in glyptic art from the Akkadian period onwards; often found in connection with another of Tiamat's monstrous progeny, the **Lahmu**. Ugallu, sometimes identified as a type, sometimes as a named creature, is usually shown with a raised dagger in one hand and a war-club in the other and guarded doorways, as in the North Palace at Nineveh, for example. See also the 'lion-man', **Urmahlilu**; the god Lahmu also had lion characteristics. (Green, 'Neo-Ass. Apo. Fig.', 87–96; Green, 'Note Lion-Dem.', 167–8; Ornan, 'Exp. Dem.', 83–92.)

UNICORN

From Latin, *uni-*, 'one', *cornu*, 'horn'. The legend of the unicorn begins with Ctesias (*Indica*, 25, 33), a Greek physician at the court of the Persian King Darius in the late fifth century BCE: 'Among the Indians, he proceeds, there are wild asses as large as horses, some being even larger. Their head is of a dark red colour, their eyes blue, and the rest of their body white. They have a horn on their forehead, a cubit in length [the filings of this horn, if given in a potion, are an antidote to poisonous drugs]. This horn for about two palm-breadths upwards from the base is of the purest white, where it tapers to a sharp point of a flaming crimson, and, in the middle, is black. These horns are made into drinking cups, and such as drink from them are attacked neither by convulsions nor by the sacred disease [epilepsy]. Nay, they are not even affected by poisons, if either before or after swallowing them they drink from these cups wine, water, or anything else. While other asses moreover, whether wild or tame, and indeed all other solid-hoofed animals have neither huckle-bones [ankle-bones], nor gall in the liver, these one-horned asses have both. Their huckle-bone is the most beautiful of all I have ever seen, and is, in appearance and size, like that of the ox. It is as heavy as lead, and of the colour of cinnabar both on the surface, and all throughout; It is exceedingly fleet and strong, and no creature that pursues it, not even the horse, can overtake it.' Ctesias also described the particular problems of trying to catch unicorns: 'On first starting it scampers off somewhat leisurely, but the longer it runs, it gallops faster and faster till the pace becomes most furious.' These animals therefore can only be caught at one particular time – that is when they lead out their little foals to the pastures in which they roam. They are then hemmed in on all sides by a vast number of hunters mounted on horseback, and being unwilling to escape while leaving their young to perish, stand their ground and fight, and by butting with their horns and kicking and biting kill many horses and men. But they are in the end taken, pierced to death with arrows and spears, for to take them alive is in no way possible. Their flesh being bitter is unfit for food, and they are hunted merely for the sake of their horns and their huckle-bones' (*Indica*, 26–7). Aristotle (384–322 BCE) included Ctesias' Indian ass in his influential *Historia Animalium* (II.2.8 and VI.36), adding a single horned **Oryx**, a type of large antelope normally having two horns. Into the first century CE, Pliny's unicorn takes on new features: 'a very fierce animal called the monoceros [unicorn], which has the head of the stag, the feet of the elephant, and the tail of the boar, while the rest of the body is like that of the horse; it makes a deep lowing noise, and has a single black horn, which projects from the middle of its forehead, two cubits in length. This animal, it is said, cannot be taken alive' (*Nat. Hist.*, 8.31, trans. Bostock). The unicorn is mentioned three times in the Old Testament, even God is likened to the unicorn (Numbers), at least in the King James Version. The Hebrew **Re'em** became *monoceros* in Greek; unicorn in English. According to the Jewish *Talmud*, Adam sacrificed a unicorn to God, for the same reason. Modern translations usually give 'wild ox', as it seems more plausible that the now extinct auroch was intended.

These ancient accounts were given a new lease of life when medieval Europeans started to explore the further reaches of the known world. Marco Polo's account of the unicorns of Sumatra: 'There are wild elephants in the country, and numerous unicorns, which are very nearly as big.

Unicorn (Medieval)

They have hair like that of a buffalo, feet like those of an elephant, and a horn in the middle of the forehead, which is black and very thick. They do no mischief, however, with the horn, but with the tongue alone; for this is covered all over with long and strong prickles [and when savage with any one they crush him under their knees and then rasp him with their tongue]. The head resembles that of a wild boar, and they carry it ever bent towards the ground. They delight much to abide in mire and mud. 'Tis a passing ugly beast to look upon, and is not in the least like that which our stories tell of as being caught in the lap of a virgin; in fact, 'tis altogether different from what we fancied' (*Travels*, II, 3.9). Marco Polo was in fact describing the rhinoceros. But his was not the only sighting: Bernard of Breydenbach (*Peregrinatio in Terram Sanctum*, Mainz 1486) on a pilgrimage from Mainz in Germany to the Holy Land saw a unicorn in Sinai. The animal continued to be included in works of nautral history, such as the famous Swiss encyclopedist Conrad Gessner's *Bibliotheca Universalis* (1551) and *Icones Animalium* (1560), and Edward Topsell *Histories of Foure-Footed Beastes* (1607).

AFRICAN UNICORN

The Dark Continent once harboured many tales of monsters, including, unsurprisingly, the unicorn. Here they were known by several names. The earliest account comes from the Elizabethan privateer Sir James Lancaster, who heard it called **Abath** in the Strait of Malacca in 1592. A certain Baron von Müller claimed to have seen one in Kordofan in 1848, being called an **A'nasa** (Gosse, *Rom. Nat. Hist.*). This creature is mentioned by Rupell, under the name of Nillekma or Arase (surely the same as A'nasa), as indigenous to Kordofan, and, by Cavassi, as known in Congo under that of **Abada**; and the **Ndzoodzoo**, the male of which had a soft flexible horn, was said to be 'not uncommon in Makooa' (Freeman, *Sth. Afr. Ch. Rec.*). A detailed first-hand description was made by the Jesuit missionary Jerome Lobo (*c.*1593–1678), writing in the early seventeenth century. To begin with, he was simply convinced by what others had reported and wrote to Henry Oldenburg, Secretary of the Royal Society, to tell him about it: 'These testimonies, particularly that of the good old man, John Gabriel, with what the father, my companion, affirmed also of his own knowledge, confirms me that this so celebrated *Unicorn* is found in this province, there foaled, and bred' (Lobo, *Short Relation*, 47). Some time later he saw it for himself: 'In the province of Agaus has been seen the unicorn, that beast so much talked of, and so little known: the prodigious swiftness with which this creature runs

from one wood into another has given me no opportunity of examining it particularly, yet I have had so near a sight of it as to be able to give some description of it. The shape is the same with that of a beautiful horse, exact and nicely proportioned, of a bay colour, with a black tail, which in some provinces is long, in others very short: some have long manes hanging to the ground. They are so timorous that they never feed but surrounded with other beasts that defend them' (*Voyage*, 69). Lobo was bitten by a snake during his travels and apparently used what he called 'horn of the unicorn' as an antidote, to no effect; luckily, he found a more efficacious remedy. In the early nineteenth century, Conrad Malte-Brun in his ground-breaking work, *Universal Geography* (IV, 375–7), seriously considered fifteenth- and sixteenth-century sightings of the unicorn along the south-east coast of Africa as evidence of its existence. (Gould, *Myth. Mon.*, 346–7; Reade, *Savage*, 32–3.)

AMERICAN UNICORN

As explorers were discovering the Americas, there were frequent reports of unicorns. Sir John Hawkins (1532–95) 'discovered' the American unicorn in 1564. In Florida he saw natives wearing necklaces of unicorn horn, observing: 'Of these unicornes they have many; for that they doe affirm it to be a beast with one horne, which coming to the river to drinke, putteth the same into the water before he drinketh. Of this unicorne horne there are of our company, that having gotten the same of the Frenchmen, brought horne thereof to show' (quoted in Haklyut, *Princ. Nav.*, X, 59). Searching for that elusive north-west passage to India, the explorer John Davis found himself off the east coast of North America where, on 14 June 1584, the natives offered him 'a darte with a bone in it, of a piece of Unicornes horne; as I did judge'. The Dutch geographer Arnoldus Montanus (1625–83) described the beast in his important work, *De Nieuwe en onbekende Weereld*, published in Amsterdam in 1671 (with an English edition also in 1671 and a German one in 1673). Along with an engraving of the animal was the description: 'On the borders of Canada animals are now and again seen, somewhat resembling a horse; they have cloven hoofs, shaggy manes, a horn right out of the forehead, a tail like that of a wild pig, black eyes, a stag's neck and love the gloomiest wildernesses; are shy of each other so that the male never feeds with the female except when they associate for the purposes of increase. Then they lay aside their ferocity; as soon as the rutting season is past, they again not only become wild but even attack their own' (quoted in Lutz, 'Am. Uni.', 135–9). The apparent range of the American unicorn extended from Florida, up the east coast, to Canada.

MODERN UNICORNS

'Unicorns no longer belong wholly in the doubtful twilight of mythology,' wrote Dr Frank Thone ('Unicorn', 312–13), 'There is a live unicorn right here in the USA in this modern year 1936.' He was reporting on an operation performed by Dr W. Franklin Dove, a biologist at the University of Maine, on a day-old calf, transplanting both horn buds to sit close together on the animal's brow-ridge. The article carried a picture of the Ayrshire calf, then about two and a half years old, sporting an enormous single horn bursting from its head. Dr Dove noted that this mighty horn made the calf the dominant beast, whilst at the same time giving him a placid nature. He was not content with his monster, but sought to develop a wide-ranging historical theory concerning the ancients' ability to create unicorns of their own. He offered references from Pliny to more recent anthropology to the effect that the manipulation of horn buds had been practised since ancient times, from Africa to Nepal.

UNICORN STAG

In his account of his campaigns against the Gauls in the first century BCE, Julius Caesar described an extraordinary beast roaming the extensive Hercynian Forest (Germany's Black Forest is a remnant of this): 'There is an ox of the shape of a stag, between whose ears a horn rises from the middle of the forehead, higher and straighter than those horns which are known to us. From the top of this, branches, like palms, stretch out a considerable distance. The shape of the female and of the male is the, same; the appearance and the size of the horns is the same' (*Caes. Gal.* 6.26). For another fabulous Hercynian creature, see **Hercynia**.

URAEUS

From the Greek for '**Serpent**'. As a symbol of divinity and royalty in Ancient Egypt, the god Ra wore two uraei on his forehead and kings are depicted with a uraeus. The uraeus was also a diety known as **Uatchet**, the uraeus-goddess. The uraeus was later associated with the goddesses Isis and Nephthys as they absorbed the functions of the older Uatchet. It is possible that the Ancient Greek snake-haired Gorgons derive from Egyptian goddesses crowned with uraei. (Alexander, 'Ev. Bas.', 174; Budge, *Gods*, 377.)

URIDIMMU

A Mesopotamian monster, with either a) a dog's head (*ur* means 'dog'), representing the 'howling dog' or 'rabid dog monster' created by **Tiamat** (Wiggerman, *Mes. Prot. Sp.*, 50); or b) the upper part of a man and the lower part of a lion (Green, 'Note Ass. "Goat-Fish"', 25–30). A depiction of an uridimmu was found on a limestone relief slab from the North palace of Assurbanipal at Nineveh (OD VII 10). Clay figures of the monster were buried to bring well-being and prosperity to the household.

URMAHLILU

Also *urmaḫlullû*, the rare Mesopotamian 'lion-man', or lion-centaur, having the body and four legs of a lion and the torso and head of a man. It first appears on an Assyrian seal from the thirteenth century BCE. Magical rituals prescribe the urmahlilu as the special guardian of the toilet; his half-lion representation makes him the ideal opponent of the special demon of the toilet, the completely lion-shaped Šulak. (Wiggerman, *Mes. Prot. Sp.*, 98, 181.)

V

VATNA-GEDDA

The Icelandic 'loch pike': 'It is of a flaming gold colour, about the size and shape of a small flounder. A very rare fish indeed it is, and seldom seen except in fog and thick weather before a violent storm. Whoever will catch it must bait his hook with gold, and wear gloves of human skin. It makes the best protection against the assaults of ghosts, and never was there a ghost so powerful as to be able to rise again, if a loch-pike was laid on the spot where it was made to sink into the earth. So venomous is this creature that though it is put into a bottle, and the bottle wrapped up in many coverings, any horse which carries it will lose all the hair on the place touched by the parcel, and will never be good for much after. On one occasion when a specimen was caught, it was wrapped up in two horse-skins, but it bored its way through both and disappeared into the earth. The only absolutely certain method of securing it is to wrap it first in the caul of a child and then in that of a calf.' (Davidson, *Folk-Lore*, 330.)

VATTENHÄST, SEE BÄCKAHÄST

VEDRFOLNIR

In Norse mythology, the hawk that sits between the eyes of an eagle ('he has understanding of many a thing') that perches on a branch of the World Tree, Yggdrasill. ('The Beguiling of Gylfi' in Sturluson, *Prose Edda*.)

VEGETABLE LAMB OF TARTARY

Also known as the Scythian Lamb and 'the Barometz', and by the Latin names *Agnus scythicus* and *Planta Tartarica Barometz*: supposedly, a lamb growing like a plant. News of this wonder reached the West in the fourteenth century CE with the publication of Sir

The Vegetable Lamb of Tartary (1887)

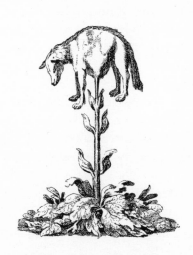

John Mandeville's *Travels*: 'there growethe a maner of Fruyt as though it weren Gowrdes: and whan thei ben rype men kutten hem ato, and men fynden with inne a lytylle Best, in Flesche, in Bon and Blode, as though it were a lytylle Lomb with outen Wolle. And Men eten both the Frut and the Best; and that is a great Marveylle. Of that Frute I have eaten; alle thoughe it were wondirfulle, but that I knowe wel that God is marveyllous in his Werkes'. Variations of the tale were reported as fact up until the eighteenth century. Carolus Linnaeus included it as one of the **Animalia Paradoxa** in the 1740 edition of his *Systema Naturae*: 'is reckoned with plants, and is similar to the lamb; whose stalk coming out of the ground enters an umbilicus; the same is said to be provided with blood by devouring wild animals by chance. It is composed artificially from the roots of American ferns. Naturally, however, it is an allegorical description of the embryo of a sheep, as all evidence has shown' (66). The Chinese did manufacture fake lambs and other animals out of ferns as a sort of **Jenny Haniver**, but Linnaeus had missed the more obvious point: it was an allegory of the cotton plant (genus *Gossypium*), the fluffy white fibres of which – looking for all the world like little lambs – could be spun like wool. The British Museum has a specimen of one of these Chinese fakes dating from 1698. (Lee, *Veg. Lamb*, passim.)

VICHSCHELM

An evil spirit in the form of a starved bull heard bellowing in the mountains of Bavaria and Austria. It apparently prayed on cattle and local tradition held that feeding them 'Bibemell' (*Pimpinella saxifraga*) would protect them from its power. (Schmid, *Bav. High.*, 178.)

VIDOFNIR

Also *Viðópnir*, *Vidopnir*, *Vidrof-nir*, the 'tree-**Serpent**'; in Norse mythology, the cock whose feathers glitter like gold, or are gold, and shines like lightning. Identified with *Gollinkambi* ('Gold Comb'), he perches atop the World Tree, Yggdrasill, in eternal watchfulness to wake the gods to battle (against the giants). As many may have noticed, he now sits on top of the church steeple, waiting for the old gods to return. ('Voluspa' and 'The Lay of Fjolsvith' in Sturluson, *Prose Edda*.)

VITRYSK STRANDMUDDLARE

The Swedish 'White-Russian Shore Muddler', known by its fictitious scientific name as *Lirpa lirpa* (Münchhausen). A single female specimen is known, supposedly from 'Zscicvzoskaija' in the Ukraine. It has the head and foreparts of a wild boar piglet, augmented with two 'tusks', the rear and tail of a squirrel, and the hind legs of a duck. It was at one point exhibited every year at the Natural History Museum in Göteborg, Sweden, on 1 April. The creature had been stuck together out of various animals – the 'tusks' were alligator teeth; the menacing eyes possibly from some raptor – in 1960 as means of boosting museum attendance. It is, of cource, a species of **Jenny Haniver**. (Dance, *Animal Fakes*, 118.)

WADJET, SEE UATCHET

WARG

Old High German, 'wolf', Old English *wearg*, 'a criminal' (the similar *werg* means 'accursed'), Old Norse, *vargr*; compare Gothic *vargs*, a fiend. The connection between the wolf and anti-social behaviour was an old one: in Norman law, outlaws were 'Wargus esto', 'to be a wolf'; in the *Lex Ripuaria*, this was 'Wargus sit, hoc est expulsus', 'whoever is a wolf, is expelled'. Hence the association of the wolf and the Devil, the Devil in the form of a wolf: in the laws of Canute, the Devil is a 'Vodfrea verewulf'; in the Middle Ages, the Devil is the arch-wolf, *Archilupus*, and often took the shape of a wolf. Grimm (*Teut. Myth.*, III, 996) saw *warg* as the origin of certain Slavic names for the Devil: Russian *vorog*, Polish *wrog*, Serbo-Croat *vrag*, etc. Angela de Labarthe has the unfortunate distinction as being, allegedly, the first woman to be burned at the stake for having sexual intercourse with the Devil in Toulouse in 1275. The spawn of this unholy union was said to be a monster with the head of a wolf and a serpent's tail that lived on a diet of babies. The association between the Devil and the wolf is traced back to the Norse **Fenrir**, the monstrous wolf unleashed at Ragnarok. (Jones, *Nightmare*, 152, 186–77.)

WATER-HORSE

A malevolent water spirit common in European folklore, regional types include **Bäckahäst** (Swedish), Cabbylushtey (Manx), Ceffly Dŵr (Welsh), **Kelpie** (Scottish), Lutin (French), **Nicker** (English and Germanic), Nuggle or **Njogel** (Shetland), **Shoopiltee** and **Tangie** (both also of the Shetlands). In his *Natural History* (9.2), Pliny wrote of several sea-adapted land animals: 'there be found in the sea certaine strange beasts like sheepe, which goe foorth to land, feed upon the roots of plants and hearbes, and then returne againe into the sea. Others also which are headed like Horses, Asses, and Buls: and those many times eat downe in the standing corne upon the ground.'

WATERTON'S NONDESCRIPT

It was said that Charles Waterton made his fourth expedition to British Guiana on the coast of South America with the express purpose 'of obtaining a specimen of that hitherto unknown animal, the Nondescript'. It was an odd-looking thing: '"The features of this animal are quite of the Grecian cast," says the Squire [Waterton], whose assertion may be checked by reference to the engraving of the Nondescript. He brought back "only the head and shoulders," because he was "pressed for daylight" and also found him too heavy to carry. In his heavy style of joking, he suggests that somebody else should go out and secure another specimen.' Some people were of the opinion that Waterton 'had slain and stuffed some "native Indian" in order to make an arrogant display of his "stuffing powers"'. There was nothing at all 'Grecian' about the horrible thing: Waterton's Nondescript was 'the skin of a Red Howler monkey from Guiana, manipulated with such skill that it appeared to be a stuffed specimen of a hirsute late Georgian gentleman'. Waterton also created the **Noctifer**. See also **Jenny Haniver**. (Aldington, *Strange Life*, 110–13.)

WEREWOLF

Writing in the first century CE, Pliny the Elder, although happy to communicate all sort of stories about the **Catoblepes** and **Licorne**, was no believer in *Versipelles*, Latin, 'turn-coats'. 'That men have been turned into wolves, and again restored to their original form,' he wrote, 'we must confidently look upon as untrue, unless, indeed, we are ready to believe all the tales, which, for so many ages, have been found to be fabulous. But,

as the belief of it has become so firmly fixed in the minds of the common people, as to have caused the term "Versipellis" to be used as a common form of imprecation, I will here point out its origin. Euanthes, a Grecian author of no mean reputation, informs us that the Arcadians assert that a member of the family of one Anthus is chosen by lot, and then taken to a certain lake in that district, where, after suspending his clothes on an oak, he swims across the water and goes away into the desert, where he is changed into a wolf and associates with other animals of the same species for a space of nine years. If he has kept himself from beholding a man during the whole of that time, he returns to the same lake, and, after swimming across it, resumes his original form, only with the addition of nine years in age to his former appearance. To this Fabius adds, that he takes his former clothes as well. It is really wonderful to what a length the credulity of the Greeks will go! There is no falsehood, if ever so barefaced, to which some of them cannot be found to bear testimony. So too, Agriopas, who wrote the *Olympionics*, informs us that Demænetus, the Parrhasian, during a sacrifice of human victims, which the Arcadians were offering up to the Lycæan Jupiter, tasted the entrails of a boy who had been slaughtered; upon which he was turned into a wolf, but, ten years afterwards, was restored to his original shape and his calling of an athlete, and returned victorious in the pugilistic contests at the Olympic games' (*Nat. Hist.*, 8.34). What makes

A German Werewolf (c.1685)

Pliny interesting is that he included the werewolf in a book on natural history; that is, he was seriously considering the possibility of their being real, even if, in the end, he decided it was a lot of Greek hogwash. However, the association of ideas between cannibalism, the breaking of a strong taboo, and becoming bestial, or wolfish, continued to inform thinking about criminality and demonology, as can be seen under the heading **Warg**.

WHALE

If nature had not supplied so many wonderful examples of this creature, one would surely have ranked it among the impossible. Its great size has amazed and terrified sailors, and engendered a wealth of folklore. Before the word zoology was coined, several notable early writers, such as Pliny the Elder, attempted to describe the whale, often unable to separate the factual from the fantastical; see **Balaena** and **Physeter**. At the other end of history, just as the rich traditions of the common people were about to be extinguished by modern education and modern entertainment, and modern living, generally, the folklorists recorded their stories about such creatures, such as the Icelandic **Illhvel**, or 'wicked whales', and the self-explanatory **Island Fish**. Where only heather grows on the Icelandic version, a Slavonic folktale tells of a forest that grew on the back of whale that swallowed a whole fleet and found itself weighted to the spot in consequence. (Gubernatis, *Zoo. Myth.*, 345; Waugh, 'Folk. Whale', 361–71.)

WHIRLEPOOLE

Philemon Holland, in what was the first English translation of Pliny the Elder's *Natural History*, used this word to denote a species of 'mightie fish' called **Physeter** and included the **Balaena** in the same order; i.e., the **Whale**.

WHISTLER

Also *Seven Whistlers*: 'Some nocturnal bird having a whistling note believed to be of ill omen: when flying in a flock called the seven whistlers' (*New Eng. Dict.*). In popular tradition, the flock of seven were seen either as the souls of the Jews who took part in the crucifixion of Jesus and condemned thus never to find rest, or the souls of unbaptised children. Legends vary across Britain. In Shropshire and Worcesterhire six birds fly about looking for the seventh; when they find him, the world will end. They have been connected to **Gabriel's Hounds** and so with the Wild Hunt, largely on account of being some aerial troop. In the south and west of England, the bird is identified as the whimbrel (*Numenius phoeopus*) whose 'rippling whistle' is repeated seven times; in Kent and Gaelic tradition, generally, the bird is the common curlew (*Numenius arquata*); and in other parts of the British Isles flocks of widgeon and plover have been given the name. (Harrison, 'Whistler', 539–41; Wright, *Rust. Sp.*, 197.)

WHITE HORSE OF SPEY

A **Kelpie** haunting the region of Speyside in Scotland. It loved storms and when the thunder rolled between the Cairngorms and the Haughs of Cromdale, its whinnying could be heard and in the lightning flash its white shape seen. It would accost the weary traveller, who, glad of the chance of a ride, would mount the animal only to be carried off and drowned in the deep places of the River Spey. The horse would sing a song, the locals said; one version goes: 'And ride weel, Davie, | And by this night at ten o'clock | Ye'll be in Pot Cravie'. (MacGregor, *Peat-Fire Flame*, 68.)

WIGHT

In Germanic folklore, wights (*wight*, Danish *vætte*) are a class of pre-Christian spirits, usually male, often associated with specific places and somewhat distinct from the fairies. They take the shape of calves, cats, dogs or dwarves with red pointed-caps (derived from ancient rustic dress). They are mischievous and easily offended. An old Icelandic law prohibited ships returning to Iceland from decorating their bows with dragons' heads so as not to affront the land-wights; there was no such prohibition on sailing to foreign lands with dragons' heads on display. In Jutland, for example, a cat or snake would be buried under the threshold of a house so that its spirit would became a protective wight (*vare* in Jutland); compare the **Kirkegrim**. Malevolent wights (Danish *Menvætter*), the souls of the murdered, suicides and the executed, demanded regular offerings, but were also countered with 'wight-fires' (Danish *Vætte-ild*) at springtime. The most famous wight is the *nisse* who brings children presents on

Yule; the same *nisse* who has been Christianised as St Nicholas (and Santa Claus); see **Nicker**. An offering of food (porridge) is left out for him in return. (Schütte, 'Dan. Pag.', 363–4.)

WILD BEAST OF BARRISDALE

In 1937 Alasdair Alpin MacGregor wrote 'Less than sixty years ago there lived at Barrisdale, by the shores of Loch Hourn, a crofter who once encountered this monster. He assured his neighbours that this ungainly creature had gigantic wings, and was three-legged. He often saw it in flight across the hills of Knoydart, especially about Barrisdale itself; and he averred that on one occasion, when it was making for him with evil design, he rushed for the shelter of his cottage. As the crofter himself used to relate up until the time of his death, he just succeeded in slamming the door in the monster's face. The dwellers by the more remote shores of Loch Hourn frequently heard the terrifying roar of the Wild Beast of Barrisdale; and an old man living in this locality, called Ranald MacMaster, ofttimes discovered the tracks of this three-legged creature on the hills, and also about the sandy stretches fringing Barrisdale Bay'. (MacGregor, *Peat-Fire Flame*, 82–3.)

WINGED CAT, SEE CAT, WINGED

WIRRY-COW

Also *wirry-cowe*, *wurry-cow*, or *worry-cow*; a malevolent spirit of Scottish folklore. Defined as both a bugbear and also another name for the scarecrow (Henderson, *Scot. Prov.*, 252), but also a ghost or the Devil; popularly thought to derive from 'worry' and 'to cow' as in harrass, but probably a corruption of the Gaelic *uruisg*, 'goblin' (Mackay, *Dict. Low. Scot.*, 283).

WISH HOUND, SEE YETH HOUND

WOLF

Canis lupus: normally found in possible zoos, the wolf has its impossible subspecies, too. According to Pliny the Elder (*Nat. Hist.*, 8.34), writing in the first century CE: 'It is commonly thought likewise in Italie, that the eye-sight of wolves is hurtfull; in so much, as if they see a man before he espie them, they cause him to loose his voice for the time.' Pliny passed no judgement on this, but was less inclined to believe in the **Werewolf**. He also reported the magical uses of the wolf's tail: 'it is commonly thought and verily beleeved, that in the taile of this beast, there is a little string or haire that is effectuall to procure love, and that when he is taken at any time, hee casteth it away from him, for that it is of no force and vertue unlesse it be taken from him whiles he is alive.' Pliny also described two variations: the 'hart-wolf' and the 'hind-wolfe'; see **Chama**. See also **Fenrir** and **Warg**.

WOLPERTINGER

The *Chimæra bavarica*, Bavarian **Chimæra**, a taxidermical fantasy comprising several species of animal grafted together. The base is typically a hare or rabbit and the

Albrecht Dürer's *Feldhase* (1502) as a Wolpertinger

simplest models are horned rabbits like the **Lepus Cornutus** and American **Jackalope**. The documented history of the Wolpertinger cannot be traced back to an illustration of a rabbit with horns and duck wings foisted on the famous German artist Albrecht Dürer in 1502. The horned hare, *Lepus conutus*, was first described in Conrad Gessner's *Historiae Animalium* ('History of the Animals'), his monumetal work of natural history published in Zurich in five volumes from 1551 to 1558 and 1587. This led to the animal being included in many other important early works of natural history until it was finally rejected as a fantasy. In 2013 the Deutsches Jagd- und Fischereimuseum (German Hunting and Fishing Museum) in Munich put on a specical exhibition, 'Living with the Wolpertinger'. They have a similar creature in Sweden called the *skvader*. (Kirein, *Wolpertinger*, *passim*.)

WOOFEN-POOF

A rare bird identified by Augustus C. Fotheringham in 1928, who named it *Eoörnis pterovelox gobiensis*. An inhabitant of the Gobi Desert, in appearance it lies midway between the pelican and pterodactyl, and can reach a top speed of 600 km (about 370 miles) per hour. It always hatches twins, one of each sex, which later pair-bond. 'Fotheringham' was, in fact, Cornell University's professor of botany, Lester W. Sharp. In a thirty-four-page pamphlet he made up much additional useless nonsense about the bird, all amply illustrated with photographs and diagrams. The woofen-poof may or may not be related to the whiffenpoof mentioned in Victor Herbert's 1908 operetta *Little Nemo*. (Anon., 'Brief Notices', 112.)

WORM

The **Dragon** of northern England and the Scottish Lowlands, from the Old Norse *Ormr*, a **Serpent** or dragon. Notable specimens are the **Lambton Worm**, the **Laidley Worm**, the **Linton Worm**, the Pollard Worm, the Worm of Sockburn, and the **Stoorworm**. In 1873, Henderson remarked that these were yet living legends among the people. Sir Walter Scott suggested that these worms were the remnants of folk memory of giant serpents that he said formerly infested the primordial forest of Britain, if you can believe it. Of the same stock, see also **Lindworm**, **Tatzelwurm**; and from further afield, the **Mongolian Death Worm**. (Henderson, *Notes*, 281; Scott, *Minstrelsy*, III, 291.)

WULVER

A wolf-headed creature of the Shetland Islands. The earliest mention seems to be by the Scottish folklorist Jessie Saxby (*Shet. Trad.*, 141), Vice-President and Hon. Dist. Sec. of the Viking Club Society for Northern Research in the early twentieth century, who described it as being covered in short brown hair and fond of fishing. It reputedly lived in a cave and gave its name to Wulver's Stane. Saxby's address was 'Wulver's Hool', Baltasound, Unst. (Viking Club, *Saga-Bk*, III, x.)

WURRUM

An Irish freshwater demi-**Dragon**. The writer W.R. Le Fanu (*Seventy Years*) described it as 'That dreadful beast, the Wurrum – half-fish, half-dragon – still survives in many a mountain lake – seldom seen, indeed, but often heard'. One individual named **Bran** is said to haunt Lough Brin, County Kerry Ireland. The Irish poet W.B. Yeats (*Celt. Twilight*, 108) wrote that 'there are of a certainty, mightier creatures, and the lake hides what neither line nor net can take'. See also **Piast**.

Wyvern (Fifteenth Century)

WYRM, SEE WORM

WYVERN

A winged serpentine creature with two eagle's legs and a barbed tail, usually depicted as curled or interwoven. An early example can be seen as one of the standards shown in the Bayeux Tapestry. It symbolises pestilence, viciousness and envy, but when used in a coat of arms means the overthrow of tyranny or of an especially evil enemy. There are several examples in heraldry. It is visually related to the **Dragon** and often confused with the same. (Vinycomb, *Fict. Sym.*, n.p.)

X

XECOTCOVACH

A monstrous primeval bird of the mythology of the Kichés, a people of Central America (particularly Guatemala), forming one of a four-fold group of destroying spirits. The chief gods created the earth and animals, and peopled their new world with wooden manikins. However, gods and manikins came to loggerheads, and the god resolved to destroy them. A great flood drowned them, a thick resin fell from heaven (and presumably smothered them), the bird Xecotcovach pecked out their eyes, the bird Camulatz tore off their heads, the bird Cotzbalam ate their flesh, the bird Tecumbalam ground their bones, and then the rest of creation turned on them. (Spence, *Popol Vuh*, 10–11.)

XIUHCOATL

Mesoamerican, literally, the 'turquoise **Serpent**', interpreted as 'fire snake'. This creature was a weapon created by the god Uitzilopochtli ('Humming-Bird Wizard') and used against his rebellious siblings, destroying them. It was a metaphor for the 'red dawn'. The fire-god Xiuhtecutli wears a fire-snake dress and **Quetzalcoatl** is represented wearing the turquoise snake-mask. (Spence, *Gods Mexico*, 66, 211, 324.)

Y

YACU MAMA

'Mother of the Waters', a somewhat supernatural **Serpent** of South America. It is of great size and primarily infests the lakes abounding the mouth of the river Amazon. It is able to raise a tempest on the waters to overturn the natives' canoes and thereby swallow them whole. Consequently, the natives make a great noise by blowing on horns to drive off the monster before venturing into the water. In 1845, Father Manuel Castrucci de Yemazza described the beast in his account of his mission to the Oivaros and Zaparos tribes along the river Pastaza: 'The sight alone of this monster confounds, intimidates, and infuses respect into the heart of the boldest man. He never seeks or follows the victims upon which he feeds; but, so great is the force of his inspiration, that he draws in with his breath whatever quadruped or bird may pass him, within from twenty to fifty yards of distance, according to its size. That which I killed from my canoe upon the Pastaza (with five shots of a fowling-piece) had two yards of thickness and fifteen yards of length; but the Indians of this region have assured me that there are animals of this kind here of three or four yards diameter, and from thirty to forty long. These swallow entire hogs, stags, tigers, and men, with the greatest facility'. It is supposed that the monster is in fact, the boa-constrictor, although the reported size is much greater than that so far measured by naturalists. (Herndon, *Exploration*, 168–9.)

YAHOO

Also *Yowie*, among the Australian Aborigines, an ape-like monster described as being of the same height and general shape as a human, with long white hair growing down from the head, unusually long arms, claws instead of hands, and backwards pointing feet. Yahoo is the earlier word for this creature, first recorded in 1842, although Yowie is now the more common term. Yowie is probably a corruption of Yahoo, which itself undoubtedly comes from the fictional Yahoos described by Jonathan Swift in his 1726 book *Gulliver's Travels*, a term subsequently applied to unkempt and uncouth people in general. (Anon., 'Super. Aus. Abo.', 92–6.)

Yahoo (1913)

YALE

From the Latin *eale*, of uncertain meaning. A hippopotamus-sized creature having an elephant's tale and the head of a wild boar with independently moveable horns. It was first described by Pliny the Elder in the first century CE (*Nat. Hist.* 8.30), who located it in Ethiopia: 'They have among them besides all these, another beast named Eale, for bignesse equal to the river-horse, tailed like to an Elephant, either blacke or reddish tawnie of colour: his mandibles or chawes resemble those of a bore: he hath hornes above a cubit long, which he can stirre or moove as hee list; for being in fight, hee can set them both or one of them as hee will himselfe, altering them every way; one while streight forward to offend, other whiles bending byas, as he hath reason to nort or push, to ward or avoid his enemie.' The animal is found in heraldry, as in the badge of the Earl of Yarborough, for example.

YETH HOUND

In Devon, *Yeth Hounds*, meaning 'death-hounds'; also *Yell Hounds*; also *Wish Hounds*: headless dogs believed to be the souls of unbaptised children. Having no admittance to heaven, they roam the countryside at night and despite the lack of the normal means of vocalisation are said to be heard wailing. Occasionally, they are also led by a headless huntsman, the Wistman (derived from *Wusc* or *Wisc*, a name for the god Odin). Dewerstone, a rocky promontory on the edge of Dartmoor, is said to be the meeting place of the hounds, and the ancient road of Abbot's Way, their hunting ground.

Yale (Medieval)

The folklorist Robert Hunt remembered being told that 'Sir Francis Drake drove a hearse into Plymouth at night with headless horses, and that he was followed by a pack of "yelling hounds" without heads. If dogs hear the cry of the wish hounds they all die' (Hunt, *Pop. Rom.*, 29, 145). See also **Dandy-Dog** and **Gabriel's Hounds**. (Anon. *Dial. Dev.*, 97; Norway, *High. By.*, 149.)

YETI

Also known as the 'Abominable Snowman', a mountain-dwelling, ape-like creature supposed to inhabit the Himalayas. One of the earliest accounts came from Major Lawrence Austine Waddell of the British Indian Army, formerly Professor of Chemistry and Pathology at the Medical College of Kolkata. He was exploring the route to the Dong-kia pass in the highlands of Sikkim, making observations on local floral and fauna, and taking notes on the effects of altitude, among other things, and had reached a place called Jarwa at an elevation of 5,200 m (17,000 ft): 'Some large footprints in the snow led across our track, and away up to the higher peaks. These were alleged to be the trail of the hairy wild men who are believed to live amongst the eternal snows, along with the mythical white lions, whose roar is reputed to be heard during storms. The belief in these creatures is universal among Tibetans.' A snow-storm blew in and Waddell was prevented from following the tracks. He was also disappointed in his later enquiries: 'None, however, of the many Tibetans I have interrogated on this subject could ever give me an authentic case. On the most superficial investigation it always resolved itself into something that somebody heard tell of.' He concluded that 'these so-called hairy wild men are evidently the great yellow snow-bear (*Ursus isabellinus*), which is highly carnivorous, and often kills yaks' – the bear in question is now known as the Himalayan brown bear (*Ursus arctos isabellinus*), locally called Dzu-Teh. (Waddell, *Am. Him.*, 223.) Since then, there have been further reports of footprints and sightings, with hair specimens sent for analysis – Khumjung monastry in Nepal even boasts a supposed Yeti scalp and has it on display in a locked glass case; none of

Supposed Footprint of a Yeti (Left) in the Himalayas (1976)

these has resolved the matter, although speculation continues (Sanderson, *Abominable*, passim.). The term 'Abominable Snowman' came into popular use in the 1950s; one of the earliest usages was in *Life* magazine for 31 December 1951.

Z

ZAHHAK, SEE AZI DAHAK

ŽALTYS

A magical green **Serpent** (grass snake) of Lithuanian folklore, 'the sentinel of the gods'. It was considered lucky to have one in the house, tucked away in a corner, under the bed, or even sitting at the table. It brought happiness and prosperity, ensuring the fertility of both land and family. (Gimbutas, *Balts*, 38.)

ZIZ

In Jewish folklore, Ziz is the king of the birds, created by Yahweh on the sixth day in juxtaposition to **Leviathan**, king of the fish, and **Behemoth**, king of the animals on land. Like the others, he is of monstrous size: 'His ankles rest on the earth, and his head reaches to the very sky [...] His wings are so huge that unfurled they darken the sky'. Again like the others, Ziz prevents the creatures under his rule from entirely devouring each other by yearly frightening them into submission: 'in Tishri, at the time of the autumnal equinox, the great bird ziz flaps his wings and utters his cry, so that the birds of prey, the eagles and the vultures, blench, and they fear to swoop down upon the others and annihilate them in their greed.' Its name comes from the different flavours of its flesh: 'it tastes like this, *seh*, and like that, *seh*'. At the end of time, Ziz will be served to the pious as a reward for their abstaining from unclean birds. (Ginzberg, *Legends Jews*, I, 4–5, 28–9.)

ZU BIRD

In other readings, *Anzu*: Babylonian, 'the divine storm bird', called 'the flesh-eating bird, the lion or giant bird, the bird of prey, the bird with the sharp beak'. Zu was a god – the words *Zu*, also *Za* and *Zi*, are Assyrian – who committed some obscure outrage (referred to as 'The Sin of the God Zu') and, hunted by the other gods, 'fled away and concealed himself in his own country' and there transformed himself into this ravenous bird of prey (Smith, *Chaldean*, 113–22). He is a Satanic figure, the 'worker of evil, who raised the head of evil' and led a rebellion against the other gods; his 'sin' was to steal the Tablets of Destiny, which gave him power over the universe. The Zu Bird symbolised the summer sandstorms that blew in from the Arabian desert and takes its place in the night sky as the constellations we now call Pegasus and Taurus; mythologically, it is cognate with the Indian **Garuda**. (Mackenzie, *Myth. Bab.*, 75.)

Enlil and the Zu Bird (Assyrian)

BIBLIOGRAPHY

MANUSCRIPTS

'Aberdeen Bestiary', Aberdeen University Library, Univ. Lib. MS 24.

'*Bestiaire of Pierre de Beauvais*', Bibliothèque Nationale de France, Nouv. acq. fr. 13521.

[Bestiary], British Library, Harley MS 4751.

Folieto, Hugo de, '*Aviarium / Dicta Chrysostomi*', British Library, London, MS Sloane 278 (published in Druce, 'Elephant').

'Marvels of the East', British Library, Cotton Tiberius B. v, ff.78v-87v.

'Rochester Bestiary', British Library, Royal MS 12 F xiii.

PUBLISHED SOURCES

Abercromby, John, 'Magic Songs of the Finns', *Folk-Lore*, vol. I (1890), pp. 17–46.

Abercromby, John, *The Pre- and Proto-Historica Finns Both Eastern and Western with The Magic Songs of the West Finns*, vol. II. London: David Nutt, 1898.

Adam, Alexander, *A Summary of Geography and History, Both Ancient and Modern*, London: A. Strahan, 1802.

Ælian, *De Natura Animalium*, Latin trans. Friedrich Jacobs. Jena: Frommann, 1832.

Aeschylus, Fragment 155, in Aristophanes, *The Frogs of Aristophanes*, trans. W.C. Green. Cambridge: Cambridge University Press, 1888.

Alcock, Elizabeth A., 'Pictish Stones Class I: Where and How?', *Glasgow Archaeological Journal*, Vol. 15 (1988–9), pp. 1–21.

Aldington, Richard, *The Strange Life of Charles Waterton*. London: Evans Brothers, 1949.

Aldrovandi, Ulyssis, *Ornithologiae*, 4 vols. Bologna, 1599–1603.

Aldrovandi, Ulyssis, *De Piscibus libri V*. Bononiae: Bellagambam, 1613.

Aldrovandi, Ulyssis, *Serpentum et Draconum Historiae libri duo*. Bononiae: C. Ferronium, 1640.

Alexander, R. M., 'The Evolution of the Basilisk', *Greece & Rome*, Vol. 10, No. 2 (Oct., 1963), pp. 170–81.

Almqvist, Bo, 'Waterhorse Legends (MLSIT 4086 & 4086B): The Case For and Against a Connection between Irish and Nordic Tradition', 'The Fairy Hill Is on Fire! Proceedings of the Symposium on the Supernatural in Irish and Scottish Migratory Legends', *Béaloideas*, 59 (1991), pp. 107–20.

Ananikian, M.H., 'Armenia (Zoroastrianism)', in *The Encyclopedia of Religion and Ethics*, vol. 1. Edinburgh: T. & T. Clark, 1908.

Andrews, Roy Chapman, *On the Trail of Ancient Man: A Narrative of the Field Work of the Central Asiatic Expeditions*. New York and London: G.P. Putnam's Sons, 1926.

Anglicus, Bartholomaeus, *Medieval Lore from Bartholomew Anglicus*, ed. Robert Steele. London: The De La More Press, 1905.

Anichkof, Eugene, 'St. Nicolas and Artemis', *Folklore*, 5.2 (June, 1894), pp. 108–20.

Anon. [Mary Reynolds Palmer], *A Dialogue in the Devonshire Dialect*. London: Longman, Rees, Orme, Brown, Green and Longman, 1837.

Anon., *Beowulf*, trans. John M. Kemble. London: William Pickering, 1837.

Anon., 'Brief Notices', *The Quarterly Review of Biology*, Vol. 5, No. 1 (March 1930), pp. 98–131.

Anon., 'Superstitions of the Australian Aborigines: The Yahoo', *Australian and New Zealand Monthly Magazine*, 1.2 (February 1842), pp. 92–6.

Anon., 'Tales of the Water-Kelpie', *Celtic Magazine*, XII (1887), 511–15.

[Pseudo-]Apollodorus, *Apollodorus, The Library*, trans. Sir James George Frazer. London: William Heinemann, 1921.

Apollonius Rhodius, *Argonautica*, trans. E.V. Rieu. Harmondsworth: Penguin, 1959.

Aristotle, *Aristotle's History of Animals*, trans. Richard Cresswell. London: George Bell & Sons, 1878.

Aristotle, *Historia Animalium*, trans. D'Arcy Wentworth Thompson, *The Works of Aristotle*, vol. 4. Oxford: Clarendon Press, 1910.

Arnoldson, Torild Washington, *Parts of the Body in Older Germanic and Scandinavian*. Chicago: University of Chicago Press, 1915.

[Arrian], *Arrian*, trans. E. Iliff Robson, 2 vols. London: Heinemann, 1933.

Artedi, Peter, *Philosophia Ichthyologica*. Grypeswaldiae: Ant. Ferdin. Röse, 1738.

Baily, James Thomas Herbert, [No Title], *The Connoisseur*, 203, 1980, p. 108.

Barandiarán, J.M. de, 'Die prähistorischen Höhlen in der baskischen Mythologie', *Paideuma* (July 1941).

Barnum, P.T., *The Life of P.T. Barnum*. Buffalo: Courier, 1888.

Barton, George A., 'Tiamat', *Journal of the American Oriental Society*, 15, 1893, pp. 1–27.

Bassett, Fletcher, *Legends and Superstitions of the Sea and of Sailors*. Chicago and New York: Belford, Clarke & Co., 1885.

Bassett, M.G., '"Formed Stones", Folklore and Fossils', *Amgueddfa*, 7, 1971, pp. 2–17.

Belon, Pierre, *De Aquatilibus*. Paris: C. Stephanum, 1553.

Bertholin, Thomas, *Historiarum Anatomicarum Rariorum*, vol. 1, Amsterdam: Joannes Henrici, 1654.

Binns, Ronald, *The Loch Ness Mystery Solved*, Open Books, 1983.

Black, G.F., *Country Folk-Lore, vol. III: Orkney and Shetland Islands*, ed. Northcote W. Thomas. London: David Nutt, 1903.

Blanchet, A., 'Recherches sur les "grylles"', *Revue des études anciennes*, XXIII (1921), pp. 43–51.

Blind, Karl, 'Scottish, Shetlandic and Germanic Water Tales', The Contemporary Review, vol. XL (July–December, 1881), pp. 186–207.

Boer, Richard Constant, (ed.), *Orvar-Odds Saga*. Leiden: E.J. Brill, 1888.

Bonnaterre, Pierre Joseph, *Tableau Encyclopedique et Methodique*. Paris: Panckoucke, 1789.

Bossewell, John, *Works of Armorie*. London: Richard Totelli, 1572.

Boswell, James, *The Journal of a Tour to the Hebrides with Samuel Johnson*. London: Henry Baldwin, 1785.

Brand, John, *Popular Antiquities of Great Britain: Faiths and Folklore; A Dictionary of National Beliefs, Superstitions and Popular Customs [...]*, ed. Sir Henry Ellis, 2 vols. London: Rivington et al., 1813; new ed. William Carew Hazlitt. London: Reeves and Turner, 1905.

Breiner, Laurence A., 'The Career of the Cockatrice', *Isis*, vol. 70, no. 1 (March 1979), pp. 30–47.

Brooke, Stopford A., *The History of Early English Literature*. New York: Macmillan & Co., 1892.

Brooks, John, 'The Nail of the Great Beast', *Western Folklore*, Vol. 18, No. 4 (Oct., 1959), pp. 317–21.

Brontë, Charlotte, *Jane Eyre*. London: Smith, Elder & Co., 1847.

Brown, Charles E., *Paul Bunyan Tales*. Madison WI: N.p., 1922.

Brown, Charles E., *Paul Bunyan: Natural History*. Madison, WI: N.p., 1935.

Buckland, Francis T., *Curiosities of Natural History*, vol. II. London: Richard Bextley, 1868.

Buckland, Frank [Francis], *Log-Book of a Fisherman and Zoologist*. London: Chapman & Hall, 1875.

Budge, E.A. Wallis, *The Egyptian Book of the Dead: The Papyrus of Ani*. London: British Museum, 1895.

Budge, E.A. Wallis, *The Babylonian Legends of the Creation*. London: Harrison and Sons, 1921.

Buffon, Georges Lois Leclerc, comte de, *Buffon's Natural History*, vol. VIII. London: H.D. Symonds, 1807 [1797].

Burns, Robert, *The Works of Robert Burns*, ed. James Currie, vol. III. Liverpool: J. M'Creery, 1800.

Burton, Robert, *The Anatomy of Melancholy*. Philadelphia: E. Claxton & Co., 1883 [1621].

Caesar, C. Julius, *Caesar's Gallic War*, trans. W. A. McDevitte and W. S. Bohn. New York: Harper & Brothers, 1869.

Calvert, Albert F., *The Aborigines of Western Australia*. London: Simpkin, Marshall, Hamilton, Kent & Co., 1894.

Cambrensis, Giraldus, *The Historical Works of Giraldus Cambrensis*, trans. Thomas Forester and Sir Richard Colt Hoare. London: George Bell and Sons, 1894.

Campbell, Alexander, *The History of Leith*. Leith: William Reid & Son, 1827.

Campbell, J.F. *Popular Tales of the West Highlands*, New Edition, vol. IV. London: Alexander Gardner, 1893.

Campbell, J.F., *The Celtic Dragon Myth*, trans. George Henderson. Edinburgh: J. Grant, 1911.

Campbell, John Gregorson *Superstitions of the Highlands and Islands of Scotland*. Glasgow: MacLehose and Sons, 1900.

Carmichael, Alexander, *Carmina Gadelica: Hymns and Incantations*, 2 vols. Edinburgh: T. and A. Constable, 1900; new ed., Oliver and Boyd, 1928.

Carrington, Richard, *Mermaids and Mastodons*, pp. 59–62.

Caxton, William, *Caxton's Mirrour of the World*, ed. Iliver H. Prior. London: Early English Text Society, 1913.

Chaucer, Geoffrey, *The Canterbury Tales*. London: William Caxton, 1478.

Collaert, Adriaen, *Animalium Quadrupedum*. Antwerp: n.p., 1612.

Cook, Albert Stanburrough, and James Hall Pitman (trans.), *The Old English Physiologus*. Oxford: Oxford University Press, 1821.

Costello, Peter, *In Search of Lake Monsters*. Berkeley: Medallion Books, 1974.

Cox, William T., *Fearsome Creatures of the Lumberwoods, With a Few Desert and Mountain Beasts*. Washington: Judd & Detweiler, Inc., 1910.

Craigie, William A., *Scandinavian Folk-Lore*. London: Alexander Gardner, 1896.

Crawhall, Joseph, *History of the Lambton Worm; Also, The Laidley Worm of Spindleston Heugh*. Newcastle: W. and T. Fordyce, n.d.

Ctesias, *Ancient India as Described by Ktesias the Knidian*, ed. J.W. McCrindle. London: Trübner & Co., 1882.

Curry, Andrew, 'The Dawn of Art', *Archaeology*, Vol. 60, No. 5 (September/October 2007), pp. 28–33.

Curtis, Edmund, 'Some Medieval Seals out of the Ormond Archives', *The Journal of the Royal Society of Antiquaries of Ireland*, Seventh Series, Vol. 6, No. 1 (30 June 1936), pp. 1–8.

Czaplicka, M.A., *Shamanism in Siberia*. Oxford: Clarendon Press, 1914.

Dance, Peter, *Animal Fakes and Frauds*. London: Sampson Low, 1976.

Daniel, William Barker, *Rural Sports*. London: Bunny and Gold, 1801.

Davidson, H.R. Ellis, *Pagan Scandinavia*. London: Thames & Hudson, 1967.

Davidson, Olaf, 'The Folk-Lore of Icelandic Fishes', *The Scottish Review* (July and October, 1900), pp. 312–32.

Davis, F. Hadland, *Myths and Legends of Japan*. London: George G. Harrap & Co., 1912.

Dennison, W. Traill, '326. Orkney Folklore. Sea Myths. – 4. Nuckelavee', *The Scottish Antiquary*, vol. 5 (1891), 130–3.

Dennison, W. Traill, '495. Orkney Folklore. – 11. Selkie Folk', *The Scottish Antiquary*, vol. VII (1903), 171–7.

Derrett, J. Duncan M., 'The History of Palladiaus on the Races of India and the Brahmans', Classica et Mediaevalia, 21 (1960), 64–135.

Ditchfield, Peter Hampson, *Old English Customs Extant at the Present Time*. London: George Redway, 1896.

Dixon, Roland B., *Oceanic Mythology*. Boston: Marshall Jones Company, 1916.

Doblhoff, Josef Frh. v., 'Altes und Neues vom "Tatzelwurm"', *Zeitschrift für Österreichische Volkskunde* (1896), 142–67.

O'Donoghue, Denis, *Brendaniana: St Brendan the Voyager in Story and Legend*. Dublin: Browne & Nolan, 1893.

O'Donovan, J., *Tribes and Customs of Hy Many*. Dublin: Irish Archaeological Society, 1843.

Douglas, Sir George, *Scottish Fairy and Folk Tales*. London: Walter Scott, 1901.

Druce, George C., 'The Caladrius and its Legend, Sculptured upon the Twelfth-Century Doorway of Alne Church, Yorkshire', *Archaeological Journal*, 69 (1912), 381–416.

Druce, George C., 'The Elephant in Medieval Legend and Art', *Journal of the Royal Archaeological Institute*, vol. 76 (1919).

Druce, George C., 'An Account of the Mermecoleon or Ant-Lion', *Antiquaries Journal*, 3, 1923, 347–64.

Drugulin, W.E., *Historischer Bilderatlas*. Leipzig, 1682.

Durham, M. Edith, 'High Albania and its Customs in 1908', *The Journal of the Royal Anthropological Institute of Great Britain and Ireland*, Vol. 40 (Jul.–Dec., 1910), pp. 453–72.

Dyer, T.F. Thiselton, *The Folk-Lore of Plants*. London: Chatto & Windus, 1889.

Dyer, T.F. Thiselton, *The Ghost World*. London: Ward & Downey, 1893.

Easton, M.G., *The Illustrated Bible Dictionary*. London: Thomas Nelson, 1897.

Eberhardt, George, *Mysterious Creatures: A Guide to Cryptozoology*, 2 vols. Bideford: CFZ, 2013.

Egede, Hans, *A Natural Description of Greenland*. London: C. Hitch, 1745.

Eiichirô, Ishida, 'The "Kappa" Legend: A Comparative Ethnological Study on the Japanese Water-Spirit "Kappa" and Its Habit of Trying to Lure Horses into the Water', *Folklore Studies*, 9 (1950), pp. 1–152.

Ellis, Richard S., 'The Trouble with "Hairies"', *Iraq*, Vol. 57 (1995), pp. 159–65.

Elvin, Charles Norton, *A Dictionary of Heraldry*. London: Kent and Co., 1889.

Eric, Duncan, *Rural Rhymes, and The Sheep Thief*. Toronto: W. Briggs, 1896.

L'Estrange, John, *The Eastern Counties Collectanea*. Norwich: Tallack, 1872.

Euripides. *The Complete Greek Drama*, ed. Whitney J. Oates and Eugene O'Neill, Jr., 2 vols. 1. *Heracles*, trans. E. P. Coleridge. New York. Random House, 1938.

Evershed, Samuel, 'Legend of the Dragon-Slayer of Lyminster', *Sussex Archaeological Collections*, 18 (1848), pp. 180–3.

Fanu, W.R. Le, *Seventy Years of Irish Life*. London: E. Arnold, 1893.

Farmer, John Stephen, and William Ernest Henley, *Slang and its Analogues Past and Present*. London: printed for subscribers, 1890.

Felsecker, Johann, *Abermaliger Wunders*. Nuremberg: n.p., 1683.

Forbes, Alexander Robert, *Gaelic Names of Beasts (Mammalia), Birds, Fishes, Insects,*

Reptiles, Etc. Edinburgh, Oliver and Boyd, 1905.

Fox-Davies, Arthur Charles, *A Complete Guide to Heraldry.* London: TG & EG Jack, 1909.

Freeman, J.J., *South African Christian Recorder*, vol. I (no date), p. 33.

G., M.C., 'A Sea Spider', *Magazine of Natural History*, 2 (1829), p. 211.

Gadd, C. J., 'Some Contributions to the Gilgamesh Epic', *Iraq*, 8.2 (Autumn, 1966), pp. 105–21.

Galen, *De Theriaca ad Pisonem*, in *Claudii Galeni Opera Omnia*, ed. C.G. Kühn. Leipzig: C. Cnobloch, 1821–33.

Gessner, Conrad, *Historiae Animalium, 4 vols.* Zurich, 1551–8.

Giles, J.A., (ed.), *Six Old English Chronicles.* London: George Bell & Sons, 1896.

Gimbutas, Marija, *The Balts.* London: Thames and Hudson, 1963.

Ginzberg, Louis, *The Legends of the Jews*, trans. Henrietta Szold, 7 vols. Philadelphia: Jewish Publication Society of America, 1909.

Goldsmith, Oliver, *An History of the Earth and Animated Nature*, 8 vols. London: J. Nourse, 1774.

Goodman, Steven M., 'Description of a New Species of Subfossil Eagle from Madagascar: Stephanoaetus (Aves: Falconiformes) from the Deposits of Ampasambazimba', *Proceedings of the Biological Society of Washington*, 107 (1994), pp. 421–8.

Goodrich-Freer, A., 'More Folklore from the Hebrides', *Folklore*, 13.1 (Mar. 25, 1902), pp. 29–62.

Gosse, Philip Henry, *The Romance of Natural History.* Boston: Gould and Lincoln, 1864.

Gould, Charles, *Mythical Monsters.* London: W.H. Allen & Co., 1886.

Grammaticus, Saxo, *[Gesta Danorum] The Nine Books of Danish History of Saxo Grammaticus.* New York, Norroena Society, 1905.

Graves, Robert, 'Greek Myths and Pseudo Myths', *The Hudson Review*, 8.2 (Summer, 1955), pp. 212–30.

Gray, G.A., 'Remarks on a Specimen of Kingfisher, Supposed to Form a New Species of the Tanysiptera', *Annals and Magazine of Natural History*, 6 (1841), pp. 237–8.

Gray, J. E., 'On a New Genus of Mytilidae, and on some Distorted Forms which occur among Bivalve Shells', *Proceedings of the Zoological Society of London*, 26 (1858), pp. 90–2.

Green, Anthony, 'Neo-Assyrian Apotropaic Figures: Figurines, Rituals and Monumental Art, with Special Reference to the Figurines from the Excavations of the British School of Archaeology in Iraq at Nimrud', *Iraq*, Vol. 45, No. 1, Papers of the 29 Rencontre Assyriologique Internationale, London, 5–9 July 1982 (Spring, 1983), pp. 87–96.

Green, Anthony, 'A Note on the "Scorpion-Man" and Pazuzu', *Iraq*, 47 (1985), pp. 75–82.

Green, Anthony, 'A Note on the Assyrian "Goat-Fish", "Fish-Man" and "Fish-Woman"', *Iraq*, 48 (1986), pp. 25–30.

Green, Anthony, 'A Note on the "Lion-Demon"', *Iraq*, 50 (1988), pp. 167–8.

Grimm, Jacob, *Teutonic Mythology*, trans. James Steven Stallybrass, 4 vols. London: George Bell & Sons, 1883.

Gubernatis, Angelo de, *Zoological Mythology.* London: Trübner & Co., 1872.

Gudger, E.W., 'Jenny Hanivers, Dragons and Basilisks in the Old Natural History Books and in Modern Times', *Scientific Monthly*, 38.6 (Jun. 1934), pp. 511–23

Guest, Lady Charlotte, *The Mabinogion.* London: Bernard Quaritch, 1877.

Guillim, John, *A Display of Heraldrie.* London: n.p., 1610.

Gurdon, Lady Eveline Camilla, *Suffolk*, County Folk-Lore, Printed Extracts No. 2. London, D. Nutt, 1893.

Hagen, H.A., 'The History of the Origin and Development of Museums', *The American Naturalist*, 10 (1876), pp. 80–9.

Hagen, Sivert N., 'The Origin and Meaning of the Name Yggdrasill', *Modern Philology*, 1.1 (Jun. 1903), pp. 57–69.

Hakluyt, Richard, *The Principal Navigations, Voyages, Traffiques and Discoveries of the English Nation*, 12 vols. Glasgow: James MacLehose and Sons, 1903–05.

Hansen, George P., 'The Loch Ness Monster: A Guide to the Literature', *Zetetic Scholar*, 11, 1983.

Hardiman, James, (ed.), *A Chorographical Description of West or H-Iar Connaught, Written AD 1684 by Roderic O'Flaherty*. Dublin: Irish Archaeological Society, 1846.

Hardwick, Charles, *Traditions, Superstitions and Folk-Lore, Chiefly Lancashire and the North of England*. London: Simpkin, Marshall & Co., 1872.

Harland, John, *A Glossary of Words Used in Swaledale, Yorkshire*. London: English Dialect Society, 1873.

Harrison, Jr, Thomas P., 'Two of Spenser's Birds: Nightraven and Tedula', *Modern Language Review*, 44.2 (April 1949), pp. 232–5.

Harrison, Jr, Thomas P.,'The Whistler, Bird of Omen', *Modern Language Notes*, 65.8 (Dec., 1950), pp. 539–41.

Hartland, Edwin Sidney, *English Fairy and Other Folk Tales*. London: Walter Scott, 1890.

Hatto, A.T., *Essays on Medieval German and Other Poetry*. Cambridge: Cambridge University Press, 2010 [1980].

Haussig, Hans Wilhelm (ed.), *Götter und Mythen im Alten Europa*. Stuttgart: Ernst Klett, 1973.

O'Hear, Natasha and Anthony, *Picturing the Apocalypse*. Oxford: Oxford University Press, 2015.

Henderson, Andrew, *Scottish Proverbs*. Edinburgh: Oliver & Boyd, 1832.

Henderson, George, *Survivals of Belief Among the Celts*. Glasgow: James MacLehose and Sons, 1911.

Henderson, William, *Notes on the Folk-Lore of the Northern Counties of England and the Borders*. London: W. Satchell, Peyton and Co., 1879.

Herndon, William Lewis, *Exploration of the Valley of the Amazon*. Washington: R. Armstrong, 1854.

Herodotus, *The History of Herodotus*, trans. George Rawlinson. London: John Murray, 1859.

Hesiod, *Hesiod, The Homeric Hymns and Homerica*, trans. H.G. Evelyn-White. London: William Heinemann, 1914.

Hesiod, *Theogony*, in *Hesiod, The Homeric Hymns and Homerica*, trans. H.G. Evelyn-White. London: William Heinemann, 1914, pp. 78–153.

Hippo, Augustine of, *Sermo* 316:2 – In Solemnitate Stephani Martyris; Duri Iudaei in Stephanum.

Höfler, Otto, *Kultische Geheimbünde der Germanen*. Frankfurt: Moritz Diesterweg, 1934.

Hoefnagel, Joris, *Animalia Quadrupedia et Reptilia (Terra)*. Frankfurt, 1580.

Holiday, F.W., *The Great Orm of Loch Ness*. New York: W.W. Norton, 1969.

Holmberg, Uno, *Die Wassergottheiten der finnisch-ugrischen Völker*. Helsinki: die Gesellschaft, 1913.

Homer, *The Iliad*, trans. A.T. Murray, 2 vols. London: William Heinemann, 1924.

Homer, *The Odyssey*, trans. A.T. Murray, 2 vols. London, William Heinemann, Ltd., 1919.

Homer, *The Odyssey of Homer*, trans. George Herbert Palmer. Boston: Houghton Mifflin, 1891.

[Homer], *The Homeric Hymns*, ed. Thomas W. Allen and E. E. Sikes. London. Macmillan, 1904.

Hopkins, Clark, 'Assyrian Elements in the Perseus-Gorgon Story', *American Journal of*

Archaeology, 38.3 (Jul.–Sep., 1934), pp. 341–58.

[Horace] Q. Horatius Flaccus, *Horace: Odes and Epodes*. Paul Shorey. Boston: Benj. H. Sanborn & Co., 1898.

[Horace] Q. Horatius Flaccus, *Epistles*, in *The Works of Horace*, trans. C. Smart, vol. II. London: Carnan and Newbery, 1770.

Howey, M. Oldfield, *The Horse in Magic and Myth*. London: Rider, 1923.

Huc, Évariste Régis, *Travels in Tartary, Thibet, and China*, trans. W. Hazlitt, 2 vols. London: Office of the National Illustrated Library, 1852.

Hunt, Robert, *Popular Romances of the West of England*, 3rd ed. London: Chatto & Windus, 1903.

Huxley, Margaret, 'The Gates and Guardians in Sennacherib's Addition to the Temple of Assur', *Iraq*, 62 (2000), pp. 109–37.

[Pseudo-]Hyginus, *Hygini Fabulae*, ed. Maurice Schmidt. Jena: Hermann Dufft, 1872.

Ingersoll, Ernest, *Birds in Legend, Fable and Folklore*. London and New York: Longmans, Green & Co., 1923.

Ingersoll, Ernest, *Dragons and Dragon-Lore*. New York: Payson & Clarke, 1928.

Jackson, Steven, 'Callimachean Istrus and the Guinea-Fowl on Leros', *Hermes*, 128.2 (2000), pp. 236–40.

Jacobs, Joseph, *English Fairy Tales*. New York: Grosset & Dunlap, 1895.

Jastrow, Morris, *The Religion of Babylonia and Assyria*. Boston: Ginn & Co., 1898.

Jastrow, Morris, 'Sumerian Myths of Beginnings', *American Journal of Semitic Languages*, 33 (1917), 91–144.

Kearney, 'Lake Shore', *The Hodag and Other Tales of the Logging Camps*. Madison, WI: Democrat Printing Co., 1928.

Kennedy-Fraser, Marjory, *The Songs of the Hebrides*. London: Boosey & Co., 1909.

Kinahan., G. H., 'Aughisky, or Water-Horse', *The Folk-Lore Journal*, 2.2 (Feb., 1884), pp. 61–3.

King, Leonard William, *The Seven Tablets of Creation*. London: Luzac and Co., 1902.

Kirein, Peter, *Der Wolpertinger lebt*. Munich: Lipp, 1968.

Kirk, Robert, *The Secret Commonwealth*. Mineola: Dover, 2008 [1692].

Kohl, Johann Georg, *Travels in Scotland*. London: Darling, 1849.

Korotayev, Andrey, Yuri Berezkin, Artem Kozmin and Alexandra Arkhipova, 'Return of the White Raven: Postdiluvial Reconnaissance Motif A2234.1.1 Reconsidered', *Journal of American Folklore*, 119.472 (Spring, 2006), pp. 203–35.

Kramer, Samuel Noah, *Sumerian Mythology*. Philadelphia: University of Pennsylvania Press, 1961.

Kuhns, L. Oscar, 'Bestiares and Lapidaries', in *Library of the World's Best Literature Ancient and Modern*, edited by Charles Dudley Warner, vol. 4. New York: R.S. Peale, 1896.

Kunz, George Frederick, 'Madstones and their Magic', *Science*, 18.459 (20 Nov. 1891).

L., R,. 'Spotting the Siggahfoops', *Scottish Field*, 115 (1968), p. 18.

Lambert, W. G., 'The Pair Laḥmu—Laḥamu in Cosmology', *Orientalia*, new series, 54.1/2 (1985), pp. 189–202.

Lang, Andrew, (ed.), *The Arabian Nights' Entertainments*. London: Longmans, Green & Co., 1898.

Lang, Andrew, *The Crimson Fairy Book*. London: Longmans, Green & Co., 1903.

Langdon, Stephen, *Babylonian Liturgies*. Paris: Paul Geuthner, 1913.

Langdon, S. [Stephen], 'Six Babylonian and Assyrian Seals', *Journal of the Royal Asiatic Society of Great Britain and Ireland*, 1 (Jan., 1927), pp. 43–50.

Lee, Henry, *The Vegetable Lamb of Tartary: A Curious Fable of the Cotton Plant*. London: S. Low, Marston, Searle & Rivington, 1887.

Leland, Charles G., *The Algonquin Legends of New England*. Boston and New York: Houghton, Mifflin & Co., 1884.

Linnaeus, Carolus, *Systema Naturae*, 2nd ed. Stockholm: Gottfried Kiesewetter, 1740.

Lloyd, George Thomas, *Thirty-Seven Years in Tasmania and Victoria*. London: Houlston and Wright, 1862.

[Lobo, Jerónimo], *A Short Relation of the River Nile: Of Its Source and Current*. London: Lackington, Allen & Co, 1798.

Lobo, Jerónimo, *A Voyage to Abyssinia*, trans. Samuel Johnson. London and Edinburgh: Elliot and Kay, 1789.

Lover, Samuel, *Legends and Stories of Ireland*. Westminster: Archibald Constable & Co., 1899.

Lucan, *Pharsalia (The Civil War)*, trans. Edward Ridley. London: Longmans, Green, and Co., 1986.

Lucian, *Lucian*, trans. A. M. Harmon, vol. IV. Cambridge MA: Harvard University Press, 1992.

Lutz, Cora E., 'The American Unicorn', *The Yale University Library Gazette*, 53.3 (Jan., 1979), pp. 135–9.

Macalister, R.A. Stewart, *The Philistines: Their History and Civilization*. London: British Academy, 1913.

MacDougall, J.M., *Waifs and Strays of Celtic Tradition, Argyllshire Series, No. III: Folk and Hero Tales*. London: David Nutt, 1891.

MacDougall, James, and George Calder, *Folk Tales and Fairy Lore in Gaelic and English*. Edinburgh: J. Grant, 1910.

MacGregor, Alasdair Alpin, *The Peat-Fire Flame: Folk-Tales and Traditions of the Highlands and Islands*. Edinburgh: The Moray Press, 1937.

M'Kenzie, Dan, 'Children and Wells', *Folklore*, 18.3 (Sep., 1907), pp. 253–82.

Mackay, Charles, *A Dictionary of Lowland Scotch*. London: Whittaker, 1888.

Mackenzie, Donald A., *Myths of Babylonia and Assyria*. London: Gresham, 1915.

Mackenzie, Donald A., *Myths of China and Japan*. London: Gresham, 1923.

Mackinlay, James Murray, *Folklore of Scottish Lochs and Springs*. Glasgow: W. Hodge, 1893.

Macleod, Fiona, *Wind and Wave, Collection of British Authors*, 3609. Leipzig: Tauchnitz, 1902.

MacRitchie, David, 'Memories of the Picts', *The Scottish Antiquary, or, Northern Notes and Queries*, 14.55 (Jan., 1900), pp. 121–39.

Magnus, Albertus, *De Animalibus Historia*, ed. Hermann Stadler. Münster: Aschendorff, 1916.

Malte-Brun, Conrad, *Universal Geography*, vol. IV. Edinburgh: Adam Black, 1823.

Mandeville, John, *The Travels of Sir John Mandeville*, ed. A.W. Pollard. London: Macmillan and Co., 1900.

Mantell, Gideon Algernon, *Illustrated London News* (4 Nov. 1848).

Martin, Douglas, 'Douglas Herrick, 82, Dies; Father of West's Jackalope', *New York Times* (19 Jan. 2003).

Maylam, Percy, *The Hooden Horse*. Canterbury: Privately Printed, 1909.

McCrindle, J.W., (ed.), *Ancient India as Described by Megasthenês and Arrian*. London: Trübner & Co., 1877.

Milton, John, *Paradise Lost*, Bk II, in *The Poetical Works of John Milton*, vol. II (London: Law and Gilbert, 1809).

Miles, Clement A., *Christmas in Ritual and Tradition, Christian and Pagan*. London: T. Fisher Unwin, 1912.

Miljutin, Andrei, 'Rat Kings in Estonia', *Proc. Estonian Acad. Sci. Biol. Ecol.*, 56.1 (2007), 77–81.

Misson, Francis Maximilian, *A New Voyage to Italy*, vol. I. London, 1699.

Montanus, Arnoldus, *De Nieuwe en onbekende Weereld: Of Beschryving van America en't Zuid-land*. Amsterdam: Jacob van Meurs, 1671.

Montecuccolo, Giovanni Antonio Cavazzi da, *Istorica descrizione de tre regni Congo, Matamba ed Angola*. Bologna: Giacomo Monti, 1687.

Moore, George F., *A Descriptive Vocabulary of the Language in Common Use Amongst the Aborigines of Western Australia*. London: W. S. Orr & Co., 1842.

Morris, Edward Ellis, *Austral English: A Dictionary of Australasian Words, Phrases and Usages*. London: Macmillan, 1898.

Morris, Henry, 'Features Common to Irish, Welsh, and Manx Folklore', *Béaloideas*, 7.2 (Dec., 1937), pp. 168–79.

Murray, Margaret A., *Ancient Egyptian Legends*. London: John Murray, 1920.

Murthy, K. Krishna, *Mythical Animals in Indian Art*. New Delhi: Abhinav, 1985.

A New English Dictionary, 10 vols. Oxford: Clarendon Press, 1888–1928.

Nickel, Helmut, 'And Behold, a White Horse: Observations on the Colors of the Horses of the Four Horsemen of the Apocalypse', *Metropolitan Museum Journal*, 12 (1977), pp. 179–83.

Niehoff, M. R., 'The Phoenix in Rabbinic Literature', *Harvard Theological Review*, 89.3 (July, 1996), pp. 245–65.

Nonnos, *Dionysiaca*, trans. W.H.D. Rouse, 3 vols. London: William Heinemann, 1940.

Norway, Arthur, *Highways and Byways in Devon and Cornwall*. London: Macmillan, 1897.

Nuttal, Zelia, 'A Note on Ancient Mexican Folk-Lore', *Journal of American Folklore*, 3 (1895–6), 117–29.

Oliphant, Samuel Grant, 'The Story of the Strix: Ancient', *Transactions and Proceedings of the American Philological Association*, 44 (1913), 133–49.

Ornan, Tallay, 'Expelling Demons at Nineveh: On the Visibility of Benevolent Demons in the Palaces of Nineveh', *Iraq*, 66 (2004), pp. 83–92.

Oudemans, A.C., *The Great Sea-Serpent: An Historical and Critical Treatise*. London: Luzac & Co., 1892.

Osbeck, Peter, *A Voyage to China and the East Indies*, trans. John Rheinhold Forster, 2 vols. London: Benjamin White, 1771.

Ovid, *The Fasti, Tristia, Pontic Epistles, Ibis and Halieuticon of Ovid*, trans Henry T. Riley. London: H.G. Bohn, 1876.

Ovid, *Metamorphoses*, trans. John Dryden, et al. London: J.F. Dove, 1826.

Owen, Elias, *Welsh Folk-Lore*. Oswestry and Wrexham: Wododall, Minshall and Co., 1896.

Pausanias, *Description of Greece*, trans. W.H.S. Jones, Litt. D. and H.A. Ormerod, M.A., 6 vols. London: William Heinemann, 1918.

Peacock, Edward, 'Ghostly Hounds at Horton', *Folk-Lore Journal*, 4.3 (1886), pp. 266–7.

Peck, Harry Thurston, (ed.), *Harper's Dictionary of Classical Literature and Antiquities*. New York: Harper & Brothers, 1896.

Philostratus the Elder, *Imagines*, trans. Arthur Fairbanks. London: William Heinemann, 1931.

Piccardi, L., 'Seismotectonic Origins of the Monster of Loch Ness', *Earth System Processes: Programmes with Abstracts, Geological Society of America and Geological Society of London* (2001), p. 98.

Pindar, *The Odes of Pindar*, trans. Sir John Edwin. London: William Heinemann 1915.

Pinkerton, John, *A General Collection of the Best and Interesting Voyages and Travels in all Parts of the World*, vol. XVI. London: Longman, Hurst, Rees, Orme and Brown, 1814.

Pliny, *The Historie of the World. Commonly called, The Naturall Historie of C. Plinius Secundus*, trans. Philemon Holland. London: Adam, 1601.

Plummer, Charles, (ed.), *Two of the Saxon Chronicles*. Oxford: Clarendon Press, 1897.

Plutarch, *Plutarch's Lives*, trans. Bernadotte Perrin. London: William Heinemann, 1914.

Polo, Marco, *The Travels of Marco Polo the Venetian*, ed. John Masefield. London: J.M. Dent & Sons, 1908.

Polo, Marco, *The Travels of Marco Polo: The Complete Yule-Cordier Edition*, vol. II. N.p.: Project Gutenberg, 2004.

Pontoppidan, Erich, *The Natural History of Norway*, trans. A. Berthelson. London: A. Linde, 1755.

Potapov, L.P., 'Über den Pferdekult bei den turksprachigen Völkern des Sajan-Altai-Gebirges', *Abhandlungen und Berichte des Staatlichen Museums für Völkerkunde Dresden*, 34 (1975), pp. 473–88.

Quintus Smyrnaeus, *The Fall of Troy*, trans. Arthur S. Way. London: William Heinemann, 1913.

R., A., *True and Wonderfull: A Discourse Relating a Strange and Monstrous Serpent, or Dragon, Lately Discovered and yet Living to the Great Annoyance and Divers Slaughters both Men and Cattel*. London: John Trundle, 1614.

R., J., 'Zoological Imposture', *Magazine of Natural History*, 1 (1829), p. 189.

Reade, W. Winwood, *Savage Africa*. New York: Harper & Bros., 1864.

Rhys, John, *Celtic Folklore: Welsh and Manx*, vol. I. Oxford: Oxford University Press, 1901.

Richards, Thomas, *Antiquæ Linguæ Britannicæ Thesaurus*. Dolgelly: R. Jones, 1815.

Ridgeway, Sir William, *The Early Age of Greece*. Cambridge: Cambridge University Press, 1901.

Roes, Anne, 'New Light on the Grylli', *Journal of Hellenic Studies*, 55.2 (1935), pp. 232–5.

Rondelet, Guillaume, *Libri de Piscibus Marinis*. Lugduni [Lyon]: Mattiam Bonhomme, 1554.

Rydberg, Viktor, *Teutonic Mythology: Gods and Goddesses of the Northland*, 3 vols. London: Norroena Society, 1906.

Sanderson, Ivan T., *Abominable Snowmen: Legend Come to Life*. Philadelphia and New York: Chilton, 1961.

Saxby, Jessie M.E., *Shetland Traditional Lore*. Edinburgh: Grant & Murray, 1932.

Schmid, Herman, *The Bavarian Highlands and the Salzkammergut*. London: Chapman & Hall, 1874.

Schröer, K.J., 'Mythische Gestalten im Presburger Volksglauben: Wauwau', *Zeitschrift für deutsche Mythologie und Sittenkunde* (1853).

Schütte, Gudmund, 'Danish Paganism', *Folklore*, 35.4 (31 December 1924), pp. 360–71.

Scot, Reginald, *The Discovery of Witches*, ed. Brinsley Nicholson. London: Elliot Stock, 1886 [1584].

Scott, Sir Walter, *Letters on Demonology and Witchcraft*. Edinburgh: Ballantyne and Co., 1840.

Scott, Sir Walter, *Minstrelsy of the Scottish Border*, ed. T.F. Henderson, 4 vols. Edinburgh: W. Blackwood, 1902.

Seneca, L. Annaeus, *Hercules Furens*, in *Tragoediae*, ed. by Rudolf Peiper, Gustav Richter. Leipzig: Teubner, 1921.

Servius, *Ad Aeneid*, in *Vergilii carmina comentarii. Servii Grammatici qui feruntur in Vergilii carmina commentarii*, ed. Georg Thilo and Hermann Hagen. Leipzig: Teubner, 1881.

Seville, Isidore of, *The Etymologies of Isidore of Seville,* trans. Stephen A. Barney et al. Cambridge: Cambridge University Press, 2006.

Seymour, St John D., and Harry L. Neligan. *True Irish Ghost Stories*. Dublin: Hodges, Figgis & Co., 1914.

Sharpe, R. Bowdler, *Catalogue of the Passerifotmes, or Perching Birds in the Collection of the British Museum*, part 1. London: British Museum, 1879.

Sharpe, R. Bowdler, 'Notes on Some Birds from Perak', *Proceedings of the Zoological Society of London* (1886), p. 354.

Shaw, Ian, and Paul Nicholson, *The British Museum Dictionary of Ancient Egypt*. London: British Museum, 1995.

Sheldon, J.S., 'Herodotus and the Iranian Tradition', in *Thinking Like a Lawyer*, ed. by Paul McKechnie. Leiden: Brill, 2002, pp. 167–80.

Shepard, Odell, *Lore of the Unicorn*. London: Allen & Unwin, 1930.

Shope, Richard E., and E. Weston Hurst, 'Infectious Papillomatosis of Rabbits', *J. Exp. Med.*, 58.5 (31 Oct. 1933), pp. 607–24.

Sikes, Wirt, *British Goblins: Welsh Folk-Lore, Fairy Mythology, Legends and Traditions*, London: S. Low, Marston, Searle & Rivington, 1880.

Smith, Andrew, *Illustrations of the Zoology of South Africa*. London: Smith, Elder & Co., 1838.

Smith, George, *The Chaldean Account of Genesis*. London: Thomas Scott, 1876.

Smith, William, *A Dictionary of Greek and Roman Biography and Mythology*. London: John Murray, 1873.

Solinus, Caius Julius, *Collectanea Rerum Memorabilium*, ed. Theodor Mommsen. Berlin: Friderici Nicolai, 1864.

Sorrento, Girolamo Merolla da, *Breve e succinta relazione del vaggio nel regno di Congo nell'Africa meridionale Fatto dal P. Giralamo Merolla da Sorrento 1684–1688*. Naples: F. Mollo, 1692.

Spence, Lewis, *The Popol Vuh: The Mythic and Heroic Sagas of the Kiches of Central America*. London: David Nutt, 1908.

Spence, Lewis, *The Gods of Mexico*. London: T. Fischer Unwin, 1923.

Spicer, Dorothy Gladys, *Festivals of Western Europe*. New York: H.W. Wilson Co., 1958.

Stevenson, Robert Louis, *Travels with a Donkey in the Cevennes*. Boston: Herbert B. Turner & Co., 1903.

Stewart, George, *Shetland Fireside Tales*, 2nd ed. Lerwick: T. & J. Manson, 1892.

Strabo, *The Geography of Strabo*, ed. H. L. Jones. London: William Heinemann, 1924.

Stratton, Florence, *When the Storm God Rides: Tejas and Other Indian Legends*. New York: Charles Scribner's Sons, 1936.

Sturluson, Snorri, *Prose Edda* [c.1200], trans. Arthur Gilchrist Brodeur. New York: The American-Scandinavian Foundation, 1916.

Swainson, Charles, *Provincial Names and Folklore of British Birds*. London: Trübner & Co., 1885.

Swinburne, Algernon Charles, *Border Ballads*. Boston: Bibliophile Society, 1912.

Tatlock, J.S.P., 'The Dragons of Wessex and Wales', *Speculum*, 8.2 (Apr., 1933), pp. 223–35.

Tavernier, Jean Baptiste, *Travels in India*, trans. V. Ball, vol. II. London: Macmillan and Co., 1889.

Teit, J. A., 'Water-Beings in Shetlandic Folk-Lore, as Remembered by Shetlanders in British Columbia', *The Journal of American Folklore*, 31.120 (Apr.–Jun., 1918), pp. 180–201.

Tellez, Balthazar, *The Travels of the Jesuits in Ethiopia*. London: Knapton, Bell, et al., 1710.

Tennyson, Alfred, *Poems, Chiefly Lyrical*. London: Effingham Wilson, 1830.

Tertullian, *Liber Apologeticus: The Apology of Tertullian*, ed. Henry Annesley Woodham. Cambridge: Cambridge University Press, 1843.

Theophrastus, *Theophrastou tou Eresiou Peri taon lithaon biblion: Theophrastus's History of Stones with an English version, and Critical and Philosophical Note*s. London: C. Davis, 1746.

Thomas, W. Jenkyn, *The Welsh Fairy Book*. New York: F.A. Stokes, 1908.

Thompson, R. Campbell, *The Devils and Evil Spirits of Babylonia*, vol. I. London: Luzac & Co., 1903.

Thompson, R. Campbell, (trans.), *The Epic of Gilgamesh*. London: Luzac & Co., 1928.

Thone, Frank, 'Unicorn No Longer Fabulous; Biologist Has Produced One', *The Science News Letter*, 29.788 (16 May 1936), pp. 312–13.

Thorpe, Benjamin, *Northern Mythology*, vol. II. London: Edward Lumley, 1851.

Tohall, Patrick, 'The Dobhar-Chú Tombstones of Glenade, Co. Leitrim (Cemetries of Congbháil and Cill-Rúisc)', *The Journal of the Royal Society of Antiquaries of Ireland*, 78.2 (Dec., 1948), pp. 127–9.

Topsell, Edward, *The History of Four-Footed Beasts and Serpents*. London: E. Cotes, 1658.

Trevelyan, Marie, *Folk-Lore and Folk-Stories of Wales*. London: Elliot Stock, 1909.

Triton, Henry H., *Fearsome Critters*. Cornwall, NY: Idlewild Press, 1939.

Turner, William, *Turner on Birds*, ed. by A.H. Evans. Cambridge: Cambridge University Press, 1903 [1544].

V., 'Notice of an Imposture Entitled a Pygmy Bison, or American Ox', *Magazine of Natural History*, 2 (1829), pp. 218–19.

Verein zur Hebung des Fremdenberkehrs in Lüneburg, *Führer durch Lüneburg und Umgegend*. Lüneburg: Herold and Wahlstab, 1905.

Viking Club, *Saga-Book of the Viking Club, Society for Northern Research*, 3 (1903), p. x.

Vinycomb, John, *Fictitious and Symbolic Creatures in Art*. London: Chapman and Hall, 1906.

Virgil, *The Aeneid*, trans. Robert Fagles. London: Viking (Penguin), 2006.

W., 'Remarks on the Histories of the Kraken and Great Sea Serpent', *Blackwood's Magazine*, 2 (March, 1818), pp. 645–54.

Waddell, L.A., *Among the Himalayas*. Westminster: Archibald Constable & Co., 1899.

Waterton, Charles, *Natural History Essays*, ed. Norman Moore. London: Frederick Warne and Co., *c.*1870.

Watson, E. C., 'Highland Mythology', *The Celtic Review*, 5.17 (Jul., 1908), pp. 48–70.

Waugh, Arthur, 'The Folklore of the Whale', *Folklore*, 2.2 (Jun., 1961), pp. 361–71.

Webber, W.L., *The Thunder Bird Tootooch Legends*. Seattle: Ace Printing Co., 1936.

Webster, Wentworth, *Basque Legends*. London: Griffith and Farran, 1879.

West, E.W., (trans.), *Pahlavi Texts, Part III: Dînâ-î Maînôg-î Khirad, Sikand-gûmânîk Vigâr, and the Sad Dar*, Sacred Books of the East, vol. 24. Oxford: Clarendon, 1885.

Wiggerman, F.A.M., *Mesopotamian Protective Spirits: The Ritual Texts*. Groningen: Styx, 1992.

Wilde, Lady Francesca Speranza, *Ancient Legends, Mystic Charms, and Superstitions of Ireland*. London: Ward & Downey, 1887.

Wilkins, W.J., *Hindu Mythology: Vedic and Puranic*. London and Calcutta: Thacker & Co., 1900.

Williams, Herschel. *Fairy Tales from Folk Lore*. New York: Moffat, Yard & Co., 1908.

Williams, N. J. A., 'Of Beasts and Banners the Origin of the Heraldic Enfield', *The Journal of the Royal Society of Antiquaries of Ireland*, 119 (1989), pp. 62–78.

Willughby, Francis, *Ornithology*, ed. John Ray. London: John Martyn, 1678.

Wolf, Kirsten, 'The Color Grey in Old Norse-Icelandic Literature', *Journal of English and Germanic Philology*, 108.2 (April 2009), pp. 222–38.

Wood, Ernest, and S.V. Subrahmanyam (trans.), *The Garuda Purana*. Allahabad: Panini Office, 1911.

Wood-Martin, W.G., *Traces of the Elder Faiths of Ireland*. London: Longmans, Green and Co., 1902.

Woodward, John, *A Treatise on Heraldry, British and Foreign*, 2 vols. Edinburgh and London: W. & A.K. Johnston, 1892.

Wright, Elizabeth Mary, *Rustic Speech and Folk-Lore*. London: Humphrey Milford, 1913.

Wright, Thomas, *Dictionary of Obsolete and Provincial English*. London: Henry G. Bohn, 1857.

Wulff, Winifred, 'Carnagat', *Journal of the Royal Society of Antiquaries of Ireland*, Sixth Series, 12.1 (30 Jun., 1922), pp. 38–41.

Wyman, *Proc. Boston Soc. of Nat. Hist.*, 2 (Nov., 1845), p. 65.

Yeats, William Butler, *The Celtic Twilight*. London: A.H. Bullen, 1902.

Yule, Henry, and A.C. Burnell, *Hobson-Jobson: A Glossary of Colloquial Anglo-Indian Words and Phrases*, ed. by William Crooke. London: J. Murray, 1903.

Zimmern, Helen, *The Epic of Kings: Stories Retold from Firdusi*. London: T. Fischer Unwin, 1883.

PICTURE CREDITS

Alphyn: Kelcey Swain, 'Heraldic Alphyn', 2008, digital rendering, Wikimedia Commons.

Aspidochelone: 'Bestiarius', Danish Royal Library, Copenhagen, MS, GKS 1633 4º, fol. 59v (dated 1633).

Aspis: 'Bestiary with Theological Texts', c.1200-c.1210, British Library, London, Royal MS 12 C XIX, fol. 65v.

Bäckahäst: Theodor Kittelsen, *Gutt på hvit hest* [Boy on a White Horse], c.1900, pencil on paper, Nordnorsk Kunstmuseum, Norway.

Balaena: 'Bestiary', c.1236–1250, British Library, London, Harley MS 3244, fol. 60v.

Basilisk (1): 'Bestiary with Theological Texts', c.1200–c.1210, British Library, London, Royal MS 12 C XIX, fol. 63.

Basilisk (2): Ulyssis Aldrovandi, *Serpentum et Draconum Historiae* (Bononiae: C. Ferronium, 1640), p. 363.

Basilisk (3): Wenceslas Hollar after Marcus Gheeraerts the Younger, *The Basilisk and the Weasel*, seventeenth century, print.

Beast of the Apocalypse (Sea): William Blake, *The Great Red Dragon and the Beast from the Sea*, 1805, pen and watercolour, National Gallery of Art, Washington, DC.

Beast of the Apocalypse (Earth): 'The Beast from the Earth Killing People and People Receiving the Mark of the Beast', c.1255–1260, tempera colours, gold leaf, coloured washes, pen and ink on parchment, John Paul Getty Museum, Los Angeles, MS Ludwig III 1, fol. 25v.

Behemoth: Louis Le Breton, illustration, in Collin de Plancy, *Dictionnaire Infernal* (Paris: Henri Plon, 1863).

Bonasus: 'Rochester Bestiary', c.1230–fourteenth century, British Library, London, Royal MS 12 F XIII, fol. 16r.

Bunyip: *Australian Illustrated News* (1 October 1890).

Caladrius: 'Bestiary with Theological Texts', c.1200–c.1210, British Library, London, Royal MS 12 C XIX, fol. 47v.

Centaur: 'Bestiary with Theological Texts', c.1200–c.1210, British Library, London, Royal MS 12 C XIX, fol. 8v.

Cerberus: Hans Sebald Beham, *Hercules Capturing Cerberus* (The Labours of Hercules), 1545 (1542–1548), engraving.

Ceryneian Hind: Antonio Tempesta/Nicolo Van Aelst, *Hercules and the Hind of Mount Cerynea* (The Labours of Hercules, plate 6), 1608, etching, Los Angeles County Museum of Art, Los Angeles.

Chimæra: Apulian red-figure dish, c.350–340 BCE, Louvre, Paris, K362.

Chrysomallus: Jason seizes the Golden Fleece, Roman sarcophagus, second century CE, Palazzo Altemps, National Roman Museum, Rome, 8647.

Cinnamologus: 'Bestiary', c.1236–1250, British Library, London, Harley MS 3244, fol. 54.

Colchian Dragon (Echidna): Salvator Rosa, Jason and the Dragon, c.1663–1664, etching and drypoint on laid paper, National Gallery of Art, Washington DC.

Cretan Bull: Bernard Picart, 1731, engraving.

Cynocephalus: Ulyssis Aldrovandi, *Monstrum Historia* (Bologna: 1642).

Dragon: 'Drachen Hilpoltstein 1533', *Augsburger Wunderzeichenbuch* (Augsburg: n.p., c.1550), fol. 129.

Dragon (Wyvern): Claude Paradin and Francois d'Amboise, *Dévises héroiqves et emblèmes* (Paris: R. Bovtonné, 1622).

Dragon (Head): Giovanni Battista Tiepolo, *The Immaculate Conception* (detail), 1767–1768, oil on canvas, Museo Nacional del Prado, Madrid.

Erymanthian Boar: Antonio Tempesta/Nicolo Van Aelst, *Hercules and the Boar of Erymanthus*, The Labours of Hercules plate 4, 1608, etching, Los Angeles County Museum of Art, Los Angeles.

Fearsome Critters: Coert Du Bois, 'The Splinter Cat', published in William T. Cox, *Fearsome Creatures of the Lumberwoods* (Washington, DC: Judd & Detweiler, 1910), p. 36.

Fenrir: 'Odin and Fenris', H.A. Guerber, *Myths of the Norsemen from the Eddas and Sagas* (London: Harrap, 1909) illustration facing p. 334.

Fur-Bearing Trout: Ross C. Jobe, *Fur Bearing Trout*, no date, taxidermy, photograph by Samantha Marx, 2009.

Glycon: Statue of Glycon in Tomis, Constanta, photograph by Christian Chirita, c.2009.

Griffin: 'Rochester Bestiary', c.1230–fourteenth century, British Library, London, Royal 12 F XIII, fol. 11r.

Hercynea: 'Bestiary' c.1236–1250, British Library, London, Harley MS 3244, fol. 54.

Hippocampus: Walter Crane, *Neptune's Horses*, c.1910, published in *The Greek Mythological Legend* (London: n.p., 1910).

Hydra: 'An embalmed serpent sent by the Venetians to King Francis 1560', Pierre Boaistuau, *Histoires prodigieuses*, fol. 145R, Wellcome Library, London, WMS 136 (L0025568).

Ichneumon: Egyptian, bronze, c.600–500 BCE (Late Period), Walters Art Museum, Baltimore, Accession No. 54.410.

Jörmundgandr: 'Thor, Hymir and the Midgard Serpent' from Viktor Rydberg, Teutonic Mythology, 3vols (London: Norroena Society, 1906).

Jenny Haniver: specimen made from a guitar fish, former Collection of Jules Berdoulat, Museum of Toulouse, Toulouse, photograph by Didier Descouens, 2012.

Katzenknäuel: Johann Jonathan Felsecker, *Abermaliger Wunderswürdiger und entsetzlicher Scheusal Wie vormals der Ratzen also auch jetzt der Katzen* (Nürnberg: n.p., 1683).

King Charles I's Parrot: published in Frank Buckland, *Log-Book of a Fisherman and Zoologist* (London: Chapman & Hall, 1875).

Kraken: Riov/Etherington, 'De Alecto vindt een reuzeninktvis' ('The Alecto finds a giant squid'), engraving, published in *De Aarde en Haar Volken* (Haarlem: A.C. Kruseman, 1867).

Ladon: Antonio Tempesta/Nicolo Van Aelst, *Hercules and the Serpent Ladon* (The Labours of Hercules, plate 10), 1608, etching, Los Angeles County Museum of Art, Los Angeles.

Lamassu: Façade M, Gate K, Nr 1, Palace of Sargon II, from Paul-Émile Botta and M.E. Flandin, *Les Monument de Ninive*, vol. 1 (Paris: Imprimerie Nationale, 1849).

Lamia: Edward Topsell, *The History of Four-Footed Beasts and Serpents* (London: E.Cotes, 1658).

Lepus Cornutus: Robert Bénard, *Lièvre cornu*, c.1789, engraving, in Pierre Joseph Bonnaterre, *Tableau Encyclopedique et Methodique* (Paris: Panckoucke, 1789).

Lernæan Hydra: Cornelis Cort, *Hercules Killing the Lernæan Hydra*, c.1565, engraving.

Leucrocuta: 'Rochester Bestiary', c.1230–fourteenth century, British Library, London, Royal 12 F XIII, fol. 23r.

Leviathan: H. Pisan after Gustave Doré, *The Destruction of Leviathian*, 1866, engraving, published in *The Holy Bible with Illustrations by*

Gustave Doré (London: Cassel, Petter, and Galpin, 1866).

Manticore: Joannes Jonstonus, *A Description of the Nature of Four-Footed Beasts* (London: Moses Pitt, 1678).

Mares of Diomedes: Antonio Tempesta/Nicolo Van Aelst, *Hercules and the Mares of Diomedes* (The Labours of Hercules, plate 8), 1608, Los Angeles County Museum of Art, Los Angeles.

Mari Llwyd: Thomas Christopher Evans, *The Mari Llwyd at Llangynwyd*, c.1910–1914, photograph, National Library of Wales, Aberystwyth, Photo Album 929 A.

Mermaid: *Fake Mermaid*, 1923, photograph, Gold Museum, Ballarat, Victoria, Australia, 2011.0072.

Mermaid (FeeJee): 'Mermaid Exhibited in London', published in 'The Mermaid of Legend and of Art', *The Art Journal* (1880), fig. 39.

Minotaur: Gustave Doré, 'The Minotaur on the Shattered Cliff', engraving, published in *Dante Alighieri's Inferno from the Original by Dante Alighieri and Illustrated with the Designs of Gustave Doré* (New York: Cassell Publishing Company, 1890).

Mongolian Death Worm: Pieter Dirkx, *Allghoi Khorkhoi*, c.2007.

Nautilos: Charles Bevalet, 'Argonaut Sitting in the Open Sea', engraving, published in Louis Fibuier, *Ocean World: Being a Descriptive History of the Sea and its Living Inhabitants* (New York: D. Appleton & Co., 1868).

Pictish Beast: 'The Maiden Stone', published in Alexander Inkson McConnochie, *Bennachie* (Aberdeen: D. Wyllie & Son, 1890), p. 112.

Python: 'Apollo Killing the Python', engraving after Hendrik Goltzius, published in Ovid, *Metamorphoses* (Mülbracht, Holland: 1589), Bk 1, pl 13, Los Angeles County Museum of Art, Los Angeles, 54.70.1i.

Quetzalcoatl: 'Serpent Mask of Tlaloc' [also identified with Quetzalcoatl], Mixtec-Aztec,

1400–1521 CE, turquoise mosaic on wood, British Museum, London, Am1987,Q.3, photograph by Hans Hillewaert, 2011.

Rat King: *6 Ratten Welche mit den Schweiffen sehr Verknipfft Vnd Zu Strasburg den 4/14 Julij in einem Keller gefangen wordten* (Friedrich Wilhelm Schmuck, c.1683), Universitätsbibliothek Erlangen-Nürnberg, Erlangen, Einblattdrucke A IV 88x.

River-Whale: K. Reiger, *Waller*, 1666, illus.

Roc: published in Richard F. Burton, *The Book of the Thousand Nights and a Night*, Bassorah Edition, vol. VI (N.P.: Burton Club, 1900), frontispiece.

Sea Monsters from Schotti: P. Gasparis Schotti, *Physica Curiosa, sive Mirabilia Naturæ et Artis* (Würzburg: Jobus Hertz, 1662), plate II, facing p. 401.

Sea Monsters: Sebastian Münster, *Meerwunder vnd seltzame Thier* (Basel: n.p., c.1544).

Serpent: 'Aspic ptyas [etc.]', engraving, published in Joseph Joly, *La Géographie Sacrée, et les Monuments de l'Histoire Sainte* (Paris: Alexandre Jombert, 1784), plate x.

Siren: 'Bestiary', 1225–1250, British Library, London, Harley MS 4751, fol. 47v.

Sleipnir: Tjängvidestenen ('Tjängvide Image Stone'), 700–900 CE, petroglyph, Historiska Museet, Stockholm, Gotland Runic Inscription G 110, photograph by Dr Antje Bosselmann-Ruickbie, 2015.

Sphinx: Félix Bonfils, 'Le Sphynx apres les déblaiements et les deux grandes pyramides' ('The Sphinx after excavation and the two great pyramids'), photograph, Library of Congress Prints and Photographs Division, Washington DC, LC-DIG-ppmsca-03956, published in Félix Bonfils, *Album Souvenirs d'Orient, Egypte, Palestine, Syrie et Grèce; Nubie, Temple d'Abou Simbel* (Alais, 1878).

Turtle, Giant: *Archelon ischyros*, Yale Peabody Museum of Natural History, Yale University, published in Frederic A. Lucas, *Animals of the*

Past (New York: McClure, Phillips & Co., 1901).

Typhon: Wenceslas Hollar, *The Greek Gods: Typhon*, seventeenth century, engraving.

Unicorn: 'Rochester Bestiary', c.1230–fourteenth century, British Library, London, Royal 12 F XIII, fol. 10v.

Vegetable Lamb: published in Henry Lee, *The Vegetable Lamb of Tartary: A Curious Fable of the Cotton Plant* (London: Sampson, Low, Marston, Searle & Rivington, 1887).

Werewolf: 'Der Werwolf von Neuses', undated pamphlet, c.1685.

Wolpertinger: after Albrecht Dürer, *Feldhase*, 1502, watercolour on paper, Albertina, Vienna.

Yahoo: Louis John Rhead, 'The Servants Drive a Herd of Yahoos into the Field Laden with Hay', published in Jonathan Swift, *Gulliver's Travels* (New York and London: Harper & Brothers, 1913), facing p. 316.

Yale: 'Rochester Bestiary', c.1230–fourteenth century, British Library, London, Royal 12 F XIII, fol. 27r.

Yeti: René de Milleville, untitled, March 1976, photograph, de Milleville family collection.

Zu Bird: 'Enlil Battles Anzu', line drawing of an Assyrian relief, published in Anton Nyström, *Allmän kulturhistoria eller det mänskliga lifvet i dess utveckling*, vol. I (Stockholm: C. & E. Gernandts, 1900).

INDEX